THE LITTLE BOOK OF
PSYCHOLOGY

Penguin
Random
House

DK LONDON

Senior Art Editor Gillian Andrews
Project Art Editor Amy Orsborne
Senior Editors Sam Atkinson, Sarah Tomley
Project Editor Sam Kennedy
Editors Cecile Landau, Scarlett O'Hara
Senior Managing Art Editor Lee Griffiths
Managing Editors Camilla Hallinan, Gareth Jones,
Esther Ripley
Illustrations James Graham
Picture Research Myriam Megharbi
Producers, Pre-production Tony Phipps, Gillian Reid
Production Controller Angela Graef
Art Directors Philip Ormerod, Karen Self
Publisher Liz Wheeler
Publishing Director Jonathan Metcalf

DK DELHI

Senior Art Editors Mahua Mandal, Chhaya Sajwan
Project Art Editor Shruti Soharia Singh
Art Editors Jomin Johny,
Sonali Rawat Sharma, Priyanka Singh
Assistant Art Editors Niyati Gosain, Nidhi Mehra,
Anurag Trivedi, Vidit Vashisht
Senior Editor Monica Saigal
Assistant Editor Antara Raghavan
Editorial Team Sreshtha Bhattacharya,
Gaurav Joshi, Antara Moitra
Pre-production Manager Balwant Singh
DTP Designers Nand Kishor Acharya, Rajesh Singh
Adhikari, Harish Aggarwal, Arvind Kumar, Anita Yadav
Production Manager Pankaj Sharma
Jacket Designer Suhita Dharamjit
Jackets Editorial Coordinator Priyanka Sharma
Managing Jackets Editor Saloni Singh
Deputy Managing Art Editor
Priyabrata Roy Chowdhury
Managing Art Editors Sudakshina Basu,
Arunesh Talapatra
Deputy Managing Editor Pakshalika Jayaprakash
Senior Managing Editor Rohan Sinha

styling by
studio8 design

Content previously published in The Psychology Book.
This abridged edition first published in Great Britain in
2018 by Dorling Kindersley Limited,
80 Strand, London, WC2R 0RL

6 8 10 9 7
006 - 310302 - June/2018

Copyright © 2011, 2018 Dorling Kindersley Limited
A Penguin Random House Company

All rights reserved. No part of this publication may be
reproduced, stored in a retrieval system, or transmitted
in any form or by any means, electronic, mechanical,
photocopying, recording, or otherwise, without the prior
written permission of the copyright owner.

A CIP catalogue record for this book is available
from the British Library.

ISBN: 978-0-2413-4128-5

Printed in the UK

A WORLD OF IDEAS:
SEE ALL THERE IS TO KNOW

www.dk.com

CONTRIBUTORS

CATHERINE COLLIN

A clinical psychologist, our consultant
Catherine Collin is an Associate Professor
(Senior Lecturer in Psychological Therapies)
at the University of Plymouth. Catherine's
interests lie in primary care mental health
and cognitive behaviour therapy.

NIGEL BENSON

A lecturer in philosophy and psychology, Nigel
Benson has written several bestselling books on
the subject of psychology, including Psychology
for Beginners and Introducing Psychiatry.

JOANNAH GINSBURG

A clinical psychologist and journalist, Joannah
Ginsburg works in community treatment
centres in New York City, Boston, Philadelphia,
and Dallas, and regularly contributes to
psychology publications. She is joint author
of This Book has Issues: Adventures in
Popular Psychology.

VOULA GRAND

As a business psychologist, Voula Grand
consults into international corporations on
leadership and executive performance. Her
first novel, Honor's Shadow (2011), is about
the psychology of secrets, betrayal, and
revenge. She is currently writing the
sequel, Honor's Ghost.

MERRIN LAZYAN

A writer, editor, and classical singer, Merrin
Lazyan studied psychology at Harvard
University and has worked on several
fiction and non-fiction books, spanning
a broad range of topics.

MARCUS WEEKS

A writer and musician, Marcus Weeks
studied philosophy and worked as a teacher
before embarking on a career as an author.
He has contributed to many books on the arts
and popular sciences.

CONTENTS

THE PHILOSOPHICAL ROOTS
PSYCHOLOGY IN THE MAKING

BEHAVIOURISM
RESPONDING TO OUR ENVIRONMENT

PSYCHOTHERAPY
THE UNCONSCIOUS DETERMINES BEHAVIOUR

COGNITIVE PSYCHOLOGY
THE CALCULATING BRAIN

SOCIAL PSYCHOLOGY
BEING IN THE WORLD OF OTHERS

DEVELOPMENTAL
PHILOSOPHY
FROM INFANT TO ADULT

PSYCHOLOGY OF
DIFFERENCE
PERSONALITY AND INTELLIGENCE

INTRODU

Among all the sciences, psychology is perhaps the most mysterious to the general public, and the most prone to misconceptions. Even though its language and ideas have infiltrated everyday culture, most people have only a hazy idea of what the subject is about, and what psychologists actually do. For some, psychology conjures up images of people in white coats, either staffing an institution for mental disorders or conducting laboratory experiments on rats. Others may imagine a man with a middle-European accent psychoanalysing a patient on a couch or, if film scripts are to be believed, plotting to exercise some form of mind control.

Although these stereotypes are an exaggeration, some truth lies beneath them. It is perhaps the huge range of subjects that fall under the umbrella of psychology (and the bewildering array of terms beginning with the prefix "psych-") that creates confusion over what psychology entails; psychologists themselves are unlikely to agree on a single definition of the word. "Psychology" comes from the ancient Greek *psyche*, meaning "soul" or "mind", and *logia*, a "study" or "account", which seems to sum up the broad scope of the subject, but today the word most accurately describes "the science of mind and behaviour".

The new science

Psychology can also be seen as a bridge between philosophy and physiology. Where physiology describes and explains the physical make-up of the brain and nervous system, psychology examines the mental processes that take place within them and how these are manifested in our thoughts, speech, and behaviour. Where philosophy is concerned with thoughts and ideas, psychology studies how we come to have them and what they tell us about the workings of our minds.

All the sciences evolved from philosophy, by applying scientific methods to philosophical questions, but the intangible nature of subjects such as consciousness, perception, and memory meant that psychology was slow in making the transition from philosophical speculation to scientific practice. In some universities, particularly in the USA, psychology departments started out as branches of the philosophy department, while in others, notably those in Germany, they were established in the science faculties. But it was not until the late 19th century that psychology became established as a scientific discipline in its own right.

The founding of the world's first laboratory of experimental psychology by Wilhelm Wundt at the University of Leipzig in 1879 marked the recognition of psychology as a truly scientific subject, and as one that was breaking new ground in previously unexplored areas of research. In the course of the 20th century, psychology blossomed; all of its major branches and movements evolved. As with all sciences, its history is built upon the theories and discoveries of successive generations, with many of the older theories remaining relevant to contemporary psychologists. Some areas of research have been the subject of study from psychology's earliest days, undergoing different interpretations by the various schools of thought, while others have fallen in and out of favour, but each time they have exerted a significant influence on subsequent thinking, and have occasionally spawned completely new fields for exploration.

The simplest way to approach the vast subject of psychology for the first time is to take a look at some of its main movements in roughly chronological order, as we do in this book: from its roots in philosophical thought, through behaviourism, psychotherapy, and the study of cognitive, social, and developmental psychology, to the psychology of difference.

Two approaches

Even in its earliest days, psychology meant different things to different people. In the USA, its roots lay in philosophy, so the approach taken was speculative and theoretical, dealing with concepts such as consciousness and the self. In Europe, the study was rooted in the sciences, so the emphasis was on examining mental processes such as sensory perception and memory under controlled laboratory conditions. However, even the research of these more scientifically oriented psychologists was limited by the introspective nature of their methods: pioneers such as Hermann Ebbinghaus became the subject of their own investigations, effectively restricting the range of topics to those that could be

observed in themselves. Although they used scientific methods and their theories laid the foundations for the new science, many in the next generation of psychologists found their processes too subjective, and began to look for a more objective methodology.

In the 1890s, the Russian physiologist Ivan Pavlov conducted experiments that were to prove critical to the development of psychology in both Europe and the USA. He proved that animals could be conditioned to produce a response, an idea that developed into a new movement known as behaviourism. The behaviourists felt that it was impossible to study mental processes objectively, but found it relatively easy to measure behaviour, the manifestation of those processes. They began to design experiments that could be conducted under controlled conditions, at first on animals, to gain an insight into human psychology, and later on humans.

The behaviourists' studies concentrated almost exclusively on how behaviour is shaped by interaction with the environment; this "stimulus–response" theory became well known through the work of John Watson. New learning theories began to spring up in Europe and the USA, and attracted the interest of the general public.

However, at much the same time as behaviourism began to emerge in the USA, a young neurologist in Vienna started to develop a theory of mind that was to overturn contemporary thinking and inspire a very different approach. Based on observation of patients and case histories » rather than laboratory experiments, Sigmund Freud's psychoanalytic theory marked a return to the study of subjective experience. He was interested in memories, childhood development, and interpersonal relationships, and emphasized the importance of the unconscious in determining behaviour. Although his ideas seemed shocking at the time, they were quickly and widely adopted, and the notion of a "talking cure" continues within the various forms of psychotherapy today.

New fields of study

In the mid-20th century, both behaviourism and psychoanalysis fell out of favour, with a return to the scientific study of mental processes. This marked the beginning of cognitive psychology, a movement with its roots in the holistic approach of the Gestalt psychologists, who were interested in studying perception. Their work began to emerge in the USA in the years following World War II; by the late 1950s, cognitive psychology had become the predominant approach. The rapidly growing fields of communications and computer science provided psychologists with a useful analogy; they used the model of information processing to develop theories in areas such as attention, perception, memory and forgetting, language and language acquisition, problem-solving and decision-making, and motivation.

Even psychotherapy, which mushroomed in myriad forms from the original "talking cure", was influenced by the cognitive approach. Cognitive therapy and cognitive-behavioural therapy emerged as alternatives to psychoanalysis, leading to movements such as humanist psychology, which focused on the qualities unique to human life. These therapists turned their attention from healing the sick to guiding healthy people towards living more meaningful lives.

While psychology in its early stages had concentrated largely on the mind and behaviour of individuals, there was now an increasing interest in the way we interact with our environment and other people; this became the field of social psychology. Like cognitive psychology, it owed much to the Gestalt psychologists, especially Kurt Lewin, who had fled from Nazi Germany to the USA in the 1930s. Social psychology gathered pace during the latter half of the 20th century, when research revealed intriguing new facts about our attitudes and prejudices, our tendencies towards obedience and conformity, and our reasons for aggression or altruism, all of which were increasingly relevant in the modern world of urban life and ever-improving communications.

Freud's continuing influence was felt mainly through the new field of developmental psychology. Initially concerned only with childhood development, study in this area expanded to include change throughout life, from infancy to old age. Researchers charted methods of social, cultural, and moral learning, and the ways in which we form attachments. The contribution of developmental psychology to education and training has been significant but, less obviously, it has influenced thinking about the relationship between childhood development and attitudes to race and gender.

Almost every psychological school has touched upon the subject of human uniqueness, but in the late 20th century this area was recognized as a field in its own right in the psychology of difference. As well as attempting to identify and measure personality traits and the various factors that make up intelligence, psychologists in this growing field examine definitions and measures of normality and abnormality, and look at how much our individual differences are a product of our environment or the result of genetic inheritance.

An influential science

The many branches of psychology that exist today cover the whole spectrum of mental life and human and animal behaviour. The overall scope has extended to overlap with many other disciplines, including medicine, physiology, neuroscience, computer science, education, sociology, anthropology, and even politics, economics, and the law. Psychology has become perhaps the most diverse of sciences.

Psychology continues to influence and be influenced by the other sciences, especially in areas such as neuroscience and genetics. In particular, the nature versus nurture argument that dates back to Francis Galton's ideas of the 1870s continues to this day; recently, evolutionary psychology has contributed to the debate by exploring

psychological traits as innate and biological phenomena, which are subject to the laws of genetics and natural selection.

Psychology is a huge subject, and its findings concern every one of us. In one form or another it informs many decisions made in government, business and industry, advertising, and the mass media. It affects us as groups and as individuals, contributing as much to public debate about the ways our societies are or might be structured as it does to diagnosing and treating mental disorders.

The ideas and theories of psychologists have become part of our everyday culture, to the extent that many of their findings about behaviour and mental processes are now viewed simply as "common sense". However, while some of the ideas explored in psychology confirm our instinctive feelings, just as many make us think again; psychologists have often shocked and outraged the public when their findings have shaken conventional, long-standing beliefs.

In its short history, psychology has given us many ideas that have changed our ways of thinking, and that have also helped us to understand ourselves, other people, and the world we live in. It has questioned deeply held beliefs, unearthed unsettling truths, and provided startling insights and solutions to complex questions. Its increasing popularity as a university course is a sign not only of psychology's relevance in the modern world, but also of the enjoyment and stimulation that can be had from exploring the richness of a subject that continues to examine the mysterious world of the human mind. ∎

PHILOSOPH ROOTS

PSYCHOLOGY IN THE MAKING

Many of the issues that are examined in modern psychology had been the subject of philosophical debate long before the development of science as we know it today. The very earliest philosophers of ancient Greece sought answers to questions about the world around us, and the way we think and behave. Since then we have wrestled with ideas of consciousness and self, mind and body, knowledge and perception, how to structure society, and how to live a "good life".

The various branches of science evolved from philosophy, gaining momentum from the 16th century onwards, until finally exploding into a "scientific revolution", which ushered in the Age of Reason in the 18th century. While these advances in scientific knowledge answered many of the questions about the world we live in, they were still not capable of explaining the workings of our minds. Science and technology did, however, provide models from which we could start asking the right questions, and begin to test theories through the collection of relevant data.

Separating mind and body

One of the key figures in the scientific revolution of the 17th century, the philosopher and mathematician René Descartes, outlined a distinction between mind and body that was to prove critical to the development of psychology. He claimed that all human beings have a dualistic existence – with a separate machine-like body and a non-material, thinking mind, or soul. Later psychological thinkers, among them Johann Friedrich Herbart, were to extend the machine analogy to include the brain as well, describing the processes of the mind as the working of the brain-machine.

The degree to which mind and body are separate became a topic for debate. Scientists wondered how much the mind is formed by physical factors, and how much is shaped by our environment. The "nature versus nurture" debate, fuelled by British naturalist Charles Darwin's evolutionary theory and taken up by Francis Galton, brought subjects such as free will, personality, development, and learning to the fore. These areas had not yet been fully described by philosophical inquiry, and were now ripe for scientific study.

ICAL

Meanwhile, the mysterious nature of the mind was popularized by the discovery of hypnosis, prompting more serious scientists to consider that there was more to the mental life than immediately apparent conscious thought. These scientists set out to examine the nature of the "unconscious", and its influence on our thinking and behaviour.

The birth of psychology

Against this background, the modern science of psychology emerged. In 1879, Wilhelm Wundt founded the very first laboratory of experimental psychology at Leipzig University in Germany, and departments of psychology also began to appear in universities across Europe and the USA. Just as philosophy had taken on certain regional characteristics, psychology developed in distinct ways in the different centres: in Germany, psychologists such as Wundt, Hermann Ebbinghaus, and Emil Kraepelin took a strictly scientific and experimental approach to the subject; while in the USA, William James and his followers at Harvard adopted a more theoretical and philosophical approach. Alongside these areas of study, an influential school of thought was growing in Paris around the work of neurologist Jean-Martin Charcot, who had used hypnosis on sufferers of hysteria. The school attracted psychologists such as Pierre Janet, whose ideas of the unconscious anticipated Freud's psychoanalytic theories.

The final two decades of the 19th century saw a rapid rise in the importance of the new science of psychology, as well as the establishment of a scientific methodology for studying the mind, in much the same way that physiology and related disciplines studied the body. For the first time, the scientific method was applied to questions concerning perception, consciousness, memory, learning, and intelligence, and its practices of observation and experimentation produced a wealth of new theories.

Although these ideas often came from the introspective study of the mind by the researcher, or from highly subjective accounts by the subjects of their studies, the foundations were laid for the next generation of psychologists at the turn of the century to develop a truly objective study of mind and behaviour, and to apply their own new theories to the treatment of mental disorders. ■

THERE IS A REASONING SOUL IN THIS MACHINE

RENE DESCARTES (1596–1650)

IN CONTEXT

APPROACH
Mind/body dualism

BEFORE
4th century BCE Greek philosopher
Plato claims that the body is from the
material world, but the soul, or mind,
is from the immortal world of ideas.

4th century BCE Greek philosopher
Aristotle says that the soul and body
are inseparable: the soul is the
actuality of the body.

AFTER
1710 In *A Treatise Concerning the
Principles of Human Knowledge*,
Anglo-Irish philosopher George
Berkeley claims that the body is
merely the perception of the mind.

1904 In *Does Consciousness Exist?*
William James asserts that
consciousness is not a separate entity
but a function of particular experiences.

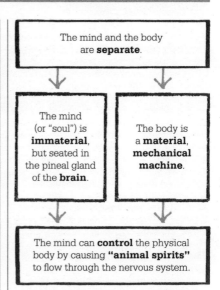

The mind and the body
are **separate**.

The mind
(or "soul") is
immaterial,
but seated in
the pineal gland
of the **brain**.

The body is
a **material**,
mechanical
machine.

The mind can **control** the physical
body by causing **"animal spirits"**
to flow through the nervous system.

T he idea that the mind and body are
separate and different dates back
to Plato and the ancient Greeks,
but it was the 17th-century philosopher
René Descartes who first described in
detail the mind-body relationship.
Descartes wrote *De Homine* ("Man"), his
first philosophical book, in 1633, in which
he describes the dualism of mind and body:
the non-material mind, or "soul", Descartes

says, is seated in the brain's pineal gland
doing the thinking, while the body is like a
machine that operates by "animal spirits",
or fluids, flowing through the nervous
system to cause movement. This idea had
been popularized in the 2nd century by
Galen, who attached it to his theory of the
humours; but Descartes was the first to
describe it in detail, and to emphasize the
separation of mind and body.

In a letter to the French philosopher Marin
Mersenne, Descartes explains that the pineal
gland is the "seat of thought", and so must
be the home of the soul, "because the one
cannot be separated from the other". This

Descartes illustrated the pineal gland, a single organ in the brain ideally placed to unite the sights and sounds of the two eyes and the two ears into one impression.

René Descartes

René Descartes was born in La Haye en Touraine (now called Descartes), France. He contracted tuberculosis from his mother, who died a few days after he was born, and remained weak for the rest of his life. From the age of eight, he was educated at the Jesuit college of La Flèche, Anjou, where he began the habit of spending each morning in bed, due to his poor health, doing "systematic meditation" – about philosophy, science, and mathematics. From 1612 to 1628, he contemplated, travelled, and wrote. In 1649, he was invited to teach Queen Christina of Sweden, but her early-morning demands on his time, combined with a harsh climate, worsened his health; he died on 11 February 1650. Officially, the cause of death was pneumonia, but some historians believe that he was poisoned to stop the Protestant Christina converting to Catholicism.

Key works

1637 *Discourse on the Method*
1662 *De Homine* (written 1633)
1647 *The Description of the Human Body*
1649 *The Passions of the Soul*

was important, because otherwise the soul would not be connected to any solid part of the body, he said, but only to the psychic spirits.

Descartes imagined the mind and body interacting through an awareness of the animal spirits that were said to flow through the body. The mind, or soul, residing in the pineal gland, located deep within the brain, was thought to sometimes become aware of the moving spirits, which then caused conscious sensation. In this way, the body could affect the mind. Likewise, the mind could affect the body by causing an outflow of animal spirits to a particular region of the body, initiating action.

An analogy for the mind

Taking his inspiration from the French formal gardens of Versailles, with their hydraulic systems that supply water to the gardens and their elaborate fountains, Descartes describes the spirits of the body operating the nerves and muscles like the force of water, and "by this means to cause motion in all the parts". The fountains were controlled by a fountaineer, and here Descartes found an analogy for the mind. He explained: "There is a reasoning soul in this machine; it has its principal site in the brain, where it is like the fountaineer who must be at the reservoir, whither all the pipes of the machine are extended, when he wishes to start, stop, or in some way alter their actions."

While philosophers still argue as to whether the mind and brain are somehow different entities, most psychologists equate the mind with the workings of the brain. However, in practical terms, the distinction between mental and physical health is a complex one: the two being closely linked when mental stress is said to cause physical illness, or when chemical imbalances affect the brain. ■

PERSONALITY IS COMPOSED OF NATURE AND NURTURE
FRANCIS GALTON (1822–1911)

IN CONTEXT

APPROACH
Bio-psychology

BEFORE
1690 British philosopher John Locke proposes that the mind of every child is a tabula rasa, or blank slate, and hence we are all born equal.

1859 Biologist Charles Darwin suggests that all human development is the result of adaptation to the environment.

1890 William James claims that people have genetically inherited individual tendencies, or "instincts".

AFTER
1925 Behaviourist John B. Watson says there is "no such thing as inheritance of capacity, talent, temperament, or mental constitution".

1940s Nazi Germany seeks to create a "master Aryan race" through eugenics.

Francis Galton counted many gifted individuals among his relatives, including the evolutionary biologist Charles Darwin. So it's not surprising that Galton was interested in the extent to which abilities are either inborn or learned. He was the first person to identify "nature" and "nurture" as two separate influences whose effects could be measured and compared, maintaining that these two elements alone were responsible for determining personality. In 1869 he used his own family tree, as well as those of "judges, statesmen, commanders, scientists, literary men… diviners, oarsmen, and wrestlers", to research inherited traits for his book *Hereditary Genius*. As predicted, he found more highly talented individuals in certain families than among the general population. However, he could not safely attribute this to nature alone, as there were also conferred benefits from growing up in a privileged home environment. Galton himself grew up in a wealthy household with access to unusually good educational resources.

A necessary balance
Galton proposed a number of other studies, including the first large survey by questionnaire, which was sent out to members of the Royal Society to enquire about their interests and affiliations. Publishing his results in *English Men of Science*, he claimed that where nature and nurture are forced to compete, nature triumphs. External influences can make an impression, he says, but nothing can "efface the deeper marks of individual character". However, he insists that both nature and nurture are essential in forming personality, as even the highest natural endowments may be "starved by defective nurture". Intelligence, he says, is inherited, but must be fostered through education.

In 1875, Galton undertook a study of 159 pairs of twins. He found that they did not

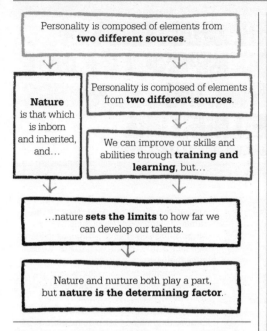

Personality is composed of elements from **two different sources**.

Nature is that which is inborn and inherited, and…

Personality is composed of elements from **two different sources**.

We can improve our skills and abilities through **training and learning**, but…

…nature **sets the limits** to how far we can develop our talents.

Nature and nurture both play a part, but **nature is the determining factor**.

follow the "normal" distribution of similarity between siblings, in which they are moderately alike, but were always extremely similar or extremely dissimilar. What really surprised him was that the degree of similarity never changed over time. He had anticipated that a shared upbringing would lessen dissimilarity between twins as they grew up, but found that this was not the case. Nurture seemed to play no role at all.

The "nature–nurture debate" continues to this day. Some people have favoured Galton's theories, including his notion – now known as eugenics – that people could be "bred" like horses to promote certain characteristics. Others have preferred to believe that every baby is a tabula rasa, or "blank slate", and we are all born equal. Most psychologists today recognize that nature and nurture are both crucially important in human development, and interact in complex ways. ■

Galton's study of twins looked for resemblances in many ways, including height, weight, hair and eye colour, and disposition. Handwriting was the only aspect in which twins always differed.

Francis Galton

Sir Francis Galton was a polymath who wrote prolifically on many subjects, including anthropology, criminology (classifying fingerprints), geography, meteorology, biology, and psychology. Born in Birmingham, England, into a wealthy Quaker family, he was a child prodigy, able to read from the age of two. He studied medicine in London and Birmingham, then mathematics at Cambridge, but his study was cut short by a mental breakdown, worsened by his father's death in 1844.

Galton turned to travelling and inventing. His marriage in 1853 to Louisa Jane Butler lasted 43 years, but was childless. He devoted his life to measuring physical and psychological characteristics, devising mental tests, and writing. He received many awards and honours in recognition of his numerous achievements, including several honorary degrees and a knighthood.

Key works

1869 *Hereditary Genius*
1874 *English Men of Science: Their Nature and Nurture*
1875 *The History of Twins*

THE BEGINNINGS OF THE MENTAL LIFE DATE FROM THE BEGINNINGS OF LIFE
WILHELM WUNDT (1832–1920)

IN CONTEXT

APPROACH
Experimental psychology

BEFORE
5th century Ancient Greek philosophers Aristotle and Plato claim that animals have a low level, distinctly non-human consciousness.

1630s René Descartes says that animals are automata without feeling.

1859 British biologist Charles Darwin links humans to animal ancestors.

AFTER
1949 Konrad Lorenz changes the way people see animals by showing their similarities to humans in *King Solomon's Ring*.

2001 American zoologist Donald Griffin argues in *Animal Minds* that animals have a sense of the future, complex memory, and perhaps consciousness itself.

The idea that non-human animals have minds and are capable of some form of thought dates back to the ancient Greek philosophers. Aristotle believed that there are three kinds of mind: plant, animal, and human. The plant mind is concerned only with nutrition and growth. The animal mind has these functions, but can also experience sensations, such as pain, pleasure, and desire, as well as initiating motion. The human mind can do all this and reason; Aristotle claims that only humans have self-awareness and are capable of higher-level cognition.

The similarity of humans to animals was a critical issue for philosophers, but even more so for psychologists. In the 15th century, the French philosopher René Descartes claimed that animals are no more than reflex-driven, complex machines. If Descartes was correct, observing animals could tell us nothing about our own behaviour. However, when Charles Darwin asserted some 200 years later that humans are linked to other animals genetically, and that consciousness operates from the creatures at the very lowest end of the evolutionary scale to ourselves, it became clear that experiments on animals might be revealing. This was the position held by the German physician, philosopher, and psychologist Wilhelm Wundt, who described a continuum of life from even the smallest animals to ourselves. In his book *Principles of Physiological Psychology*, he claimed that consciousness is a universal possession of all living organisms, and has been since the evolutionary process began.

To Wundt, the very definition of life includes having some kind of mind. He declared: "From the standpoint of observation, then, we must regard it as a highly probable hypothesis that the beginnings of the mental life date from as far back as the beginnings of life at large. The question of the origin of mental

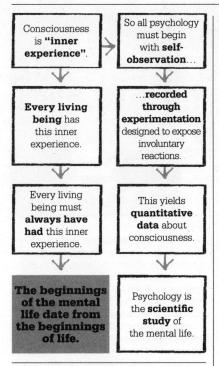

Consciousness is **"inner experience"**.

→ So all psychology must begin with **self-observation**...

↓

Every living being has this inner experience.

...**recorded through experimentation** designed to expose involuntary reactions.

↓

Every living being must **always have had** this inner experience.

This yields **quantitative data** about consciousness.

↓

The beginnings of the mental life date from the beginnings of life.

Psychology is the **scientific study** of the mental life.

Observing behaviour

Wundt believed that "the exact description of consciousness is the sole aim of experimental psychology". Although he understood consciousness as an "inner experience", he was only interested in the "immediately real" or apparent form of this experience. This ultimately led him to the study of behaviour, which could be studied and quantified by "direct observation".

Wundt said that there are two types of observation: external and internal. External observation is used to record events that are visible in the external world, and is useful in assessing relationships such as cause and effect on physical bodies – for example, in stimulus and response experiments. If a nerve fibre in a dead frog is given a small electric shock, the connecting muscles twitch, causing the legs to move. The fact that this happens even in a dead animal illustrates that such movements can occur without any consciousness. In living creatures, such actions are the basis of the automatic behaviour that we call "reflexes", such as immediately moving your hand when you touch something hot.

Wundt's second type of observation, termed "introspection" or "self-observation", is internal observation. This involves noticing and recording internal events such as thoughts and feelings. It is crucial in research because it provides information about how the mind is working. Wundt was interested in the relationship between the inner and outer worlds, which he did not see as mutually exclusive, but as interactive, describing it as "physical and psychical". He began to concentrate on the study of human sensations, such as the visual sensation of light, because **»**

development thus resolves itself into the question of the origin of life". Wundt went on to say that even simple organisms such as protozoa have some form of mind. This last claim is surprising today, when few people would expect a single-celled animal to demonstrate even simple mental abilities, but it was even more surprising when first stated more than 100 years ago.

Wundt was keen to test out his theories, and he is often called "the father of experimental psychology" because he set up the world's first formal laboratory of experimental psychology in Leipzig University, Germany, in 1879. He wanted to carry out systematic research on the mind and behaviour of humans, initially through subjecting the basic sensory processes to close examination. His laboratory inspired other universities in the USA and Europe to set up psychology departments, many of which were modelled on his original laboratory and were led by pupils such as Edward Titchener and James Cattell.

Wundt's laboratory set the style for psychology departments around the world. His experiments moved psychology out of the domain of philosophy and into that of science.

Our sensations provide details of shape, size, colour, smell, and texture, but when these are internalized, Wundt says, they are compounded into complex representations, such as a face.

these are the agencies that link the external physical world and the internal mental world.

In one experiment, Wundt asked individuals to report on their sensations when shown a light signal – which was standardized to a specific colour and a certain level of brightness, and shone for a fixed length of time. This ensured that each participant experienced exactly the same stimulus, enabling responses of different participants to be compared and the experiment to be repeated at a later date, if required. In insisting upon this possibility for replication, Wundt set the standard for all future psychological experiments.

In his sensory experiments, Wundt set out to explore human consciousness in a measurable way. He refused to see it as an unknowable, subjective experience that is unique to each individual. In the light-response experiments, he was particularly interested in the amount of time between a person receiving some form of stimulus and making a voluntary reaction to it (rather than an involuntary one), and he used various instruments to measure this response exactly. He was also just as interested to hear what his participants reported in common as he was in apparent individual differences.

Pure sensations, Wundt suggested, have three components: quality, intensity, and "feeling-tone". For example, a certain perfume may have a sweet odour (quality) that is distinct but faint (intensity) and is pleasant to smell (feeling-tone), while a dead rat might give off a nauseating (quality), strong (intensity) stench (feeling-tone). All consciousness originates in sensations, he said, but these are not internalized as "pure" sensory data; instead, they are perceived as already collected or compounded into representations, such as a dead rat. Wundt called these "images of an object or of a process in the external world". So, for example, if we see a face with certain features – mouth shape, eye colour, nose size, and so on – we may recognize the face as a person we know.

Categories of consciousness

Based on his sensory experiments, Wundt claimed that consciousness consists of three major categories of actions – representation, willing, and feeling – which together form an impression of a unitary flow of events. Representations are either "perceptions", if they represent an image in the mind of an object perceived in the external world (such as a tree within eyesight), or "intuitions" if they represent a subjective activity (such as remembering a tree, or imagining a unicorn). He named the process through which a perception or intuition becomes clear in consciousness "apperception" So, for example, you may perceive a sudden loud noise and then apperceive that it is a warning sign, meaning that you are about to be hit by a car if you don't get out of the way quickly enough.

The willing category of consciousness is characterized by the way it intervenes in the external world; it expresses our volition, or "will", from raising an arm to choosing to wear red. This form of consciousness is beyond experimental control or measurement. However, Wundt found that the third category of consciousness, feeling, could be measured through subjective reports from experimental participants, or through measuring levels of behaviour such as tension and relaxation or excitement.

Cultural psychology

For Wundt, the psychological development of a person is determined not only by sensations but also by complex social and cultural influences, which cannot be replicated or controlled in an experimental situation. He included religion, language, myths, history, art, laws, and customs among these influences, discussing them in a ten-volume work, *Cultural Psychology*, which he wrote during the last 20 years of his life.

Wundt saw language as an especially important part of culture's contribution to consciousness. Any verbal communication begins with a "general impression", or unified idea of something we wish to say. Having "apperceived" this general starting point, we then choose words and sentences to express it. While speaking, we monitor the accuracy of the intended meaning. We might say, "No, that's not right, I mean...", and then choose a different word or phrase to express ourselves better. Whoever is listening has to understand the meaning that the speaker is trying to convey, but the actual words may not be as important as the general impression, especially if strong emotions are involved. As evidence of the fact that we use this process, Wundt points out that we often remember the general meaning of what a person has said long after we've forgotten the specific words that were used.

The ability to use true language, as opposed to just exchanging limited signs and signals, is today considered by many psychologists to be a key difference between human beings and the rest of the animal kingdom. There may be a few exceptions, including non-human primates such as chimpanzees, but language is generally considered to be a human ability that is very important in consciousness.

Consciousness and species

The definition of consciousness continues to be debated, but it has not fundamentally changed since Wundt. The level of consciousness within animals has not yet been established, and this has led to the formation of special Codes of Ethics for animal experiments, intensive farming, and blood sports such as fox hunting and bull fighting. Of particular concern is whether animals experience discomfort, fear, and pain in ways that resemble the form in which we feel them ourselves. The fundamental question of which animals have self-awareness or consciousness remains unanswered, although few psychologists today would assume, as Wundt did, that it applies even to the microscopic protozoa. ∎

Wilhelm Wundt

Born in Baden (now Mannheim, Germany), Wilhelm Wundt was the fourth child in a family with a long history of intellectual achievement. His father was a Lutheran minister. The young Wundt was allowed little time for play, as he was pushed through a rigorous educational regime, attending a strict Catholic school from the age of 13. He went on to study at the universities of Berlin, Tübingen, and Heidelberg, graduating in medicine in 1856.

Two years later, Wundt became assistant to the physician Hermann von Helmholtz, who was famous for his work on visual perception. While at Heidelberg, Wundt started teaching the world's first course in experimental psychology, and in 1879 opened the first psychology laboratory. Wundt wrote over 490 works and was probably the world's most prolific scientific writer.

Key works

1863 *Lectures on the Mind of Humans and Animals*
1896 *Outline of Psychology*
1873 *Principles of Physiological Psychology*

WE KNOW THE MEANING OF "CONSCIOUSNESS" SO LONG AS NO ONE ASKS US TO DEFINE IT
WILLIAM JAMES (1842–1910)

IN CONTEXT

APPROACH
Analysis of consciousness

BEFORE
1641 René Descartes defines consciousness of self in terms of the ability to think.

1690 English philosopher and physician John Locke defines consciousness as "the perception of what passes in a man's own mind".

1781 German philosopher Immanuel Kant states that simultaneous events are experienced as a "unity of consciousness".

AFTER
1923 Max Wertheimer in *Laws of Organization in Perceptual Forms* shows how the mind actively interprets images.

1925 John B. Watson dismisses consciousness as "neither a definite nor a usable concept".

The term "consciousness" is generally used to refer to an individual's awareness of his or her own thoughts, including sensations, feelings, and memories. We usually take this awareness for granted, except when we are having difficulties – such as trying to do something when we are very tired. But if you focus your thoughts on your consciousness, you soon become aware that your conscious experiences are constantly changing. While reading this book, for example, you may be reminded of past experiences or present discomforts that interrupt your concentration; plans for the future may spontaneously spring to mind. Thinking about your conscious experiences makes you realize just how much your thoughts are changing, and yet they seem to come together, merging and carrying on smoothly as a whole.

American psychologist William James compared these everyday experiences of consciousness to a stream that continuously flows, despite the odd interruption and change of direction. He declared: "A 'river' or a 'stream' are the metaphors by which it is most naturally described. In talking of it hereafter, let us call it the stream of thought, of consciousness...".

James's famous description of the "stream... of consciousness" is one that almost everyone can identify with, because we all experience it. Yet, at the same time, James points out that it is very hard to actually define: "When I say every thought is part of a personal consciousness, 'personal consciousness' is one of the terms in question... to give an accurate account of it is the most difficult of philosophic tasks".

This "most difficult of philosophic tasks" has a long history. The ancient Greeks discussed the mind, but did not use the term "consciousness" or any equivalent. However, there was debate as to whether something separate from the body exists at all. In the 4th century BCE, Plato made a

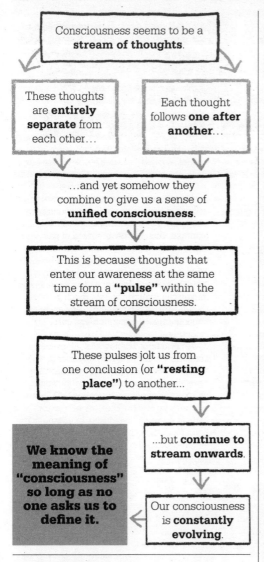

Consciousness seems to be a **stream of thoughts**.

These thoughts are **entirely separate** from each other…

Each thought follows **one after another**…

…and yet somehow they combine to give us a sense of **unified consciousness**.

This is because thoughts that enter our awareness at the same time form a **"pulse"** within the stream of consciousness.

These pulses jolt us from one conclusion (or **"resting place"**) to another…

…but **continue to stream onwards**.

We know the meaning of "consciousness" so long as no one asks us to define it.

Our consciousness is **constantly evolving**.

William James

William James was born in 1842 to a wealthy and influential New York family, and travelled widely as a child, attending schools in both Europe and the USA. James showed early artistic ability and initially pursued a career as a painter, but his growing interest in science eventually led to him to enrol at Harvard University in 1861. By 1864, he had moved to Harvard Medical School, although his studies were interrupted by bouts of physical illness and depression. He finally qualified as a physician in 1869, but never practised medicine.

In 1873, James returned to Harvard, where he became a professor of both philosophy and psychology. He set up the first experimental psychology courses in the USA, playing a key role in establishing psychology as a truly scientific discipline. He retired in 1907, and died peacefully at his home in New Hampshire in 1910.

Key works

1890 *The Principles of Psychology*
1892 *Psychology*
1897 *The Will to Believe*

distinction between the soul and the body, but Aristotle argued that even if there is a distinction, the two cannot be separated.

Early definitions

René Descartes, in the mid-17th century, was one of the first philosophers to attempt to describe consciousness, proposing that it resides in an »

> No-one ever had a simple sensation by itself: consciousness…is of a teeming multiplicity of objects and relations.
> **William James**

immaterial domain he called "the realm of thought", in contrast to the physical domain of material things, which he called "the realm of extension". However, the first person accredited with the modern concept of consciousness as an ongoing passage of individual perceptions is the 17th-century English philosopher John Locke. James was drawn to Locke's idea of passing perceptions and also to the work of the 18th-century German philosopher Immanuel Kant. Kant was impressed by the way our experiences come together, noting that if we hear a noise and feel pain at the same time, we typically experience these as one event. He called this the "unity of consciousness", a concept that influenced many later philosophers, including William James.

James felt the most important point about consciousness is that it is not a "thing" but a process – it is what the brain does to "steer a nervous system grown too complex to regulate itself". It allows us to reflect upon the past, present, and future, to plan and adapt to circumstances and so fulfil what he believed was the prime purpose of consciousness – to stay alive.

But James found it hard to imagine the structure of a unified consciousness. He likened it to a group of 12 men: "Take a dozen words, take twelve men, and to each give one word. Then stand the men in a row or jam, and let each think of his word as intently as he will; nowhere will there be a consciousness of the whole sentence". If consciousness is a stream of distinct thoughts, James struggled to see how these combine. As he said, "The idea of a plus the idea of b is not identical with the idea of $(a + b)$". Two thoughts added together cannot be made into one idea. They are more likely to form an entirely new idea. For example, if thought a is "it's nine o'clock", and thought b is "the train leaves at 9:02", thought c – "I'm going to miss my train!" – might follow.

Combining thoughts

James concluded that the simplest way to understand how thoughts within the stream of consciousness might combine to make sense is to suppose "that things

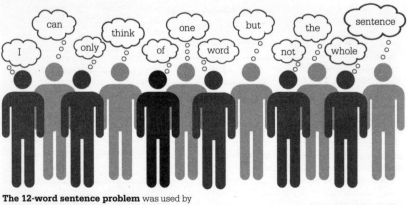

The 12-word sentence problem was used by James to illustrate his difficulty in grasping how a unified consciousness stems from separate thoughts. If each man is aware of just one word, how can there be a consciousness of the whole sentence?

that are known together are known in single pulses of that stream". Some thoughts, or sensations, he believed, are unavoidably connected, like Kant's example of hearing a noise and feeling pain at precisely the same time, because any thoughts that enter our awareness during the same moment of time combine to form a pulse, or current, within the stream. We may have many of these currents flowing through our consciousness, some fast and some slow. James stated that there are even resting points, where we pause to form pictures in our minds, which can be held and contemplated at length. He called the resting places "substantive parts", and the moving currents the "transitive parts", claiming that our thinking is constantly being dislodged from one substantive part towards another, propelled by the transitive parts, or current. We are, therefore, effectively "bumped" from one conclusion to another by the constant stream of thoughts, whose purpose is to pull us ever forwards in this way. There is no final conclusion; consciousness is not a thing but process, which is constantly evolving.

James also drew attention to the personal nature of consciousness, stating that thoughts do not exist independently of a thinker – they are your thoughts or mine. Each one is "owned" by someone, and never "comes into direct sight of a thought in another personal consciousness than its own". And it is these thoughts "connected as we feel them to be connected" that form the self. As thoughts cannot be divided from the self, James said that investigating this self should be the starting point of psychology. Experimental psychologists did not agree, because "the self" cannot be offered up for experimentation, but James thought it was enough to work with our understanding of a self that does certain things and feels in certain ways. He called this the "empirical self", which manifests itself through its behaviour, and suggested that it consists of several parts – the material self, spiritual self, and social self – each of which can be studied through introspection.

Dots of pure colour make up this work by the French, Post-Impressionist painter Georges Seurat. Yet our brain combines these separate elements so that what we see is a human figure.

Theory of emotion

In the early stages of his research into consciousness, James realized that the emotions play an important role in our daily lives, and went on to develop, with his colleague Carl Lange, a theory about how they relate to our actions and behaviour. What was to become known as the James–Lange Theory of Emotion states that emotions arise from your conscious mind's perception of your physiological condition. To illustrate this theory, James used the example of seeing a bear, then running away. It is not the case that you see the bear, feel afraid, and then run away because of the fear. What is really happening is that you see the bear and run away, and the conscious feeling of fear is caused by the action of running. This contradicts what most people might think, but James's view was that the mind's perception of the physical effects of running – rapid breathing, increased heartbeat, and perspiring heavily – is translated into the emotion of fear. »

Another example, according to James's theory, would be that you feel happy because you are conscious that you are smiling; it is not that you feel happy first, and then smile.

Pragmatism

Related to James's theories about consciousness is his approach to the way we believe things to be true or not. He stated that "truths emerge from facts... but... the 'facts' themselves meanwhile are not true; they simply are. Truth is the function of the beliefs that start and terminate among them". James defined "true beliefs" as those that the believer finds useful. This emphasis on the usefulness of beliefs lies at the heart of the American philosophical tradition of pragmatism, which was central to James's thinking.

In the course of our lives, James claimed that we are continually testing "truths" against each other, and our conscious beliefs keep changing, as "old truths" are modified, and sometimes replaced by "new truths". This theory is particularly relevant to the way that all scientific research, including psychology, progresses. James cited the discovery of the radioactive element radium by Pierre and Marie Curie in 1902 as an example. In the course of their investigations, the Curies found that radium appeared to give off unlimited amounts of energy, which "seemed for a moment to contradict our ideas of the whole order of nature". However, after conscious consideration of this revelation, they concluded that "although it extends our old ideas of energy, it causes a minimum of alteration in their nature". In this instance, the Curies' scientific knowledge had been questioned and modified, but its core truths remained intact.

Further studies

The period following James's death saw the rise of the behaviourist movement, and a decline of interest in consciousness. Consequently, little theorizing on the subject happened from around the start of the 1920s up until the 1950s. One important exception was the German-based Gestalt movement, which emphasized that the brain operates in a holistic way, taking account of whole conscious experiences, rather than separate events – just as when we look at a picture, we see not just separate dots, lines, and shapes, but a meaningful whole. This concept is behind the now famous Gestalt phrase: "The whole is greater than the sum of the parts".

Since the 1980s, however, psychologists and neuroscientists have developed a new field of research called "consciousness studies", focusing on two main areas of interest: the content of consciousness, as reported by people who are considered to be normal and healthy; and the consciousness of people whose state of awareness has been impaired in some way. The latter group includes cases, such as when the subject is in a "persistent vegetative state" (PVS) – in which patients in a coma are awake and breathing independently, but have apparently lost all higher brain functions. The goal with both paths of research is to try to find ways of assessing consciousness as objectively as possible, and to understand its underlying mechanisms – both physical and psychological.

Modern neuroscience has demonstrated that there are mechanisms of consciousness. By the closing years of the 20th century, the British molecular biologist and biophysicist Francis Crick was claiming that

Pierre and Marie Curie's research, like most scientific work, modified, rather than totally contradicted, earlier theories. New "truths", James claimed, constantly modify our basic beliefs in a similar way.

consciousness is related to a specific part of the brain – the prefrontal cortex area, which is involved in thought processes such as planning, problem-solving, and the control of behaviour.

Research carried out by the Colombian neuroscientist Rodolfo Linas links consciousness to the activities of the thalamus in conjunction with the cerebral cortex. The thalamus, a structure embedded deep in the centre of the brain, is responsible for regulating vibrations inside the brain at certain frequencies; if these regular rhythms are disrupted – by an infection or genetic causes – then an individual may experience neurological disorders, such as epilepsy and Parkinson's disease, as well as psychological conditions, such as depression.

But when it comes to definitions of consciousness, modern attempts still remain vague and difficult to apply. For example, the American neuroscientist Antonio Damasio calls consciousness "the feeling of what happens", and defines it as "an organism's awareness of its own self and its surroundings". As William James suggested, more than 100 years earlier, consciousness is hard to define.

Lasting legacy

An edited version of James's 1890 book, *The Principles of Psychology*, is still in print, and his ideas have been a major influence on many psychologists, as well as other scientists and thinkers. The application of his pragmatic philosophy to facts – concentrating not on what is "true" but on what it is "useful to believe" – has helped psychology move on from the question of whether the mind and body are separate or not to a more useful study of mental processes, such as attention, memory, reasoning, imagination, and intention. James claimed his approach helped to move philosophers and psychologists "away from abstraction, fixed principles, closed systems, and pretended absolutes and origins, towards facts, action, and power". His insistence on focusing on the wholeness of events, including the effects of different environments on our actions – in contrast to the introspective, structuralist approach of

MRI scans of the brain have helped to identify structures such as the thalamus, seen in the centre of this scan, that appear to have links to consciousness.

breaking down our experiences into small details – has also shaped our understanding of behaviour.

Before James started teaching the subject at Harvard in 1875, there were no independent psychology courses available in any American university. But within 20 years, around 24 universities and colleges in the USA had recognized psychology as a distinct academic discipline, and were offering degrees in the subject. Three specialist psychology journals were also founded in that time, and a professional organization – the American Psychological Association – was formed.

James introduced experimental psychology to America, despite claiming to "hate experimental work". He did so because he had come to realize that it was the best way to prove or disprove a theory. But he continued to value the use of introspection as a tool of discovery, especially of mental processes.

The shift in the perception of psychology and its concerns from being considered, "a nasty little subject" (in James's words) into a vastly beneficial discipline owes much to his work. In 1977, in a speech celebrating the 75th anniversary of the formation of the American Psychological Association, David Krech, then Professor Emeritus in psychology at the University of California at Berkeley, referred to James as the "father of psychology". ∎

24 HOURS AFTER LEARNING SOMETHING, WE FORGET TWO-THIRDS OF IT
HERMANN EBBINGHAUS (1850–1909)

IN CONTEXT

APPROACH
Memory studies

BEFORE
5th century BCE The ancient Greeks make use of "mnemonics" – techniques, such as key words or rhymes, that aid memory.

1582 Italian philosopher Giordano Bruno in *The Art of Memory* gives methods for memorizing, using diagrams of knowledge and experience.

AFTER
1932 Frederick Bartlett says that every memory is a blend of knowledge and inference.

1949 Donald Hebb, in *The Organization of Behavior*, describes how learning results from stimulated brain cells linking up into "assemblies".

1960 US psychologist Leo Postman finds that new learning can interfere with previous learning, causing "retroactive interference".

In 1885, Hermann Ebbinghaus became the first psychologist to systematically study learning and memory, by carrying out a long, exhausting experiment on himself. Philosophers such as John Locke and David Hume had argued that remembering involves

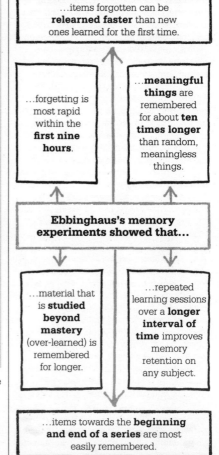

...items forgotten can be **relearned faster** than new ones learned for the first time.

...forgetting is most rapid within the **first nine hours**.

...**meaningful things** are remembered for about **ten times longer** than random, meaningless things.

Ebbinghaus's memory experiments showed that...

...material that is **studied beyond mastery** (over-learned) is remembered for longer.

...repeated learning sessions over a **longer interval of time** improves memory retention on any subject.

...items towards the **beginning and end of a series** are most easily remembered.

association–linking things or ideas by shared characteristics, such as time, place, cause, or effect. Ebbinghaus decided to test the effect of association on memory, recording the results mathematically to see if memory follows verifiable patterns.

Memory experiments

Ebbinghaus started by memorizing lists of words and testing how many he could recall. To avoid the use of association, he then created 2,300 "nonsense syllables", all three letters long and using the standard word format of consonant–vowel consonant: for example, "ZUC" and "QAX". Grouping these into lists, he looked at each syllable for a fraction of a second, pausing for 15 seconds before going through a list again. He did this until he could recite a series correctly at speed. He tested different list lengths and different learning intervals, noting the speed of learning and forgetting.

Ebbinghaus found that he could remember meaningful material, such as a poem, ten times more easily than his nonsense lists. He also noted that the more times the stimuli (the nonsense syllables) were repeated, the less time was needed to reproduce the memorized information. Also, the first few repetitions proved the most effective in memorizing a list.

Learning material and committing it to memory within an hour of hearing it, Ebbinghaus showed, will mean that we remember it for longer and can recall it more easily.

When looking at his results for evidence of forgetting, Ebbinghaus found, unsurprisingly, that he tended to forget less quickly the lists that he had spent the most time memorizing, and that recall is best performed immediately after learning. Ebbinghaus also uncovered an unexpected pattern in memory retention. He found that there is typically a very rapid loss of recall in the first hour, followed by a slightly slower loss, so that after nine hours, about 60 per cent is forgotten. After 24 hours, about two-thirds of anything memorized is forgotten. Plotted on a graph, this shows a distinct "forgetting curve" that starts with a sharp drop, followed by a shallow slope.

Ebbinghaus's research launched a new field of enquiry, and helped establish psychology as a scientific discipline. His meticulous methods remain the basis of all psychological experimentation to this day. ∎

Hermann Ebbinghaus

Hermann Ebbinghaus was born in Barmen, Germany, to a family of Lutheran merchants. At 17, he began to study philosophy at Bonn University, but his academic career was disrupted in 1870 by the Franco-Prussian War. In 1873, he completed his studies and moved to Berlin, later travelling to France and England, where he carried out research on the power of his own memory, starting in 1879. He published *Memory* in 1885, detailing the "nonsense syllable" research, and in the same year became a professor at Berlin University, where he set up two psychology laboratories and founded an academic journal. Ebbinghaus later moved to Breslau University, where he also established a laboratory, and finally to Halle, where he taught until his death from pneumonia at the age of 59.

Key works

1885 *Memory: A Contribution to Experimental Psychology*
1897–1908 *Fundamentals of Psychology* (2 volumes)
1908 *Psychology: An Elementary Textbook*

THE INTELLIGENCE OF AN INDIVIDUAL IS NOT A FIXED QUANTITY
ALFRED BINET (1857–1911)

IN CONTEXT

APPROACH
Intelligence theory

BEFORE
1859 English naturalist Charles Darwin proposes that intelligence is inherited in *On the Origin of Species*.

From 1879 Wilhelm Wundt applies scientific methods to psychology, seeking objective ways of measuring mental abilities such as intelligence.

1890 US psychologist James Cattell devises tests to measure differences in individual mental abilities.

AFTER
1920s English educational psychologist Cyril Burt claims intelligence is mainly genetic.

1940s Raymond Cattell defines two types of intelligence: fluid (inborn) and crystallized (shaped by experience).

In 1859, Charles Darwin set out his theory of evolution in *On the Origin of Species*, providing a framework for the debate over whether intelligence was fixed by genetic inheritance or could be modified by circumstances. His cousin, Francis Galton, carried out tests on the cognitive abilities of around 9,000 people in London in the early 1880s, and concluded that basic intelligence was fixed at birth. Around the same time, Wilhelm Wundt proposed the idea of an intelligence quotient (IQ), and made attempts to measure it. Wundt's work inspired studies into the measurement of mental abilities by the America psychologist James Cattell, and were also to form the basis of Alfred Binet's research into human intelligence.

Fascination with learning
Binet studied law and natural science before psychology captured his interest. He was largely self-taught, although working with Jean-Martin Charcot at Paris's Salpêtrière Hospital for more than seven years gave him a firm grasp of experimental procedures, with their need for precision and careful planning. His desire to study human intelligence grew out of his fascination with the development of his own two daughters. He noted that the speed and ease with which his children absorbed new information varied according to how much they were paying attention. Context, and the child's frame of mind, seemed to be critical to learning.

On hearing of Francis Galton's testing in London, Binet decided to carry out his own large-scale research on assessing differences in individual abilities between various special-interest groups, such as mathematicians, chess players, writers, and artists. At the same time, he continued his study of the functional intelligence of children, noting that they became capable of certain skills at specific ages. For example, very young children were not capable of abstract

Intelligence testing can only measure…

↓

…an individual's mental abilities at a **particular time** and in a **particular context**.

↓

Abilities change within short periods of time; they also change over the long-term as part of the **developmental process**.

↓

Intelligence will alter during **a person's lifetime**.

↓

The intelligence of an individual is not a fixed quantity.

Alfred Binet

Alfred Binet was born in Nice, France, but moved to Paris at a young age after his parents separated. He gained a law degree in 1878, then studied sciences at the Sorbonne, in preparation for taking up medicine. But Binet decided that his real interest lay in psychology, and although he was largely self-taught, in 1883 he was offered a post at Paris's Salpêtrière Hospital by Jean-Martin Charcot. After his marriage the following year, and the birth of two daughters, he began to take an interest in intelligence and learning. In 1891, Binet was appointed associate director of the Sorbonne's Laboratory of Experimental Psychology, becoming director in 1894.

Many honours have been heaped upon Binet since his untimely death in 1911. These include changing the name of La Société Libre pour l'Etude Psychologique de l'Enfant to La Société Alfred Binet in 1917.

Key works

1903 *Experimental Study of Intelligence*
1905 *The Mind and Brain*
1911 *A Method of Measuring the Development of Intelligence*

thought –this seemed to be a hallmark of an increased level of intelligence that was directly attributable to age.

In 1899, Binet was invited to join a new organization dedicated to educational research, La Société Libre pour L'Etude Psychologique de l'Enfant (The Free Society for the Psychological Study of the Child). Within a short time, he became the group's leader, and began to publish articles and information useful to teachers and education officials. Around the same time, it became mandatory for all children in France to attend school between the ages of six and 12, and Binet was asked to consider how to develop a test that would identify children who might have learning disabilities, so that they could receive schooling that was appropriate to their needs. In 1904, this work led to Binet being asked to join a government commission to devise a method of assessing learning potential in infants, and he made it his mission to establish the differences between normal and intellectually challenged children, and to find a way of measuring these differences. »

Taking intelligence tests, which are still largely based on the Binet–Simon Scale, has become an almost standard way of predicting a child's potential to be successful at school.

The Binet–Simon Scale

Binet was joined in his task by Théodore Simon, a research scientist at the Sorbonne's Laboratory of Experimental Psychology, where Binet had been director since 1894. It was to be the beginning of a long and fruitful collaboration between the two scientists.

By 1905, Binet and Simon had created their first test, labelled "New Methods for Diagnosing Idiocy, Imbecility, and Moron Status". Soon after, they introduced a revised version, for children aged 3 to 13, which was simply called the Binet–Simon Scale. It was revised once more in 1908, and then again in 1911.

Based on their many years of observing children, Binet and Simon put together 30 tests of increasing difficulty, using a range of tasks that reflected the average abilities of children at different ages. The easiest tasks included following a beam of light, or engaging in basic conversation with the person who was testing them. Slightly more difficult tasks included pointing to various named body parts, repeating a series of two digits, repeating simple

sentences, and defining basic words such as "house" or "fork". In the more difficult tests, children were asked to describe the difference between pairs of similar objects, to reproduce drawings from memory, and to construct sentences around three given words. The very hardest tasks included repeating seven random digits, finding three rhymes for the French word "obéisance"; and answering questions such as "My neighbour has been receiving strange visitors. He has received in turn a doctor, a lawyer, and then a priest. What is taking place?"

Binet and Simon tested their scale on a sample of 50 children, divided equally between five age groups. These children had been selected by their school teachers as being average for their age, providing a baseline measure of normality against which children of all abilities could be measured.

Binet and Simon's 30 tasks, arranged in order of difficulty, were to be carried out under carefully controlled conditions. Binet had learned from observing his daughters that children are easily distracted, and that their level of attention plays a critical role in their ability to perform. He saw intelligence as a mixture of multifaceted mental faculties that operate within a real world of ever-changing circumstances, and are controlled by practical judgment.

Intelligence is not fixed

Binet was always frank about the limitations of the Binet–Simon Scale. He was keen to point out that the scale simply ordered children from their performance of intellectual tasks in relation to other children of a similar age. The tests of 1908 and 1911 placed greater

> 66 There is in intelligence…
> a fundamental agency, the
> lack or alteration of which has
> the greatest importance for
> practical life: that is judgment.
> **Alfred Binet** 99

emphasis on tests for different age groups, and it was this that eventually led to the concept of "mental age".

Binet also stressed that mental development progressed at different rates and could be influenced by environmental factors. He preferred to think of his tests as a way of assessing mental level at a particular point in time, because this allowed for an individual's level to change as their circumstances changed. This was in opposition to the views of the influential English psychologist Charles Spearman, who later proposed that intelligence was based on biological factors alone. Binet maintained that a child's "intelligence is not a fixed quantity", but grows just as the child does, and that even though he had devised a way of quantifying it, no number could ever give an accurate measure of a person's intelligence. A complete picture, Binet thought, could only be formed from an accompanying case study. Ultimately, Binet did not believe that it was possible to measure intellectual aptitude as if it were a length or a capacity; it was only possible to classify it.

Uses and abuses

In 1908, the American psychologist Henry H. Goddard travelled to Europe, where he discovered the Binet–Simon tests. He translated them, distributing around 22,000 copies across the USA to be used for testing in schools. Unfortunately, while Binet had been careful not to attribute intelligence to hereditary factors, Goddard thought that it was genetically determined. He saw the Binet–Simon Scale as a way of rooting out "feebleminded people" for compulsory sterilization.

In 1916, yet another American psychologist, Lewis Terman, modified the Binet–Simon Scale. Using test results from a large sample of American children, he renamed it the Stanford–Binet Scale. It was no longer used solely to identify children with special needs, but to pick out those who might be suitable for streaming off into more vocational, or job-oriented, education, effectively condemning them to a lifetime of menial work. Terman, like

66 I have not sought to sketch a method of measuring... but only a method of classification of individuals.
Alfred Binet 99

Goddard, believed that intelligence was inherited and unchangeable, so no amount of schooling could alter it.

Binet was probably unaware of these uses of his work for quite some time. He was an isolated figure, who rarely concerned himself with professional developments outside his immediate sphere. He never travelled outside France, where the Binet–Simon Scale was not adopted during his lifetime, so he was never confronted by any modifications of his work. When he eventually became aware of the "foreign ideas being grafted on his instrument" he strongly condemned those who with "brutal pessimism" and "deplorable verdicts" promoted the concept of intelligence as a single constant.

Binet's concept of the "IQ test" remains the basis of intelligence today. Despite its shortcomings, it has, nevertheless, generated a body of research that has advanced our knowledge of human intelligence. ∎

Binet–Simon tests generate an IQ (intelligence quotient) number, representing an overall level of performance. This can be plotted on a graph to reveal IQ variations across groups or populations.

THE UNCONSCIOUS SEES THE MEN BEHIND THE CURTAINS
PIERRE JANET (1859–1947)

IN CONTEXT

APPROACH
Neurological science

BEFORE
1878 Jean-Martin Charcot in *Diseases of the Nervous System* describes the symptoms of hysteria, then considered to be a distinct, biological illness.

AFTER
1895 Sigmund Freud suggests that dissociation is one of the mind's defence mechanisms.

1900s American neurologist Morton Prince suggests that there is a spectrum of dissociative disorders.

1913 French naturalist J.P.F. Deleuze describes dissociation as being like the formation of two distinct people – one of them fully awake, and the other in a trance-like state.

1977 Ernest R. Hilgard's *Divided Consciousness* discusses the splitting up of consciousness by hypnosis.

If someone shows **physiological signs of terror** or distress for no apparent reason…

↓

…they may be caused by a **subconscious idea**…

↓

…that therapy reveals to be related to an **earlier traumatic incident**.

↓

This may in severe cases lead to **dissociation** – the existence of two separate consciousnesses.

Between around 1880 and 1910, there was a great deal of interest in the condition of "dissociation" – the separation of some mental processes from a person's conscious mind, or normal everyday personality. Mild dissociation, in which the world seems "dreamlike" and "unreal", is common, and affects most people at some time or other. It is often caused by illnesses, such as flu, or drugs, including alcohol, and may lead to a partial or complete loss of memory during and after the period of dissociation. In rare cases of what was then described as multiple personality disorder, a person appears to have two or more distinct personalities. Such extreme examples are now classified as "dissociative identity disorder".

The French philosopher and physician Pierre Janet is credited with being the first person to study and describe dissociation as a psychiatric condition. In the late 1880s and early 1890s, he worked at the Salpêtrière hospital in Paris, where he treated patients who were suffering from "hysteria". He published case studies of several women who showed extreme symptoms. A patient called "Lucie", for example, would usually be calm, but then suddenly became agitated, crying and looking terrified for no apparent reason. She seemed to have three distinct personalities, which Janet named "Lucie 1", "Lucie 2", and "Lucie 3", and would change between them unexpectedly, especially when hypnotized. Lucie 1 had only "her own" memories, as did Lucie 2, but Lucie 3 could remember events relating to all three personalities. Significantly, Lucie 3 could recall a traumatic experience, while on holiday at the age of seven, when she was terrified by two men who were hiding behind a curtain.

Subconscious trauma

Lucie's childhood trauma, Janet concluded, was the cause of her dissociation. As he wrote in *Psychological Automatism*: "To have one's body in the posture of terror is to feel the emotion of terror; and if this posture is determined by a subconscious idea, the patient will have the emotion alone in his consciousness without knowing why he feels this way." As her terror took hold, Lucie would say, "I'm afraid and I don't know why." "The unconscious," said Janet, "is having its dream; it sees the men behind the curtains, and puts the body in a posture of terror." Janet added that he believed traumatic

events and stress could cause dissociation in anyone with that predisposition.

Janet described the part of the mind that he believed was behind uncharacteristic and disturbed behaviour as "the subconscious". But Sigmund Freud thought this term was too vague, and instead labelled the source of his patients' mental traumas as the "unconscious". Freud also developed Janet's ideas, stating that dissociation was a universal "defence mechanism".

Janet's work was neglected for decades, as the use of hypnotism to investigate and treat mental illness was discredited. However, since the late 20th century, it has again attracted interest from psychologists studying dissociative disorders. ∎

Childhood traumas may appear to be forgotten, but according to Pierre Janet, they can often remain in the "subconscious" part of the mind, giving rise to mental problems in later life.

Pierre Janet

Pierre Janet was born into a cultured, middle-class family in Paris, France. As a child he loved the natural sciences, and began collecting and cataloguing plants. His philosopher uncle, Paul Janet, encouraged him to study both medicine and philosophy, and after attending the elite École Normale Supérieure in Paris, he went on to receive a master's degree in philosophy from the Sorbonne. Aged just 22, Janet was appointed Professor of Philosophy at the Lycée in Le Havre, where he launched his research into hypnotically induced states.

Influenced by Jean-Martin Charcot, Janet extended his studies to include "hysteria", becoming director of Charcot's laboratory at Paris's Salpêtrière Hospital in 1898. He also taught at the Sorbonne, and was made Professor of Psychology at the Collège de France in 1902.

Key works

1893 *The Mental State of Hystericals*
1902 *Neuroses*
1907 *The Major Symptoms of Hysteria*

BEHAVIO

RESPONDING TO OUR ENVIRONMENT

By the 1890s, psychology was accepted as a scientific subject separate from its philosophical origins. Laboratories and university departments had been established in Europe and the USA, and a second generation of psychologists was emerging.

In the USA, psychologists anxious to put the new discipline on an objective, scientific footing reacted against the introspective, philosophical approach taken by William James and others. Introspection, they felt, was by definition subjective, and theories based on it could be neither proved nor disproved; if psychology was to be treated as a science, it would have to be based on observable and measurable phenomena. Their solution was to study the manifestation of the workings of the mind–behaviour – under strictly controlled laboratory conditions. As John B. Watson put it, psychology is "that division of Natural Science which takes human behaviour – the doings and sayings, both learned and unlearned – as its subject matter". Early "behaviourists", including Edward Thorndike, Edward Tolman, and Edwin Guthrie, designed experiments to observe the behaviour of animals in carefully devised situations, and from these tests inferred theories about how humans interact with their environment, as well as about learning, memory, and conditioning.

Conditioning responses

Behaviourist experiments were influenced by similar experiments devised by physiologists studying physical processes, and it was a Russian physiologist, Ivan Pavlov, who unwittingly provided a basis for the emergent behaviourist psychology. In his now famous study of salivation in dogs, Pavlov described how an animal responds to a stimulus in the process of conditioning, and gave psychologists the foundation on which to build the central idea of behaviourism. The notion of conditioning, often referred to as "stimulus–response" (S–R) psychology, shaped the form behaviourism was to take.

The behaviourist approach concentrated on observing responses to external stimuli, ignoring inner mental states and processes, which were thought to be impossible to examine scientifically and therefore could not be included in any analysis of behaviour. The shift from "mind" to "behaviour" as a basis for the

URISM

study of psychology was revolutionary, and was even accompanied by a "behaviourist manifesto" – the paper *Psychology as the Behaviorist Views It*, delivered in 1913 by Watson.

In the USA, which was leading the field in psychology, behaviourism became the dominant approach for the next 40 years. Evolving from the idea of Pavlovian or classical conditioning came Watson's assertion that environmental stimuli alone shape behaviour; innate or inherited factors are not involved. The next generation included the "radical behaviourist" B.F. Skinner, who proposed a rethink of the stimulus–response notion in his theory of "operant conditioning" – which stated that behaviour was shaped by consequences, not by a preceding stimulus. Although the concept was similar to ideas proposed by William James, it radically altered the course of behaviourism, taking into account genetic factors and explaining mental states as a result (rather than as a cause) of behaviour.

The cognitive revolution
By the mid-20th century, however, psychologists were questioning the behaviourist approach. Ethology, the study of animal behaviour, showed the importance of instinctive as well as learned behaviour – a finding that sat uncomfortably with strict ideas of conditioning. A reaction to Skinner's ideas also sparked the "cognitive revolution", which turned attention once again from behaviour back to the mind and mental processes. A key figure at this time was Edward Tolman, a behaviourist whose theories had not dismissed the importance of perception and cognition, due to his interest in German-based Gestalt psychology. Advances in neuroscience, explored by another behaviourist, Karl Lashley, also played a part in shifting the emphasis from behaviour to the brain and its workings.

Behaviourism had now run its course, and was superseded by the various branches of cognitive psychology. However, its legacy, particularly in establishing a scientific methodology for the subject, and in providing models that could be used in psychological experimentation, was a lasting one. Behavioural therapy is also still in use today, as an essential part of cognitive-behavioural therapy. ■

THE SIGHT OF TASTY FOOD MAKES A HUNGRY MAN'S MOUTH WATER

IVAN PAVLOV (1849–1936)

IN CONTEXT

APPROACH
Classical conditioning

BEFORE
Early 12th century Arab physician Avenzoar (Ibn Zuhr) performs experiments on animals in order to test surgical procedures.

1890 In *Principles of Psychology*, William James states that in animals "the feeling of having executed one impulsive step is an indispensable part of the stimulus of the next one".

AFTER
1920 John B. Watson's "Little Albert" experiment demonstrates classical conditioning in humans.

1930s B.F. Skinner shows that rats can be "conditioned" to behave in a specific way.

1950s Psychotherapists employ "conditioning" as part of behaviour therapy.

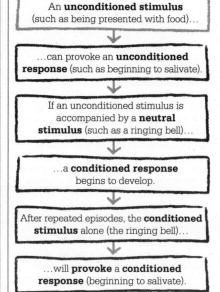

An **unconditioned stimulus** (such as being presented with food)…

↓

…can provoke an **unconditioned response** (such as beginning to salivate).

↓

If an unconditioned stimulus is accompanied by a **neutral stimulus** (such as a ringing bell)…

↓

…a **conditioned response** begins to develop.

↓

After repeated episodes, the **conditioned stimulus** alone (the ringing bell)…

↓

…will **provoke** a **conditioned response** (beginning to salivate).

Many of the key discoveries made when modern psychology was still in its infancy were the result of research by scientists working in other fields. Ivan Pavlov, a Russian physiologist, is one of the best known of these early pioneers, whose investigations into the secretion of saliva during digestion in dogs led him to some unexpected conclusions.

During the 1890s, Pavlov carried out a series of experiments on dogs, using various surgically implanted devices to measure the flow of saliva when these animals were being fed. He noted that the dogs salivated not only when they were actually eating, but also whenever they could just smell or see some appetizing food. The dogs would even salivate, in anticipation of food being produced, when they were simply being approached by one of their keepers.

Pavlov's dogs would salivate simply at the sight of someone in a white lab coat. They had become "conditioned" to associate the coat with eating, as whoever fed them always wore one.

Pavlov's observations led him to investigate the links between various stimuli and the responses they elicited. In one experiment, he set off a clicking metronome just before offering food to the dogs, repeating this process until the animals always associated the sound with a good meal. This "conditioning" eventually resulted in the dogs salivating in response to the click of the metronome alone.

In further experiments, Pavlov replaced the metronome with a bell or buzzer, a flashing light, and whistles of different pitches. However, regardless of the nature of the stimulus used, the result was the always same: once an association between the neutral stimulus (bell, buzzer, or light) and food had been established, the dogs would respond to the stimulus by salivating.

Conditioned response

Pavlov concluded that the food offered to the dogs was an "unconditioned stimulus" (US), because it led to an unlearned, or "unconditioned" response (UR) – in this case, salivation. The click of the metronome, however, only became a stimulus to salivation after its association with food had been learned. Pavlov then called this a "conditioned stimulus" (CS). The salivation in response to the metronome was also learned, so was a "conditioned response" (CR).

In later experiments, Pavlov showed that conditioned responses could be repressed, or "unlearned," if the conditioned stimulus was given repeatedly without being followed by food. He also demonstrated that a conditioned response could be mental as well as physical, by carrying out experiments in which various stimuli were associated with pain or some form of threat and began to elicit a conditioned response of fear or anxiety.

The principle of what is now known as classical or Pavlovian conditioning, as well as Pavlov's experimental method, marked a ground-breaking step in the emergence of psychology as a truly scientific, rather than philosophical, discipline. Pavlov's work was to be hugely influential, particularly on US behaviourist psychologists, such as John B. Watson and B.F. Skinner. ■

Ivan Pavlov

Ivan Pavlov, the eldest son of a village priest in Ryazan, Russia, was initially destined to follow in his father's footsteps. However, he quickly abandoned his training at a local seminary, transferring to the University of St Petersburg to study natural science. After graduation in 1875, he enrolled at the Academy of Medical Surgery, where he gained a doctorate and later a fellowship. In 1890, Pavlov became a professor at the Military Medical Academy, and was also made director of the physiology department at the Institute of Experimental Medicine. It was here that he carried out his famous research into the digestive secretions of dogs, which won him the Nobel Prize in 1904. Pavlov retired officially in 1925, but continued his experiments until his death from pneumonia in February 1936.

Key works

1897 *Lectures on the Work of the Principal Digestive Glands*
1928 *Lectures on Conditioned Reflexes*
1941 *Conditioned Reflexes and Psychiatry*

PROFITLESS ACTS ARE STAMPED OUT

EDWARD THORNDIKE (1874–1949)

IN CONTEXT

APPROACH
Connectionism

BEFORE
1885 In his book *On Memory*, Hermann Ebbinghaus describes the "forgetting curve" – the rate at which human memories fade.

1890s Ivan Pavlov establishes the principle of classical conditioning.

AFTER
1918 John B. Watson's "Little Albert" experiments apply conditioning to a human baby.

1923 English psychologist Charles Spearman proposes a single general factor – the "g factor" – in measurements of human intelligence.

1930s B.F. Skinner develops a theory of conditioning from consequences – "operant conditioning".

> Psychology helps to measure the probability that an aim is attainable.
> **Edward Thorndike**

A t much the same time as Pavlov was conducting his experiments on dogs in Russia, Edward Thorndike began researching animal behaviour for his doctoral thesis in the US. He was perhaps the first true "behaviourist" psychologist, although his research took place long before the term was adopted.

Scientific psychology was emerging as a fresh field of study in universities when Thorndike graduated in the 1890s, and he was attracted by the prospect of applying this new science to his interest in education and learning. Thorndike's original intention had been to study learning in humans, but when he was unable to obtain a suitable subject for his research, he turned his attention to animals, with the aim of examining the processes of intelligence and learning through observation in a series of controlled experiments. Thorndike's results went much further than this, however, laying down the foundations of behaviourist psychology.

Learning environments
Thorndike's first studies were of chicks learning to negotiate mazes that he designed and built specifically for his experiments. This later became a hallmark of behaviourist experimental technique – the use of a specially created environment in which a subject is given specific stimuli or tasks, now known as "instrumental conditioning" or "instrumental learning". As his research progressed, Thorndike

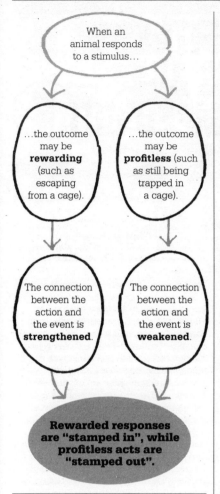

When an animal responds to a stimulus...

...the outcome may be **rewarding** (such as escaping from a cage).

...the outcome may be **profitless** (such as still being trapped in a cage).

The connection between the action and the event is **strengthened**.

The connection between the action and the event is **weakened**.

Rewarded responses are "stamped in", while profitless acts are "stamped out".

noted how long it took for the cat to open the puzzle box each time; this indicated how quickly the animal was learning about its environment.

The experiment was carried out using several different cats, placing each one in a series of puzzle boxes that were opened by different devices. What Thorndike noticed was that although the cats had all discovered the escape mechanism by trial and error in their first attempt, on successive occasions the amount of trial and error gradually decreased as the cats learned which actions were going to be fruitless and which would lead to a reward.

The Law of Effect

As a result of these experiments Thorndike proposed his Law of Effect, which states that a response to a situation that results in a satisfying outcome is more likely to occur again in the future; and conversely, that a response to a situation that results in an unsatisfying outcome is less likely to occur again. This was the first formal statement of an idea that lies behind all behaviourist psychology, the connection between stimulus and response and its relevance to the process of learning and behaviour. Thorndike proposed that when a connection is made between a stimulus (S) and a response (R), a corresponding neural connection is made in the brain. He referred to his brand of S-R learning as "connectionism", asserting that the connections made during learning are "stamped in" the circuitry of the brain.

What Thorndike proposed was that it is the outcome of an action that determines how strongly or weakly the stimulus-response connection is stamped in; in the case of the puzzle boxes, whether pulling a string or pushing a panel resulted in escape or frustration. In other words, when particular stimulus-response sequences are followed by a satisfying or pleasant state of affairs (such as escape or a reward), those responses tend to become "more firmly connected with the situation, so that, when it recurs, they will be more likely to recur". They become "stamped in" as a neural connection. When stimulus-response sequences are followed by an »

turned his attention to cats, inventing "puzzle boxes" to observe their ability to learn mechanisms for escape.

A hungry cat was locked inside a puzzle box, and by exploring its environment would come across various devices, such as a loop of string, or a ring, or a button or panel to be pressed, only one of which would be connected to the latch that would open the door of the box. In time, the cat would discover the device, which would allow it to escape and receive a reward of food. The process was repeated and it was

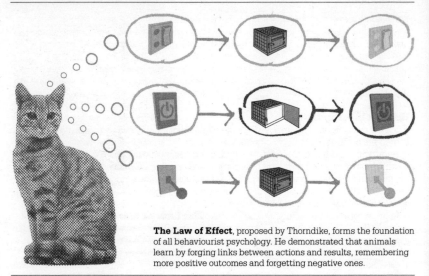

The Law of Effect, proposed by Thorndike, forms the foundation of all behaviourist psychology. He demonstrated that animals learn by forging links between actions and results, remembering more positive outcomes and forgetting negative ones.

annoying or unpleasant state of affairs (such as continued imprisonment or punishment), the neural connections between the situation and response are weakened, until eventually "profitless acts are stamped out".

This focus on the outcome of a stimulus and its response, and the idea that the outcome could work back to strengthen the stimulus-response connection, is an example of what would later be called a reinforcement theory of learning. Reinforcement, and the importance of outcomes, was virtually ignored by psychologists in the next generation of behaviourists, such as John B. Watson, but the Law of Effect brilliantly anticipated the work of B.F. Skinner and his theory of "operant conditioning".

> The intellect, character, and skill possessed by any man are the product of certain original tendencies and the training which they have received.
> **Edward Thorndike**

In later research, Thorndike refined the Law of Effect to take into account other variables, such as the delay between response and reward, the effect of repetition of a task, and how quickly a task was forgotten when it was not repeated. From this, he derived his Law of Exercise, which states that stimulus-response connections that are repeated are strengthened, while those that are not used again are weakened. Moreover, the rate at which connections strengthen or weaken can vary. According to Thorndike, "the greater the satisfaction or discomfort, the greater the strengthening or weakening of the bond".

Interestingly, although Thorndike was studying animal behaviour using what were to become standard behaviourist methods – and authoring a book, *Animal Intelligence* (1911), which was to become a classic of early behaviourism – he considered himself primarily an educational psychologist. He had originally intended to examine animal intelligence, not behaviour. He wanted to show, for example, that animals learned by simple trial and error rather than by using a faculty of insight, an idea that was prevalent in psychology at the time: "In the first place, most of the books do not give us a psychology, but rather a eulogy of animals. They have all been about animal intelligence, never about animal stupidity," he wrote. The fact that his cats in puzzle boxes learned gradually, rather than suddenly gaining an insight into how to escape, confirmed his theories. The animals were forced to learn by trial and error, because they were unable to use reason to work out the link between the door and the operating handle.

Human intelligence

After the publication of *Animal Intelligence*, Thorndike turned his attention to human intelligence. In his opinion, the most basic intelligence is characterized by simple stimulus and response association, resulting in a neural connection. The more intelligent an animal, the more capable it will be of making such connections. Therefore, intelligence can be defined in terms of the ability to form neural bonds, which is dependent not only on genetic factors, but also on experience.

To find a measurement of human intelligence, Thorndike devised his CAVD (Completion, Arithmetic, Vocabulary, and Directions) test. It became the model for all modern intelligence tests, and assessed mechanical intelligence (understanding of how things work), as well as abstract intelligence (creative ability) and social intelligence (interpersonal skills). Thorndike was especially interested in how age might affect learning, and also proposed a theory of learning that remains at the heart of educational psychology to this day, a contribution that is perhaps what Thorndike would have wished more than anything else to be remembered for. However, it is for his enormous influence on the behaviourist movement that Thorndike is most often lauded. ∎

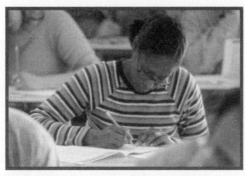

Adult learners were once thought to be less capable of retaining information than children. Thorndike showed that the only significant difference was in speed of learning, not memory.

Edward Thorndike

The son of a Methodist minister, Edward Thorndike was born in Williamsburg, Massachusetts, USA, in 1874. He graduated in sciences from Wesleyan University in 1895, proceeding to Harvard to study psychology under William James. In 1897, Thorndike moved to Columbia University in New York City, where he completed his doctorate thesis in 1898.

Thorndike's interest in educational psychology led to a teaching post at the College for Women of Case Western Reserve in Cleveland, Ohio, but he returned to Columbia just a year later, in 1899, teaching there until his retirement in 1939. In 1912, his peers elected him President of the American Psychological Association. Thorndike continued to research and write until his death, aged 74, in Montrose, New York.

Key works

1905 *The Elements of Psychology*
1910 *The Contribution of Psychology to Education*
1911 *Animal Intelligence*
1927 *The Measurement of Intelligence*

ANYONE, REGARDLESS OF THEIR NATURE, CAN BE TRAINED TO BE ANYTHING
JOHN B. WATSON (1878–1958)

IN CONTEXT

APPROACH
Classical behaviourism

BEFORE
1890s German-born biologist Jacques Loeb (one of Watson's professors) explains animal behaviour in purely physical-chemical terms.

1890s The principle of classical conditioning is established by Ivan Pavlov using experiments on dogs.

1905 Edward Thorndike shows that animals learn through achieving successful outcomes from their behaviour.

AFTER
1932 Edward Tolman adds cognition into behaviourism in his theory of latent learning.

1950s Cognitive psychologists focus on understanding the mental processes that both lie behind and produce human behaviour.

B y the beginning of the 20th century, many psychologists had concluded that the human mind could not be adequately studied through introspective methods, and were advocating a switch to the study of the mind through the evidence of behaviour in controlled laboratory experiments.

John Watson was not the first advocate of this thoroughgoing behaviourist approach, but he was certainly the most conspicuous. In a career cut short by his marital infidelity, he became one of the most influential and controversial psychologists of the 20th century. Through his work on the stimulus–response learning theory that had been pioneered by Thorndike, he became regarded as the "founding father" of behaviourism, and he did much to popularize the use of the term. His 1913 lecture, Psychology as the *Behaviorist Views It*, put forward the revolutionary idea that "a truly scientific psychology would abandon talk of mental states… and instead focus on prediction and control of behavior". This lecture became known to later psychologists as the "behaviourist manifesto".

Before Watson's research at Johns Hopkins University, in Baltimore, USA, the majority of experiments on behaviour had concentrated on animal behaviour, with the results extrapolated to human behaviour. Watson himself studied rats and monkeys for his doctorate but (perhaps influenced by his experience working with the military during World War I) was keen to conduct experiments using human subjects. He wanted to study the stimulus–response model of classical conditioning and how it applied to the prediction and control of human behaviour. He believed that people have three fundamental emotions – fear, rage, and love – and he wanted to find out whether a person could be conditioned into feeling these in response to a stimulus.

Little Albert

With his research assistant, Rosalie Rayner, Watson began a series of experiments involving "Albert B", a nine-month-old baby chosen from a local children's hospital. The tests were designed to see whether it is possible to teach an infant to fear an animal by repeatedly presenting it at the same time as a loud, frightening noise. Watson also wanted to find out whether such a fear would transfer to other animals or objects; and how long this fear would persist. Today, his methods would be considered unethical and even cruel, but at the time they were seen as a logical and natural progression from previous animal studies.

In the now famous "Little Albert experiment", Watson placed the healthy but "on the whole, stolid and unemotional" baby Albert on a mattress and then observed his reactions when introduced to a dog, a white rat, a rabbit, a monkey, and some inanimate objects, including human masks and burning paper. Albert showed no fear of any of these animals or objects and even reached out to touch them. In this way, Watson established a baseline from which he could measure any change in the child's behaviour towards the objects.

On a separate occasion, while Albert was sitting on the mattress, Watson struck

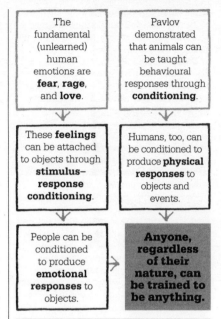

The fundamental (unlearned) human emotions are **fear**, **rage**, and **love**.

Pavlov demonstrated that animals can be taught behavioural responses through **conditioning**.

These **feelings** can be attached to objects through **stimulus–response conditioning**.

Humans, too, can be conditioned to produce **physical responses** to objects and events.

People can be conditioned to produce **emotional responses** to objects.

Anyone, regardless of their nature, can be trained to be anything.

a metal bar with a hammer to make a sudden loud noise; unsurprisingly, Albert became frightened and distressed, bursting into tears. Watson now had an unconditioned stimulus (the loud noise) that he knew elicited a response of fear »

John B. Watson

Born into a poor family in South Carolina, John Broadus Watson's childhood was unhappy; his father was a hard-drinking womanizer who left when Watson was 13, and his mother was devoutly religious. Watson became a rebellious and violent teenager, but was a brilliant scholar, attending nearby Furman University at the age of 16. After gaining a PhD from Chicago, he became associate professor at Johns Hopkins University, where his 1913 lecture became known as the "behaviourist manifesto". He worked for a short time for the military during World War I, then returned to Johns Hopkins. Forced to resign after an affair with his research assistant, Rosalie Rayner, he turned to a career in advertising while still publishing books on psychology. After Rayner's early death in 1935 aged 37, Watson became essentially a recluse.

Key works

1913 *Psychology as the Behaviorist Views It*
1920 *Conditioned Emotional Reactions (with Rosalie Rayner)*
1924 *Behaviorism*

in the child. By pairing this with the sight of the rat, he hypothesized that he would be able to condition little Albert to become afraid of the animal.

When Albert was just over 11 months old, Watson carried out the experiment. The white rat was placed on the mattress with Albert, then Watson hit the hammer on the steel bar when the child touched the rat. The child burst into tears. This procedure was repeated seven times over two sessions, one week apart, after which Albert became distressed as soon as the rat was brought into the room, even when it was not accompanied by the noise.

By repeatedly pairing the rat with the loud noise, Watson was applying the same kind of classical conditioning as Pavlov had in his experiments with dogs. The child's natural response to the noise – fear and distress – had now become associated with the rat. The child had become conditioned to respond to the rat with fear. In terms of classical conditioning, the rat was initially a neutral stimulus eliciting no particular response; the loud noise was an "unconditioned stimulus" (US) that elicited an "unconditioned response" (UR) of fear. After conditioning, the rat had become a "conditioned stimulus" (CS), eliciting the "conditioned response" (CR) of fear.

However, this conditioning seemed to go deeper than simply a fear of the white rat, and appeared to be far from temporary. In order to test whether Albert's fear had "generalized", or spread to other, similar objects, he was reintroduced to white furry things – including a rabbit, a dog, and a sheepskin coat – five days after the original conditioning. Albert showed the same distressed and fearful response to these as to the rat.

In these experiments, Watson demonstrated that human emotions are susceptible to classical conditioning. This was a new finding, because previous stimulus–response experiments had focused on testing the learning of physical behaviours. Watson had discovered that not only can human behaviour be predicted – given certain stimuli and conditions – it can also be controlled and modified. A further check of Albert's reactions to the rat, rabbit, and dog one month later suggested that

the effects of this conditioning were long-lasting, but this could not be proven as Albert was soon after removed from the hospital by his mother. It has been suggested that this was a sign of the mother's distress, but according to Watson and Rayner's own account, it occurred on a prearranged date.

Infinitely malleable

Watson's career was abruptly brought to an end shortly after the Little Albert experiments when he was forced to resign his professorship amid the scandal of his affair with his researcher, Rosalie Rayner. Despite the incompleteness of his research, Watson felt vindicated in his belief in behaviourism, and more particularly the application of classical stimulus–response conditioning to humans. Perhaps because of his forced ejection from the academic world (into advertising, where he was hugely successful) he developed a tendency to overstate the scope of his findings, and with a natural gift for self-publicity continued to publish books on the subject of psychology.

Not content, for example, to claim that it is possible to condition emotional responses, he boasted that on the same principle it would be possible to control

Watson saw the child as the ultimate "blank slate". He claimed that behaviourist principles could be used to mould children into any kind of specialist, from artist to doctor, regardless of nature.

or modify almost any aspect of human behaviour, no matter how complex.

Just as Little Albert had been conditioned to fear certain white furry objects against his natural inclination, Watson believed that "Anyone, regardless of their nature, can be trained to be anything". He even boasted in his 1924 book *Behaviorism*: "Give me a dozen healthy infants, well-formed, and my own specified world to bring them up in and I'll guarantee to take any one at random and train him to become any type of specialist I might select – doctor, lawyer, artist, merchant-chief, and, yes, even beggar-man and thief, regardless of his talents, penchants, tendencies, abilities, vocations, and race of his ancestors". In the "nature versus nurture" debate, Watson was firmly on the side of nurture.

Unemotional parenting

Unable to continue his university research, Watson popularized his ideas on behaviourism by turning his attention to the business of childcare. It was in this that his views proved to be most publicly influential, and eventually most controversial. Predictably, he advocated a strictly behaviourist approach to bringing up children, and throughout the 1920s and 30s, his many books on childcare became immensely popular. In retrospect, it is easy to see that his approach, based on extreme emotional detachment, was at best misguided and potentially damaging, but his methods were adopted by millions of parents, including Watson and Rosalie Rayner themselves.

The child, Watson believed, is shaped by its environment, and that environment is controlled by the parents. In essence, he saw child-raising as an objective exercise in behaviour modification, especially of the emotions of fear, rage, and love. Perhaps understandably, given his own unhappy childhood, he dismissed affection as sentimental, leading to over-dependence of the child on the parent. But he also advised against the opposite emotional extreme and was an opponent of physical punishment.

Watson's questionable application of stimulus–response conditioning to childcare eventually drew criticism. Later generations viewed the approach as manipulative and uncaring, with an emphasis on efficiency and results rather than on the wellbeing of the child. The long-term damage to children brought up according to Watson's behaviourist model became apparent only gradually, but was significant. The popularity of his books as childcare "bibles" meant that a whole generation was affected by what can now be seen as a dysfunctional upbringing. Even Watson's own family suffered: Rosalie eventually saw the flaws in her husband's child-rearing theories and wrote a critical article for *Parents' Magazine* entitled "I Am the Mother of a Behaviorist's Sons", and Watson's granddaughter, the actor Mariette Hartley, gave an account of her disturbed family background in her autobiographical book *Breaking the Silence*.

Alternative approaches to childcare soon appeared, even among committed behaviourists. While accepting the basic principle of conditioning established by Watson (despite the dubious ethics of the Little Albert experiment), and using that as a starting point for his own "radical behaviourism", the psychologist B.F. Skinner was to apply behaviourism to the business of childcare in a much more benign (if eccentric) manner. ∎

Watson applied his understanding of human behaviour to advertising in the 1920s, demonstrating that people can be influenced into buying products through their image, not content.

THAT GREAT GOD-GIVEN MAZE WHICH IS OUR HUMAN WORLD

EDWARD TOLMAN (1886–1959)

IN CONTEXT

APPROACH
Cognitive ("purposive") behaviourism

BEFORE
1890s Ivan Pavlov's experiments with dogs establish the theory of classical conditioning.

1920 John B. Watson conducts behaviourist experiments on humans, notably "Little Albert".

AFTER
1938 B.F. Skinner's research into operant conditioning uses pigeons in place of rats, and becomes more sophisticated.

1950s Cognitive psychology replaces behaviourism as the dominant movement in psychology.

1980s Joseph Wolpe's behavioural therapy and Aaron Beck's cognitive therapy merge into cognitive behavioural therapy.

As a rat explores a maze…

↓

…it builds up a **"cognitive map"** of the area…

↓

…which can be used to **reach a goal**.

↓

Humans think in a similar way to rats.

↓

Humans create a cognitive map of their environment, which is like a "God-given maze".

A lthough considered one of the leading figures of US behaviourist psychology, Edward Tolman took a very different approach from that of Thorndike and Watson. He agreed with the basic methodology of behaviourism – that psychology could only be studied by objective, scientific experiments – but was also interested in ideas about mental processes, including perception, cognition, and motivation, which he had encountered while studying Gestalt psychology in Germany. By bridging these two previously separate approaches, he developed a new theory about the role of conditioning, and created what he called "purposive behaviourism", now called cognitive behaviourism.

Tolman questioned the basic premise of conditioned learning (that behaviour was learned simply by an automatic response to a stimulus). He believed that animals could learn about the world around them without the reinforcement of a reward, and later use that knowledge in decision-making.

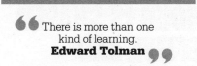

> There is more than one kind of learning.
> **Edward Tolman**

He designed a series of experiments using rats in mazes to examine the role of reinforcement in learning. Comparing a group of rats that were rewarded with food daily for successfully negotiating the maze, with another group who were only rewarded after six days, and a third group rewarded after two days, Tolman's ideas were confirmed. The second and third groups made fewer errors when running the maze the day after they had been rewarded with food, demonstrating that they already "knew" their way around the maze, having learned it prior to receiving rewards. Once rewards were on offer, they were able to use the "cognitive map" they had built in order to negotiate the maze faster.

Latent learning

Tolman referred to the rats' initial learning period, where there was no obvious reward, as "latent learning". He believed that as all animals, including humans, go about their daily lives, they build up a cognitive map of the world about them – the "God-given maze" – which they can apply to locate specific goals. He gave the example of how we learn the locations of various landmarks on our daily journeys, but only realize what we have learned when we need to find somewhere along the route. Further experiments showed that the rats learned a sense of location rather than merely the turns required to reach a particular place.

In *Purposive Behavior in Animals and Men*, Tolman outlined his theory of latent learning and cognitive maps, bringing together the methodology of behaviourism with Gestalt psychology, and introducing the element of cognition. ∎

A cognitive map of our surroundings develops in the course of our daily lives. We may not be aware of this until we need to find somewhere that we have passed without noticing.

Edward Tolman

Edward Chace Tolman was born into a well-to-do family in West Newton, Massachusetts, USA. He studied at the Massachusetts Institute of Technology, graduating in electrochemistry in 1911, but after reading works by William James opted for a postgraduate degree at Harvard in philosophy and psychology. While studying, he travelled to Germany and was introduced to Gestalt psychology. After gaining his doctorate, he taught at Northwestern University, but his pacifist views lost him his job, and he moved to the University of California at Berkeley.

It was here that he experimented with rats in mazes. During the McCarthy period, he was threatened with dismissal for not signing a loyalty oath that he felt restricted academic freedom. The case was overturned in 1955. He died in Berkeley, aged 73, in 1959.

Key works

1932 *Purposive Behavior in Animals and Men*
1942 *Drives Toward War*
1951 *Collected Papers in Psychology*

BEHAVIOUR IS SHAPED BY POSITIVE AND NEGATIVE REINFORCEMENT

B.F. SKINNER (1904–1990)

IN CONTEXT

APPROACH
Radical behaviourism

BEFORE
1890 William James outlines the theories of behaviourism in *The Principles of Psychology*.

1890s Ivan Pavlov develops the concept of conditioned stimulus and response.

1924 John B. Watson lays the foundations for the modern behaviourist movement.

1930s Zing-Yang Kuo claims that behaviour is continually being modified throughout life, and that even so-called innate behaviour is influenced by "experiences" as an embryo.

AFTER
1950s Joseph Wolpe pioneers systematic desensitization as part of behaviour therapy.

1960s Albert Bandura's social learning theory is influenced by radical behaviourism.

Burrhus Frederic Skinner, better known as B.F. Skinner, is possibly the most widely known and influential behaviourist psychologist. He was not, however, a pioneer in the field, but developed the ideas of his predecessors, such as Ivan Pavlov and John B. Watson, by subjecting theories of behaviourism to rigorous experimental scrutiny in order to arrive at his controversial stance of "radical behaviourism".

Skinner proved to be an ideal advocate of behaviourism. Not only were his arguments based on the results of scrupulous scientific methodology (so evidence-based and provable), but his experiments tended to involve the use of novel contraptions that the general public found fascinating. Skinner was an inveterate "gadget man" and a provocative self-publicist. But behind the showman image was a serious scientist, whose work helped to finally sever psychology from its introspective philosophical roots and establish it as a scientific discipline in its own right.

Skinner had once contemplated a career as an author, but he had little time for the philosophical theorizing of many of the early psychologists. Works by Pavlov and Watson were his main influence; he saw psychology as following in the scientific tradition, and anything that could not be seen, measured, and repeated in a rigorously controlled experiment was of no interest to him.

Processes of the mind, therefore, were outside Skinner's interest and scope. In fact, he reached the conclusion that they must be utterly subjective, and did not exist at all separately from the body. In Skinner's opinion, the way to carry out psychological research was through observable behaviour, rather than through unobservable thoughts.

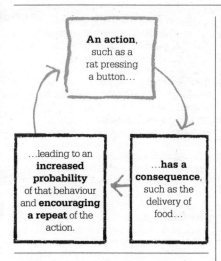

An action, such as a rat pressing a button…

…**has a consequence**, such as the delivery of food…

…leading to an **increased probability** of that behaviour and **encouraging a repeat** of the action.

To Skinner, it seemed that the consequences of an action were more important in shaping behaviour than any stimulus that had preceded or coincided with it. He concluded from his experiments that behaviour is primarily learned from the results of actions. As with so many great insights, this may appear to be self-evident, but it marked a major turning point in behaviourist psychology.

Skinner boxes

While working as a research fellow at Harvard, Skinner carried out a series of experiments on rats, using an invention that later became known as a "Skinner box". A rat was placed in one of these boxes, which had a special bar fitted on the inside. Every time the rat pressed this bar, it was presented with a food pellet. The rate of bar-pressing was automatically recorded. Initially, the rat might press the bar accidentally, or simply out of curiosity, and as a consequence receive some food. Over time, the rat learned that food appeared whenever the bar was pressed, and began to press it purposefully in order to be fed. Comparing results from rats given the "positive reinforcement" of food for their bar-pressing behaviour with those that were not, or were presented with food at different rates, it became »

Although a strict behaviourist from the outset of his career, Skinner differed from earlier behaviourists in his interpretation of conditioning – in particular, the principle of "classical conditioning" as described by Pavlov. While not disagreeing that a conditioned response could be elicited by repeated training, Skinner felt that this was something of a special case, involving the deliberate, artificial introduction of a conditioning stimulus.

B.F. Skinner

Burrhus Frederic Skinner was born in 1904 in Susquehanna, Pennsylvania. He studied English at Hamilton College, New York, intending to be a writer, but soon realized that the literary life was not for him. Influenced by the works of Ivan Pavlov and John B. Watson, he studied psychology at Harvard, gaining his doctorate in 1931 and becoming a junior fellow. He moved to the University of Minnesota in 1936, and from 1946 to 1947 ran the psychology department at Indiana University. In 1948, Skinner returned to Harvard, where he remained for the rest of his life. He was diagnosed with leukaemia in the 1980s, but continued to work, finishing an article from his final lecture on the day he died, 18 August 1990.

Key works

1938 *The Behavior of Organisms: An Experimental Analysis*
1948 *Walden Two*
1953 *Science and Human Behavior*
1957 *Verbal Behavior*
1971 *Beyond Freedom and Dignity*

Skinner boxes were one of many ingenious devices that the psychologist created, giving him total control over the environment of the animals whose behaviour he was observing.

clear that when food appeared as a consequence of the rat's actions, this influenced its future behaviour.

Skinner concluded that animals are conditioned by the responses they receive from their actions and environment. As the rats explored the world around them, some of their actions had a positive consequence (Skinner was careful to avoid the word "reward" with its connotations of being given for "good" behaviour), which in turn encouraged them to repeat that behaviour. In Skinner's terms, an "organism" operates on its environment, and encounters a stimulus (a food pellet), which reinforces its operant behaviour (pressing on the bar). In order to distinguish this from classical conditioning, he coined the term "operant conditioning"; the major distinction being that operant conditioning depends not on a preceding stimulus, but on what follows as a consequence of behaviour. It is also different in that it represents a two-way process, in which an action, or behaviour,

is operating on the environment just as much as the environment is shaping that behaviour.

In the course of his experiments, Skinner began to run short of food pellets, forcing him to reschedule the rate at which they were being given to the rats. Some rats now received a food pellet only after pressing the bar a number of times repeatedly, either at fixed intervals or randomly. The results of this variation reinforced Skinner's original findings, but they also led to a further discovery: that while a reinforcing stimulus led to a greater probability of a behaviour occurring, if the reinforcing stimulus was then stopped, there was a decrease in the likelihood of that behaviour occurring – the pattern of which was determined by the pattern of its withdrawal.

Skinner continued making his experiments ever more varied and sophisticated, including changes of schedule to establish whether the rats could distinguish and respond to differences in the rate of delivery of food pellets. As he suspected, the rats adapted very quickly to the new schedules.

Negative reinforcement
In later experiments, the floors of the Skinner boxes were each fitted with an electric grid, which would give the rats an unpleasant shock whenever they were activated. This allowed for the investigation of the effect of negative reinforcement on behaviour. Again, just as Skinner avoided the word "reward", he

Positive reinforcement can stimulate particular patterns of behaviour, as Skinner demonstrated by placing a rat in one of his specially designed boxes, fitted with a lever or bar. Pellets of food appeared every time the animal pressed the bar, encouraging it to perform this action again and again.

Winning at gambling often boosts the compulsion to try again, while losing lessens it, just as changes in the rate at which Skinner's rats were fed made them modify their behaviour.

was careful not to describe the electric shock as "punishment", a distinction that became increasingly important as he examined the implications of his research.

Negative reinforcement was not a new concept in psychology. As early as 1890, William James had written in *Principles of Psychology*: "Animals, for example, awaken in a child the opposite impulses of fearing and fondling. But if a child, in his first attempts to pat a dog, gets snapped at or bitten, so that the impulse of fear is strongly aroused, it may be that for years to come no dog will excite in him the impulse to fondle again". Skinner was to provide the experimental evidence for this idea.

Positive reinforcement

As expected, Skinner found that whenever a behaviour resulted in the negative consequence of an electric shock, there was a decrease in that behaviour. He went on to redesign the Skinner boxes used in the experiment, so that the rats inside were able to switch off the electrified grid by pressing a bar, which provided a form of positive reinforcement arising from the removal of a negative stimulus. The results that followed confirmed Skinner's theory – if a behaviour leads to the removal of a negative stimulus, that behaviour increases.

However, the results also revealed an interesting distinction between behaviour learned by positive reinforcement and behaviour elicited by negative stimuli. The rats responded better and more quickly to the positive stimuli (as well as the removal of negative stimuli), than when their behaviour resulted in a negative response. While still careful to avoid the notions of "reward" and "punishment", Skinner concluded that

behaviour was shaped much more efficiently by a programme of positive reinforcement. In fact, he came to believe that negative reinforcement could even be counter-productive, with the subject continuing to seek positive responses for a specific behaviour, despite this leading to a negative response in the majority of cases.

This has implications in various areas of human behaviour too; for example, in the use of disciplinary measures to teach children. If a boy is continually being punished for something he finds enjoyable, such as picking his nose, he is likely to avoid doing so when adults are around. The child may modify his behaviour, but only so far as it enables him to avoid punishment. Skinner himself believed that ultimately all forms of punishment were unsuitable for controlling children's behaviour.

Genetic predisposition

The "shaping" of behaviour by operant conditioning has striking parallels with Charles Darwin's theory of natural selection – in essence, that only organisms suited by their genetic make-up to a particular environment will survive to reproduce, ensuring the "success" of their species. The likelihood of a rat behaving in a way that will result in a reinforcing stimulus, triggering the process of operant conditioning, is dependent on the level of its curiosity and intelligence, both of which are determined by genetic make-up. It was this combination of predisposition and conditioning that led Skinner to conclude that "a person's »

Skinner's pigeon experiments proved that the positive reinforcement of being fed on the achievement of a task helped to speed up and reinforce the learning of new behaviour patterns.

behaviour is controlled by his genetic and environmental histories" – an idea that he explored further in his article *The Selection by Consequences,* written for the journal *Science* in 1981.

In 1936, Skinner took up a post at the University of Minnesota, where he continued to refine his experimental research in operant conditioning and to explore practical applications for his ideas, this time using pigeons instead of rats. With the pigeons, Skinner found that he was able to devise more subtle experiments. Using what he described as a "method of successive approximations", he could elicit and investigate more complex patterns of behaviour.

Skinner gave the pigeons positive reinforcement for any behaviour that was similar to that he was trying to elicit. For example, if he was trying to train a pigeon to fly in a circle clockwise, food would be given for any movement the pigeon made to the right, however small. Once this behaviour had been established, the food was only given for longer flights to the right, and the process was repeated until the pigeon had to fly a full circle in order to receive some food.

Teaching programme

Skinner's research led him to question teaching methods used in schools. In the 1950s, when his own children were involved in formal education, students were often set long tasks that involved several stages, and usually had to wait until the teacher had marked work carried out over the entire project before getting

Praise or encouragement given at frequent intervals during the progress of a piece of work, rather than one large reward at the end, has been shown to boost the rate at which children learn.

any response. This approach ran contrary to Skinner's findings about the process of learning and, in his opinion, was holding back progress. In response, Skinner developed a teaching programme that gave incremental feedback at every stage of a project – a process that was later incorporated into a number of educational systems. He also invented a "teaching machine" that gave a student encouraging feedback for correct answers given at every stage of a long series of test questions, rather than just at the end. Although it only achieved limited approval at the time, the principles embodied in Skinner's teaching machine resurfaced decades later in self-education computer programs.

It has to be said that many of Skinner's inventions were misunderstood at the time, and gained him a reputation as an eccentric. His "baby tender", for example, was designed as a cot alternative to keep his infant daughter in a controlled, warm, and draught-free environment. However, the public confused it with a Skinner box, and it was dubbed the "heir conditioner" by the press, amid rumours that Skinner was experimenting on his own children. Nevertheless, the baby tender attracted publicity, and Skinner was never shy of the limelight.

War effort

Yet another famous experiment called "Project Pigeon" was met with scepticism and some derision. This practical application of Skinner's work with pigeons was intended as a serious contribution to the war effort in 1944. Missile guidance systems were yet to be invented, so Skinner devised a nose cone that could be attached to a bomb and steered by three pigeons placed inside it. The birds had been trained, using operant conditioning, to peck at an image of the bomb's target, which was projected into the nose cone via a lens at the front. This pecking controlled the flight-path of the missile. At least the military took his idea seriously; the National Defense Research Committee helped fund the project, even though it was never used in combat. The suspicion was that Skinner, with his passion for gadgets, was more interested in the

Classical conditioning creates an automatic behavioural response to a neutral stimulus, such as salivating in expectation of food when a bell is rung

Operant conditioning creates a higher probability of repeated behaviour through positive reinforcement, such as releasing food by pulling a lever.

invention than in its application. When asked if he thought it right to involve animals in warfare, he replied that he thought it was wrong to involve humans.

In later life as an academic at Harvard, Skinner also expanded on the implications of his findings in numerous articles and books. *Walden Two* (1948) describes a utopian society based on behaviour learned with operant conditioning. The book's vision of social control achieved by positive reinforcement caused controversy, and despite its benign intent was criticized by many as totalitarian. This was not a surprising reaction, given the political climate in the aftermath of World War II.

Radical behaviourism

Skinner remained true to his behaviourist approach, coining the term "radical behaviourism" for the branch of psychology he espoused. Although he did not deny the existence of thought processes and mental states, he believed that psychology should be concerned solely with the study of physical responses to prevailing conditions or situations.

In his book *Beyond Freedom and Dignity*, Skinner took the concept of shaping behaviour even further, resurrecting the philosophical debate between free will and determinism. For the radical behaviourist Skinner, free will is an illusion; selection by consequences controls all of our behaviour, and hence our lives. Attempts to escape this notion are doomed to failure and chaos. As he put it: "When Milton's Satan falls from heaven, he ends in hell. And what does he say to reassure himself? 'Here, at least, we shall be free.' And that, I think, is the fate of the old-fashioned liberal. He's going to

be free, but he's going to find himself in hell." Views such as these gained him notoriety, and prompted some of his fiercest critics. In particular, the application of his behaviourist ideas to the learning of language in *Verbal Behavior* in 1957 received a scathing review from Noam Chomsky, which is often credited as launching the movement known as cognitive psychology.

Some criticism of Skinner's work, however, has been based on misunderstanding of the principles of operant conditioning. Radical behaviourism has often been linked erroneously to the European philosophical movement of logical positivism, which holds the view that statements or ideas are only meaningful if they can be verified by actual experience. But it has in fact much more in common with American pragmatism, which measures the importance or value of actions according to their consequences. It has also been misinterpreted as presenting all living beings as the passive subjects of conditioning, whereas to Skinner operant conditioning was a two-way process, in which an organism operates on its environment and that environment responds, with the consequence often shaping future behaviour.

In the 1960s, the focus in psychology swung away from the study of behaviour to the study of mental processes, and for a time Skinner's ideas were discredited, or at least ignored. A reappraisal of behaviourism soon followed, however, and his work found an appreciative audience in many areas of applied psychology, especially among educationalists and clinical psychologists – the approach of cognitive behavioural therapy owes much to his ideas. ■

PSYCHOT

THE UNCONSCIOUS DETERMINES BEHAVIOUR

At the turn of the 20th century, behaviourism was becoming the dominant approach to psychology in the USA; psychologists in Europe, however, were taking a different direction. This was largely due to the work of Sigmund Freud, whose theories focused on psychopathology and treatment rather than the study of mental processes and behaviour. Unlike behaviourism, his ideas were based on observation and case histories rather than experimental evidence.

Freud had worked with the French neurologist Jean Martin Charcot, and was much influenced by the latter's use of hypnosis for the treatment of hysteria. From his time with Charcot, Freud realized the importance of the unconscious, an area of non-conscious thought that he felt was key to our behaviour. Freud believed that accessing the unconscious by talking to his patients would bring painful, hidden memories into conscious awareness where the patient could make sense of them, and so gain relief from their symptoms.

New psychotherapies

Freud's ideas spread across Europe and the USA. He attracted a circle at his Vienna Psychoanalytic Society, which included Alfred Adler and Carl Jung. However, both these men came to disagree with elements of Freud's theories, going on to develop their own distinct psychodynamic approaches based on Freud's groundwork. Well-known therapists Melanie Klein and Karen Horney, and even Freud's daughter Anna, also broke away from Freud. Despite these differences of opinion, however, Freud's basic ideas were modified rather than rejected by the next generation of psychoanalysts, and subsequent theories place the emphasis on different areas. Erik Erikson, for example, took a more social and developmental approach, while Jung was to formulate the idea of a collective unconscious.

For the first half of the 20th century, psychoanalysis in its various forms remained the main alternative to behaviourism, and it faced no serious challenges until after World War II. In the 1950s, Freudian psychotherapy was still practised by therapists, especially in France by Jacques Lacan and his followers, but new therapies appeared that sought to bring about genuine change in patients' lives. The somewhat eclectic Gestalt therapy was developed by Fritz and Laura

HERAPY

Perls and Paul Goodman, while existential philosophy inspired psychologists such as Viktor Frankl and Erich Fromm, who gave therapy a more socio-political agenda.

Most importantly, a group of psychologists keen to explore a more humanistic approach held a series of meetings in the USA in the late 1950s, setting out a framework for an association known as "the third force", which was dedicated to exploring themes such as self-actualization, creativity, and personal freedom. Its founders – including Abraham Maslow, Carl Rogers, and Rollo May – stressed the importance of mental health as much as the treatment of mental disorders.

Perhaps the most significant threat to psychoanalysis at this time came from cognitive psychology, which criticized psychoanalysis for its lack of objective evidence – either for its theories or its efficacy as treatment. In contrast, cognitive psychology provided scientifically proven theories and, later, clinically effective therapeutic practices.

Cognitive psychotherapy
Cognitive psychologists dismissed psychoanalysis as unscientific and its theories as unprovable. One of the key concepts of Freudian analysis – repressed memory – was questioned by Paul Watzlawick, and the validity of all forms of memory was shown to be unstable by Elizabeth Loftus. Cognitive psychology instead offered evidence-based psychotherapies such as Albert Ellis's Rational Emotive Behaviour Therapy (REBT) and Aaron Beck's cognitive therapy. Freud's emphasis on childhood development and personal history inspired much developmental and social psychology, and in the late 20th century psychotherapists such as Guy Corneau, Virginia Satir, and Donald Winnicott turned their attention to the family environment; while others, including Timothy Leary and Dorothy Rowe, focused on social pressures.

Though Freud's original ideas have often been questioned over the years, the evolution from Freudian psychoanalysis to cognitive therapy and humanistic psychotherapy has led to huge improvements in mental health treatments, and has provided a model for the unconscious, our drives, and behaviour. ∎

THE UNCONSCIOUS IS THE TRUE PSYCHICAL REALITY
SIGMUND FREUD (1856–1939)

IN CONTEXT

APPROACH
Psychoanalysis

BEFORE
2500–600 BCE The Hindu Vedas describe consciousness as "an abstract, silent, completely unified field of consciousness".

1567 Swiss physician Paracelsus provides the first medical description of the unconscious.

1880s French neurologist Jean-Martin Charcot uses hypnotism to treat hysteria and other abnormal mental conditions.

AFTER
1913 John B. Watson criticizes Freud's ideas of the unconscious as unscientific and not provable.

1944 Carl Jung claims that the presence of universal archetypes proves the existence of the unconscious.

The unconscious is one of the most intriguing concepts in psychology. It seems to contain all of our experience of reality, although it appears to be beyond our awareness or control. It is the place where we retain all our memories, thoughts, and feelings. The notion fascinated Austrian neurologist and psychiatrist Sigmund Freud, who wanted to find out if it was possible to explain things that seemed to lie beyond the confines of psychology at the time. Those who had begun to examine the unconscious feared that it might be filled with psychic activity that was too powerful, too frightening, or too incomprehensible for our conscious mind to be able to incorporate. Freud's work on the subject was pioneering. He described the structure of the mind as formed of the conscious, the unconscious, and the preconscious, and he popularized the idea of the unconscious, introducing the notion that it is the part of the mind that defines and explains the workings behind our ability to think and experience.

Hypnosis and hysteria
Freud's introduction to the world of the unconscious came in 1885 when he came across the work of the French neurologist Jean-Martin Charcot, who seemed to be successfully treating patients for symptoms of mental illness using hypnosis. Charcot's view was that hysteria was a neurological disorder caused by abnormalities of the nervous system, and this idea provided important new possibilities for treatments. Freud returned to Vienna, eager to use this new knowledge, but struggled to find a workable technique.

He then encountered Joseph Breuer, a well-respected physician, who had found that he could greatly reduce the severity of one of his patient's symptoms of mental illness simply by asking her to describe her fantasies and hallucinations. Breuer began

Anna O, actually Bertha Pappenheim, was diagnosed with paralysis and hysteria. She was treated successfully, with what she described as a "talking cure", by physician Josef Breuer.

using hypnosis to facilitate her access to memories of a traumatic event, and after twice-weekly hypnosis sessions all her symptoms had been alleviated. Breuer concluded that her symptoms had been the result of disturbing memories buried in her unconscious mind, and that voicing the thoughts brought them to consciousness, allowing the symptoms to disappear. This is the case of Anna O, and is the first instance of intensive psychotherapy as a treatment for mental illness.

Breuer became Freud's friend and colleague, and together the two developed and popularized a method of psychological treatment based on the idea that many forms of mental illness (irrational fears, anxiety, hysteria, imagined paralyses and pains, and certain types of paranoia) were the results of traumatic experiences that had occurred in the patient's past and were now hidden away from consciousness. Through Freud and Breuer's technique, outlined in the jointly published *Studies in Hysteria* (1895), they claimed to have found a way to release the repressed memory from the unconscious, allowing the patient to consciously recall the memory and confront the experience, both emotionally and intellectually. The process set free the trapped emotion, and the symptoms disappeared. Breuer disagreed with what he felt was Freud's eventual overemphasis on the sexual origins and content of neuroses (problems caused by psychological conflicts), and the two parted; Freud to continue developing the ideas and techniques of psychoanalysis.

Our everyday mind

It is easy to take for granted the reality of the conscious, and naively believe that what we think, feel, remember, and experience make up the entirety of the human mind. But Freud says that the active state of consciousness – that is, the operational mind of which we are directly aware in our everyday experience – is just a fraction of the total psychological forces at work in our psychical reality. The conscious exists at the superficial level, to which we have easy and immediate access. Beneath the conscious lies the powerful dimensions of the unconscious, the warehouse from which our active cognitive state and behaviour are dictated. The »

When ideas, memories, or impulses are **too overwhelming or inappropriate** for the conscious mind to withstand, they are **repressed**…

…and **stored in the unconscious** alongside our instinctual drives, where they are not accessible by immediate consciousness.

The unconscious silently **directs the thoughts and behaviour** of the individual.

The difference between our unconscious and conscious thoughts creates **psychic tension**…

…that can only be released when repressed memories are **allowed into consciousness** through psychoanalysis.

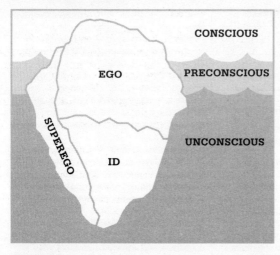

CONSCIOUS

EGO

PRECONSCIOUS

SUPEREGO

UNCONSCIOUS

ID

Our psyche, according to Freud, resembles an iceberg, with the area of primitive drives, the id, lying hidden in the unconscious. The ego deals with conscious thoughts and regulates both the id and the superego – our critical, judging voice.

conscious is effectively the puppet in the hands of the unconscious. The conscious mind is merely the surface of a complex psychic realm.

Since the unconscious is all-encompassing, Freud says, it contains within it the smaller spheres of the conscious and an area called the "preconscious". Everything that is conscious – that we actively know – has at one time been unconscious before rising to consciousness. However, not everything becomes consciously known; much of what is unconscious remains there. Memories that are not in our everyday working memory, but which have not been repressed, reside in a part of the conscious mind that Freud called the preconscious. We are able to bring these memories into conscious awareness at any time.

The unconscious acts as a receptacle for ideas or memories that are too powerful, too painful, or otherwise too much for the conscious mind to process. Freud believed that when certain ideas or memories (and their associated emotions) threaten to overwhelm the psyche, they are split apart from a memory that can be accessed

by the conscious mind, and stored in the unconscious instead.

Dynamic thought

Freud was also influenced by the physiologist Ernst Brücke, who was one of the founders of the 19th-century's "new physiology", which looked for mechanistic explanations for all organic phenomena. Brücke claimed that like every other living organism, the human being is essentially an energy system, and so must abide by the Principle of the Conservation of Energy. This law states that the total amount of energy in a system stays constant over time; it cannot be destroyed, only moved or transformed. Freud applied this thinking to mental processes, resulting in the idea of "psychic energy". This energy, he said, can undergo modification, transmission, and conversion, but cannot be destroyed. So if we have a thought that the conscious mind finds unacceptable, the mind redirects it away from conscious thought into the unconscious, in a process Freud called "repression". We may repress the memory of a childhood trauma (such as abuse or witnessing an accident), a desire we have judged as unacceptable (perhaps for your best friend's partner), or ideas that otherwise threaten our wellbeing or way of life.

Motivating drives

The unconscious is also the place where our instinctual biological drives reside. The drives govern our behaviour, directing us towards choices that promise to satisfy our basic needs. The drives ensure our survival: the need for food and water; the desire for sex to ensure the continuation of our species; and the necessity to find warmth, shelter, and companionship. But Freud claims the unconscious also holds a contrasting drive, the death drive, which is present from birth. This drive is self-destructive and impels us forward, though as we do so we are moving closer to our death.

In his later works, Freud moved away from the idea that the mind was structured by the conscious, unconscious, and preconscious to propose a new controlling structure: the id, ego, and superego. The id (formed of primitive impulses) obeys the Pleasure Principle, which says that every wishful impulse must be immediately gratified: it wants everything now. However, another part of the mental structure, the ego, recognizes the Reality Principle, which says we can't have everything we desire, but must take account of the world we live in. The ego negotiates with the id, trying to find reasonable ways to help it get what it wants, without resulting in damage or other terrible consequences. The ego itself is controlled by the superego – the internalized voice of parents and society's moral codes. The superego is a judging force, and the source of our conscience, guilt, and shame.

In fact, Freud proposes, the unconscious holds a vast amount of conflicting forces. In addition to the drives of the life and death forces, it encompasses the intensity of repressed memories and emotions, as well as the contradictions inherent in our views of conscious reality alongside our repressed reality. According to Freud, the conflict that arises from these contrasting forces is the psychological conflict that underlies human suffering. Is it any wonder that humans exist in states of anxiety, depression, neurosis, and other forms of discontent?

Psychoanalytical treatment
Since the unconscious remains inaccessible, the only way the conflicts can be recognized is through the symptoms that are present in

> ❝ A man should not strive to eliminate his complexes, but to get into accord with them; they are legitimately what directs his conduct in the world.
> **Sigmund Freud** ❞

the conscious. Emotional suffering, Freud claims, is the result of unconscious conflict. We cannot continually fight against ourselves, against the uprising of repressed material, and against the force of death, without emotional turmoil.

Freud's unique approach to the treatment of psychological ailments involved working with the conflicts that existed in the unconscious. He sought to free the patient from repressed memories and so alleviate their mental pain. His approach to treatment is called psychoanalytic psychotherapy, or psychoanalysis. This process is not easy or quick. Psychoanalysis is only performed by a therapist trained in Freud's specific approach, and it is his therapy that encourages a patient to lie on a couch and talk. From Freud's first treatments, psychoanalysis has been practised in sessions that can sometimes last for hours, take place several times per week, and continue for many years.

While unconscious thoughts cannot be retrieved through normal introspection, the unconscious can communicate with the conscious in some ways. It quietly communicates via our preferences, the frames of reference in which we tend to understand things, and the symbols that we are drawn to or create. During analysis, the analyst acts as a mediator, trying to allow unspoken thoughts or »

Freud's patients would recline on this couch in his treatment room while they talked. Freud would sit out of sight while he listened for clues to the source of the patient's internal conflicts.

unbearable feelings to come to light. Messages arising from a conflict between the conscious and the unconscious are likely to be disguised, or encoded, and it is the psychoanalyst's job to interpret the messages using the tools of psychoanalysis.

There are several techniques that allow the unconscious to emerge. One of the first to be discussed by Freud at length was dream analysis; he famously studied his own dreams in his book, *The Interpretation of Dreams*. He claimed that every dream enacts a wish fulfilment, and the more unpalatable the wish is to our conscious mind, the more hidden or distorted the desire becomes in our dreams. So the unconscious, he says, sends messages to our conscious mind in code. For instance, Freud discusses dreams where the dreamer is naked – the primary source for these dreams in most people is memories from early childhood, when nakedness was not frowned upon and there was no sense of shame. In dreams where the dreamer feels embarrassment, the other people in the dream generally seem oblivious, lending support to a wish-

Salvador Dali's *The Persistence of Memory* (1931) is a surrealist vision of time passing, leading to decay and death. Its fantastical quality suggests the Freudian process of dream analysis.

> ❝ The interpretation of dreams is the royal road to knowledge of the unconscious activities of the mind.
> **Sigmund Freud** ❞

fulfilment interpretation where the dreamer wants to leave behind shame and restriction. Even buildings and structures have coded meanings; stairwells, mine shafts, locked doors, or a small building in a narrow recess all represent repressed sexual feelings, according to Freud.

Accessing the unconscious

Other well-known ways in which the unconscious reveals itself are through Freudian slips and the process of free association. A Freudian slip is a verbal error, or "slip of the tongue", and it is said to reveal a repressed belief, thought, or emotion. It is an involuntary substitution of one word for another that sounds similar but inadvertently reveals something the person really feels. For instance, a man might thank a woman he finds desirable for making "the *breast* dinner ever", the slip revealing his true thoughts. Freud used the free-association technique (developed by Carl Jung), whereby patients heard a word and were then invited to say the first word that came into their mind. He believed that this process allowed the unconscious to break through because our mind uses automatic associations, so "hidden" thoughts are voiced before the conscious mind has a chance to interrupt.

In order to help an individual emerge from a repressed state and begin to consciously deal with the real issues that are affecting him or her, Freud believed that it is necessary to access repressed feelings. For example, if a man finds it difficult to confront others, he will choose to repress his feelings rather than deal with the confrontation. Over time, however, these repressed emotions build up and reveal themselves in other ways. Anger, anxiety, depression, drug and alcohol abuse, or eating disorders may all be the result of struggling to fend off feelings that have been repressed instead of being addressed. Unprocessed emotions, Freud asserts, are constantly threatening to break through, generating an increasingly uncomfortable tension and inciting more and more extreme measures to keep them down.

Analysis allows trapped memories and feelings to emerge, and the patient is often surprised to feel the emotion that has been buried. It is not uncommon for patients to find themselves moved to tears by an issue from many years ago that they felt they had long since "got over". This response demonstrates that the event and the emotion are still alive – still holding emotional energy – and have been repressed rather than dealt with. In Freudian terms, "catharsis" describes the act of releasing and feeling the deep emotions associated with repressed memories. If the significant event – such as the death of a parent – was not fully experienced at the time because it was too overwhelming, the difficulty and the energy remain, to be released at the moment of catharsis.

School of psychoanalysis

Freud founded the prominent Psychoanalytic Society in Vienna, from which he exerted his powerful influence on the mental health community of the time, training others in his methods and acting as the authority on what was acceptable practice. Over time, his students and other professionals modified his ideas, eventually splitting the Society into three: the Freudians (who remained true to Freud's original thoughts), the Kleinians (who followed the ideas of Melanie Klein), and the Neo-Freudians (a later group who incorporated Freud's ideas into their broader practice). Modern psychoanalysis encompasses at least 22 different schools of thought, though Freud's ideas continue to remain influential for all contemporary practitioners. ■

Sigmund Freud

Born Sigismund Schlomo Freud in Freiberg, Moravia, Freud was openly his mother's favourite child; she called him "Golden Siggie". When Freud was four years old, the family moved to Vienna and Sigismund became Sigmund. Sigmund completed a medical degree and in 1886 he opened a medical practice specializing in neurology, and married Martha Bernays. Eventually, he developed the "talking cure" that was to become an entirely new psychological approach: psychoanalysis.

In 1908, Freud established the Psychoanalytic Society, which ensured the future of his school of thought. During World War II, the Nazis publicly burned his work, and Freud moved to London. He died by assisted suicide, after enduring mouth cancer.

Key works

1900 *The Interpretation of Dreams*
1904 *The Psychopathology of Everyday Life*
1905 *Three Essays on the Theory of Sexuality*
1930 *Civilization and Its Discontents*

THE NEUROTIC CARRIES A FEELING OF INFERIORITY WITH HIM CONSTANTLY
ALFRED ADLER (1870–1937)

IN CONTEXT

APPROACH
Individual psychology

BEFORE
1896 William James says that self-esteem is about a ratio of "goals satisfied" to "goals unmet" and can be raised by lowering expectations as well as through achievements.

1902 Charles Horton Cooley describes the "looking glass self"; the way we view ourselves is based on how we imagine other people view us.

AFTER
1943 Abraham Maslow says that to feel both necessary and good about ourselves we need achievements as well as respect from others.

1960s British psychologist Michael Argyle states that comparison shapes self-esteem; we feel better when we feel more successful than others, and worse when we feel less successful than others.

F reudian thinking dominated psychotherapy in the late 19th century, but Freud's approach was limited to addressing unconscious drives and the legacy of an individual's past. Alfred Adler was the first psychoanalyst to expand psychological theory beyond the Freudian viewpoint, suggesting that a person's psychology was also influenced by present and conscious forces, and that the influence of the social realm and environment was equally vital. Adler founded his own approach, individual psychology, based on these ideas.

Adler's particular interest in inferiority and the positive and negative effects of self-esteem began early in his career, when he worked with patients who had physical disabilities. Looking at the effects that disability had on achievement and sense of self, he found huge differences between his patients. Some people with disabilities were able to reach high levels of athletic success, and Adler noted that in these personalities, the disability served as a strong motivational force. At the other extreme, he witnessed patients who felt defeated by their disability and who made little effort to improve their situation. Adler realized that the differences came down to how these individuals viewed themselves: in other words, their self-esteem.

The inferiority complex
According to Adler, feeling inferior is a universal human experience that is rooted in childhood. Children naturally feel inferior because they are constantly surrounded by stronger, more powerful people with greater abilities. A child generally seeks to emulate and achieve the abilities of its elders, motivated by the surrounding forces that propel him towards his own development and accomplishments.

Children and adults with a healthy and balanced personality gain confidence each

A paralympic athlete may be driven by a powerful desire to overcome her disabilities and reach greater levels of physical achievement. Adler described this trait as "compensation".

Alfred Adler

After coming close to death from pneumonia at the age of five, Alfred Adler expressed a wish to become a physician. Growing up in Vienna, he went on to study medicine, branching into ophthalmology before finally settling with psychology. In 1897, he married Raissa Epstein, a Russian intellectual and social activist, and they had four children.

Adler was one of the original members of the Freudian-based Vienna Psychoanalytical Society and the first to depart from it, asserting that individuals are affected by social factors as well as the unconscious drives that Freud identified. After this split in 1911, Adler flourished professionally, establishing his own school of psychotherapy and developing many of psychology's prominent concepts. He left Austria in 1932 for the USA. He died of a heart attack while lecturing at Aberdeen University, Scotland.

Key works

1912 *The Neurotic Character*
1927 *The Practice and Theory of Individual Psychology*
1927 *Understanding Human Nature*

time they realize that they are capable of meeting external goals. Feelings of inferiority dissipate until the next challenge presents itself and is overcome; this process of psychic growth is continual. However, an individual with a physical inferiority may develop more generalized feelings of inferiority – leading to an unbalanced personality and what Adler termed an "inferiority complex", where the feelings of inferiority are never relieved.

Adler also recognized the equally unbalanced "superiority complex", manifested in a constant need to strive towards goals. When attained, these goals do not instil confidence in the individual, but merely prompt him to continually seek further external recognition and achievements. ■

Every child feels **inferior** because stronger, smarter people surround them.

Inferiority **motivates** them to try to do and achieve things.

In a **balanced psyche**, success relieves feelings of inferiority…

In an **imbalanced psyche**, success doesn't relieve feelings of inferiority…

… and **confidence** develops.

…and an **inferiority complex** develops.

THE COLLECTIVE UNCONSCIOUS IS MADE UP OF ARCHETYPES
CARL JUNG (1875–1961)

IN CONTEXT

APPROACH
Psychoanalysis

BEFORE
1899 Sigmund Freud explores the nature of the unconscious and dream symbolism in *The Interpretation of Dreams*.

1903 Pierre Janet suggests that traumatic incidents generate emotionally charged beliefs, which influence an individual's emotions and behaviours for many years.

AFTER
1949 Jungian scholar Joseph Campbell publishes *Hero With a Thousand Faces*, detailing archetypal themes in literature from many different cultures throughout history.

1969 British psychologist John Bowlby states that human instinct is expressed as patterned action and thought in social exchanges.

Sigmund Freud introduced the idea that rather than being guided by forces outside ourselves, such as God or fate, we are actually motivated and controlled by the inner workings of our own minds, specifically, the unconscious. He claimed that our experiences are affected by primal drives contained in the unconscious. His protégé, the Swiss psychiatrist Carl Jung, took this idea further, delving into the elements that make up the unconscious and its workings.

Jung was fascinated by the way that societies around the world share certain striking similarities, despite being culturally very different. They share an uncanny commonality in their myths and symbols, and have done so for thousands of years. He thought that this must be due to something larger than the individual experience of man; the symbols, he decided, must exist as part of the human psyche.

It seemed to Jung that the existence of these shared myths proved that part of the human psyche contains ideas that are held in a timeless structure, which acts as a form of "collective memory". Jung introduced the notion that one distinct and separate part of the unconscious exists within each of us, which is not based on any of our own individual experiences – this is the "collective unconscious".

The commonly found myths and symbols are, for Jung, part of this universally shared collective unconscious. He believed that the symbols exist as part of hereditary memories that are passed on from generation to generation, changing only slightly in their attributes across different cultures and time periods. These inherited memories emerge within the psyche in the language of symbols, which Jung calls "archetypes".

Ancient memories

Jung believes that the archetypes are layers of inherited memory, and they constitute the entirety of the human experience. The Latin

Myths and symbols are strikingly similar in cultures around the world and across the centuries.

⬇

Therefore, they must be a result of the **knowledge and experiences we share** as a species.

⬇

The memory of this shared experience is held…

⬇

…in the **collective unconscious**, which is part of each and every person.

…in the form of **archetypes** – symbols that act as organizing forms for behavioural patterns.

⬇

Each of us is born with the innate tendency to use these archetypes to **understand the world**.

word *archetypum* translates as "first-moulded", and Jung believed that archetypes are memories from the experiences of our first ancestors. They act as templates within the psyche that we use unconsciously to organize and understand our own experience. We may fill out the gaps with details from our individual lives, but it is this pre-existing substructure in the unconscious that is the framework that allows us to make sense of our experience.

Archetypes can be thought of as inherited emotional or behavioural patterns. They allow us to recognize a particular set of behaviours or emotional expressions as a unified pattern that has meaning. It seems

that we do this instinctively, but Jung says that what seems to be instinct is actually the unconscious use of archetypes.

Jung suggests that the psyche is composed of three components: the ego, the personal unconscious, and the collective unconscious. The ego, he says, represents the conscious mind or self, while the personal unconscious contains the individual's own memories, including those that have been suppressed. The collective unconscious is the part of the psyche that houses the archetypes.

The archetypes
There are many archetypes, and though they can blend and mould into each other in different cultures, each of us contains within us the model of each archetype. Since we use these symbolic forms to make sense of the world and our experiences, they appear in all human forms of expression, such as art, literature, and drama.

The nature of an archetype is such that we recognize it instantly and are able to attach to it a specific, emotional meaning. Archetypes can be associated with many kinds of behavioural and emotional patterns, but there are certain prominent ones that are highly recognizable, such as The Wise Old Man, The Goddess, The Madonna, the Great Mother, and The Hero.

The Persona is one of the most important archetypes described by Jung. He recognized early in his own life that he had a tendency to share only a certain part of his personality with the outside world. He also recognized this trait in other people, and »

Eve is one representation of the Anima, the female part of a man's unconscious. Jung says she is "full of snares and traps, in order that man should fall… and life should be lived".

noted that human beings divide their personalities into components, selectively sharing only certain components of their selves according to the environment and situation. The self that we present to the world – our public image – is an archetype, which Jung calls the "Persona".

Jung believes that the self has both masculine and feminine parts, and is moulded into becoming fully male or female by society as much as biology. When we become wholly male or female we turn our backs on half of our potential, though we can still access this part of the self through an archetype. The Animus exists as the masculine component of the female personality, and the Anima as the feminine attributes of the male psyche. This is the "other half", the half that was taken from us as we grew into a girl or boy. These archetypes help us to understand the nature of the opposite sex, and because they contain "deposits of all the impressions ever made" by a man or woman, so they necessarily reflect the traditional ideas of masculine and feminine.

The Animus is represented in our culture as the "real man"; he is the muscle man, the commander of soldiers, the cool logician, and the romantic seducer. The Anima appears as a wood nymph, a virgin, a seductress. She can be close to nature, intuitive, and spontaneous. She appears in paintings and stories as Eve, or Helen of Troy, or a personality such as Marilyn Monroe, bewitching men or sucking the life from them. As these archetypes exist

in our unconscious, they can affect our moods and reactions, and can manifest themselves as prophetic statements (Anima) or unbending rationality (Animus).

Jung defines one archetype as representing the part of ourselves we do not want the world to see. He calls it the Shadow, and it is the opposite of the Persona, representing all our secret or repressed thoughts and the shameful aspects of our character. It appears in the Bible as the devil, and in literature as Dr Jekyll's Mr Hyde. The Shadow is the "bad" side of ourselves that we project onto others, and yet it is not entirely negative; it may represent aspects that we choose to suppress only because they are unacceptable in a particular situation.

Of all the archetypes, the most important is the True Self. This is a central, organizing archetype that attempts to harmonize all other aspects into a unified, whole self. According to Jung, the real goal of human existence is to achieve an advanced, enlightened psychological state of being that he refers to as "self-realization", and the route to this lies in the archetype of the True Self. When fully realized, this archetype is the source of wisdom and truth, and is able to connect the self to the spiritual. Jung stressed that self-realization does not happen automatically, it must be consciously sought.

Archetypes in dreams

The archetypes are of significant importance in the interpretation of dreams. Jung believed that dreams are a dialogue between the conscious self and the eternal (the ego and the collective unconscious), and that the archetypes operate as symbols within the dream, facilitating the dialogue.

The archetypes have specific meanings in the context of dreams. For instance, the archetype of The Wise Old Man or Woman may be represented in a dream by a spiritual leader, parent, teacher, or

Dr Jekyll transforms into the evil Mr Hyde in a story by Robert Louis Stevenson that explores the idea of the "darker self", through a character that embodies Jung's Shadow archetype.

The tale of Snow White can be found all over the world with slight variations. Jung attributed the universal popularity of fairy tales and myths to their use of archetypal characters.

Carl Jung

Carl Gustav Jung was born in a small Swiss village to an educated family with a fair share of eccentrics. He was close to his mother, though she suffered from bouts of depression. A talented linguist, Jung mastered many European languages as well as several ancient ones, including Sanskrit. he married Emma Rauschenbach in 1903 and they had five children.

Jung trained in psychiatry, but after meeting Sigmund Freud in 1907, he became a psychoanalyst and Freud's heir apparent. However, the pair grew estranged over theoretical differences and never met again. In the years following World War I, Jung travelled widely through Africa, America, and India, studying native people and taking part in anthropological and archaeological expeditions. He became a professor at the University of Zurich in 1935, but gave up teaching to concentrate on research.

doctor – it indicates those who offer guidance, direction, and wisdom. The Great Mother, an archetype who might appear as the dreamer's own mother or grandmother, represents the nurturer. She provides reassurance, comfort, and validation. The Divine Child, the archetype that represents your True Self in its purest form, symbolizing innocence or vulnerability, would appear as a baby or child in dreams, suggesting openness or potential. And lest the ego grow too large, it is kept in check by the appearance of the Trickster, a playful archetype that exposes the dreamer's vulnerabilities and plays jokes, preventing the individual from taking himself and his desires too seriously. The Trickster also appears as the Norse half-god Loki, the Greek god Pan, the African spider god Anansi, or simply a magician or clown.

Using the archetypes

The archetypes exist in our minds before conscious thought, and can therefore have an immensely powerful impact on our perception of experience. Whatever we may consciously think is happening, what we choose to perceive – and therefore experience – is governed by these preformed ideas within the unconscious. In this way, the collective unconscious and its contents affect the conscious state. According to Jung, much of what we generally attribute to deliberate, reasoned, conscious thinking is actually already being guided by unconscious activity, especially the organizing forms of the archetypes.

In addition to his ideas of the collective unconscious and the archetypes, Jung was the first to explore the practice of word association, and he also introduced the concepts of the extravert and introvert personality types. These ultimately inspired widely used personality tests such as the Myers–Briggs Type Indicator (MBTI). Jung's work was influential in the fields of psychology, anthropology, and spirituality, and his archetypes are so widespread that they can easily be identified in film, literature, and other cultural forms that attempt to portray universal characters. ■

Key works

1912 *Symbols of Transformation*
1934 *The Archetypes and the Collective Unconscious*
1945 *On the Nature of Dreams*

THE STRUGGLE BETWEEN THE LIFE AND DEATH INSTINCTS PERSISTS THROUGHOUT LIFE
MELANIE KLEIN (1882–1960)

IN CONTEXT

APPROACH
Psychoanalysis

BEFORE
1818 German philosopher Arthur Schopenhauer states that existence is driven by the will to live, which is constantly being opposed by an equally forceful death drive.

1910 Psychoanalyst Wilhelm Stekel suggests that social suppression of the sexual instinct is paralleled by the growth of a death instinct.

1932 Sigmund Freud claims that the most basic drive for satisfaction is in fact a striving towards death.

AFTER
2002 American psychologist Julie K. Norem introduces the idea of "defensive pessimism", suggesting that being pessimistic may in fact better prepare people to cope with the demands and stresses of modern life.

Drama's power lies in its reflection of real emotions and feelings. Great plays, such as Shakespeare's *Romeo and Juliet,* show not only love's life-affirming force, but also its deadly, toxic aspects.

The theme of opposing forces has always intrigued writers, philosophers, and scientists. Literature, religion, and art are filled with tales of good and evil, of friend and foe. Newtonian physics states that stability or balance is achieved through one force being countered by an equal and opposite force. Such opposing forces appear to be an essential part of existence, and perhaps the most powerful of them are the instinctive drives we have for life and death.

Sigmund Freud said that to avoid being destroyed by our own death instinct, we employ our narcissistic or self-regarding life instinct (libido) to force the death instinct outwards, directing it against other objects. Melanie Klein expanded on this, saying that even as we redirect the death force outwards, we still sense the danger of being destroyed by "this instinct of aggression"; we acknowledge the huge task of "mobilizing the libido" against it. Living with these opposing forces is an inherent psychological conflict that is central to human experience. Klein claimed that our tendencies towards growth and creation – from procreation to creativity – are forced to run constantly against an equally powerful and destructive force, and that this ongoing psychic tension underlies all suffering.

Klein also stated that this psychic tension explains our innate tendency towards aggression and violence. It creates a related struggle between love and hate, present

The human unconscious contains…

↓ ↓

…the **life instinct**, which drives us towards growth and creation.

…the **death instinct**, which drives us towards destruction and disintegration.

↓ ↓

Life itself is the striving against a drive towards death.

↓

This creates a constant **psychic tension** in which…

↓

…the struggle between the life and death instincts persists throughout life.

Melanie Klein

One of four children, Melanie Klein was born in Austria. Her parents, who later divorced, were cold and unaffectionate. At 17, she became engaged to Arthur Klein, an industrial chemist, casting aside her plans to study medicine.

Klein decided to become a psychoanalyst after reading a book by Sigmund Freud in 1910. She suffered from depression herself, and was haunted by death: her adored elder sister died when Klein was four; her older brother died in a suspected suicide; and her son was killed in a climbing accident in 1933. Although Klein did not have any formal qualifications, she was a major influence in the field of psychoanalysis, and is particularly revered for her work with children, and for her use of play as a form of therapy.

Key works

1932 *The Psychoanalysis of Children*
1935 *A Contribution to The Psychogenesis of Manic Depressive States*
1955 *Envy and Gratitude*
1961 *Narrative of a Child Analysis*

even in a newborn baby. This constant battle between our life and death instincts – between pleasure and pain, renewal and destruction – results in confusion within our psyches. Anger or "bad" feelings may then become directed towards every situation, whether they are good or bad.

Constant conflict

Klein believed that we never shed these primitive impulses. We maintain them throughout life, never reaching a safe, mature state, but living with an unconscious that simmers with "primitive phantasies" of violence. Given the permeating influence of such a psychic conflict, Klein thought that traditional notions of happiness are impossible to attain, and that living is about finding a way to tolerate the conflict; it is not about achieving nirvana.

As this state of tolerance is the best that we can hope for, Klein found it unsurprising that life falls short of what people desire or believe they deserve, resulting in depression and disappointment. Human experience, to Klein, is inevitably filled with anxiety, pain, loss, and destruction. People must, therefore, learn to work within the extremes of life and death. ■

TRUTH CAN BE TOLERATED ONLY IF YOU DISCOVER IT YOURSELF

FRITZ PERLS (1893–1970)

IN CONTEXT

APPROACH
Gestalt therapy

BEFORE
1920s Carl Jung says that people need to connect with their inner selves.

1943 Max Wertheimer explains the Gestalt idea of "productive thinking", which is distinctive for using personal insight.

1950 In *Neurosis and Human Growth,* Karen Horney identifies the need to reject the "shoulds" imposed by others.

AFTER
1961 Carl Rogers says that it is the client, not the therapist, who knows what form and direction therapy should take.

1973 American self-help author Richard Bandler, one of the founders of Neurolinguistic Programming (NLP), uses many of the Gestalt therapy techniques in his new therapy.

I n the 18th century, the German philosopher Immanuel Kant revolutionized our thinking about the world by pointing out that we can never really know what is "out there" beyond ourselves, because our knowledge is limited to the constraints of our minds and senses. We don't know how things are "in themselves", but only as we experience them. This view forms the basis of Gestalt therapy, which says that it is vitally important to remember that the complexity of the human experience – with its tragedies and traumas, inspirations and passions, and its nearly infinite range of possibilities – is coded by the individual "lenses" through which we view it. We do not automatically absorb all the sounds, feelings, and pictures of the world; we scan and select just a few.

Fritz Perls, one of the founders of Gestalt therapy, pointed out that this means our personal sense of reality is created through our perception; through the ways in which we view our experiences, not the events themselves. However, it is easy to forget this, or even fail to recognize it. He says we tend to mistake our viewpoint of the world for the absolute, objective truth, rather than acknowledging the role of perception and its influence in creating our perspective, together with all the ideas, actions, and beliefs that stem from it. For Perls, the only truth one can ever have is one's own personal truth.

Accepting responsibility

Perls developed his theories in the 1940s, when the dominant psychoanalytical view was that the human mind could be reduced to a series of biological drives seeking fulfilment. This approach was far too rigid, structured, simplified, and generalized for Perls; it did not allow for individual experience, which Perls held paramount. Nor did its analysts enable their patients to recognize and take responsibility for the creation of their

People believe that their viewpoint of the world is the **objective truth**.

But human experience is coloured by the **personal "lenses"** through which we view it.

As it is our perception that **shapes our experience**...

...it is possible to **change our inner realities**, and ultimately our external realities.

...we must **discard the "given" values** of society and family, and discover our own, true values.

We become aware that we are **building our own world**, or "truth".

Truth can only be tolerated if you discover it yourself.

experience. The psychoanalytical model operates on the understanding that patients are at the mercy of their unconscious conflicts until an analyst enters to save them from their unconscious drives. Perls, on the other hand, feels it is essential for people to understand the power of their own roles in creation. He wants to make us aware that we can change our realities, and in fact are responsible for doing so. No one else can do it for us. Once we realize that perception is the backbone of reality, each of us is forced to take responsibility for the life we create and the way we choose to view the world.

Acknowledging power

Gestalt theory uses the tenets of individual experience, perception, and responsibility – both for one's thoughts and feelings – to encourage personal growth by establishing a sense of internal control. Perls insists that we can learn to control our inner experience, regardless of our external environment. Once we understand that our perception shapes our experience, we can see how the roles we play and the actions we take are tools, which we can then use consciously for changing reality. Control of our own inner psychic environment gives us power through two layers of choice: in how to interpret the environment, and how to react to it. The adage, "no one can make you angry other than yourself", perfectly exemplifies this philosophy, and its truth can be seen played out in the different ways that people react to traffic jams, bad news, or personal criticism, for example.

In Gestalt therapy, a person is forced to take direct responsibility for how he or she acts and reacts, regardless of what may seem to be happening. Perls refers to this ability to maintain emotional stability regardless of the environment as "homeostasis", using a biological term normally used to describe the maintenance of a stable physical environment within the body. It implies a fine balancing of many systems, and this is how Gestalt therapy views the mind. It looks for ways of balancing the mind through the many thoughts, feelings, and perceptions that make up the whole human experience. It views a person holistically and places the focus firmly on the whole, not the parts.

Perls saw his task as helping his patients to cultivate an awareness of the power of their perceptions, and how they shape reality (or what we describe as "reality"). In this way, his patients became able to take control of shaping their interior landscape. In taking responsibility for their perceived sense of reality, they could create the reality they wanted.

Perls helped his patients achieve this through teaching them the integral processes of Gestalt therapy. The first and most important process is learning to cultivate awareness and to focus that awareness on the feelings of the present moment. This allows the individual to directly experience his or her feelings and perceived reality in the present moment. This ability, to "be here now" is critical to the »

The Gestalt prayer was written by Fritz Perls to encapsulate Gestalt therapy. It emphasizes the importance of living according to our own needs, and not seeking fulfilment through others.

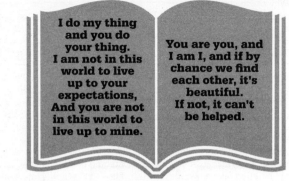

I do my thing and you do your thing. I am not in this world to live up to your expectations, And you are not in this world to live up to mine.

You are you, and I am I, and if by chance we find each other, it's beautiful. If not, it can't be helped.

Gestalt process; it is an acute emotional awareness, and one that forms the foundation for understanding how each of us creates and reacts to our own environment. It also offers a pathway for learning how to change the ways we experience ourselves and our environment.

As a tool for personal growth, the ability to get in touch with authentic feelings – true thoughts and emotions – is more important to Perls than the psychological explanations or analytic feedback of other forms of therapy. The "why" behind behaviour holds little significance for Perls; what is important is the "how" and "what". This devaluing of the need to find out "why" and the shift of responsibility for meaning from analyst to patient brought with it a profound change in the therapist–patient hierarchy. Where previous approaches in therapy generally involved a therapist manipulating the patient towards the therapeutic goal, the Gestalt approach is characterized by a warm, empathic relationship between therapist and patient, who work together as partners towards the goal. The therapist is dynamic

Like Buddhism, Gestalt therapy encourages the development of mindful awareness and the acceptance of change as inevitable. Perls called change "the study of creative adjustments".

but does not lead the patient; the Gestalt approach of Perls would later form the basis of Carl Rogers' humanistic, person-centred approach.

A denial of fate

Another component in the Gestalt method involves the use of language. One critical tool patients are given for increasing self-awareness is the instruction to notice and change the use of the word "I" within speech. Perls says that to take responsibility for our reality, we must recognize how we use language to give the illusion that we have no control when this is not the case. By simply rephrasing "I can't do that" to "I won't do that", it becomes clear that I am making a choice. This also helps to establish ownership of feeling; emotions arise in and belong to me; I cannot blame someone or something else for my feelings.

Other examples of language change include replacing the word "should" with "want", changing, for example, "I should leave now" to "I want to leave now". This also acts to reveal the element of choice. As we learn to take responsibility for our experience, Perls says, we develop authentic selves that are free from society's influence. We also experience self-empowerment as we realize that we are not at the mercy of things that "just happen". Feelings of victimization dissolve once we understand that what we accept for ourselves in our lives – what we selectively perceive and experience – is a choice; we are not powerless.

With this personal responsibility comes the obligation to refuse to experience events, relationships, or circumstances that we know to be wrong for our authentic selves. Gestalt theory also asks us to look closely at what we choose to accept among our society's norms. We may have acted under the assumption of their truth for so long that we automatically accept them. Perls says we need instead to adopt beliefs that best inspire and develop our authentic self. The ability to write our own personal rules, determine our own opinions, philosophies, desires, and interests is of the essence. As we increase our awareness of self-accountability, self-reliance, and self-insight, we understand that we are building our own world, or truth. The lives we are living become easier to bear, because "truth can be tolerated only if you discover it yourself".

The possibility of intimacy

Gestalt therapy's emphasis on "being in the present" and finding one's own path and one's own ideas fitted perfectly within the 1960s counter-culture revolution of the Western world. But this focus on individualism was seen by some psychologists and analysts as a weakness within the therapy, especially by those who view human beings as, above all, social beings. They claim that a life lived along Gestalt principles would exclude the possibility of intimacy with another, and that it focuses too much on the individual at the expense of the community. In response, supporters of Gestalt therapy have claimed that without the development of an authentic self, it would not be possible to develop an authentic relationship with another.

In 1964, Perls became a regular lecturer at the Esalen Institute in California, becoming a lasting influence on this renowned centre for spiritual and psychological development. After an explosion of popularity in the 1970s, Gestalt therapy fell out of favour, but its tenets were accepted into the roots of other forms of therapy. Gestalt is today recognized as one of many "standard" approaches to therapy. ■

Fritz Perls

Frederick "Fritz" Salomon Perls was born in Berlin at the end of the 19th century. He studied medicine, and after a short time in the German army during World War I, graduated as a doctor. He then trained as a psychiatrist, and after marrying the psychologist Laura Posner in 1930, emigrated to South Africa, where he and Laura set up a psychoanalytic institute. Becoming disenchanted with the over-intellectualism of the psychoanalytic approach, they moved to New York City in the late 1940s and became immersed in a thriving culture of progressive thought. In the late 1960s, they separated, and Perls moved to California, where he continued to change the landscape of psychotherapy. He left the USA to start a therapy centre in Canada in 1969, but died one year later of heart failure while conducting a workshop.

Key works

1946 *Ego Hunger and Aggression*
1969 *Gestalt Therapy Verbatim*
1973 *The Gestalt Approach and Eye Witness to Therapy*

The 1960s hippie culture chimed with the Gestalt idea of finding oneself, but Perls warned against the "peddlers of instant joy" and the "so-called easy road of sensory liberation".

IT IS NOTORIOUSLY INADEQUATE TO TAKE AN ADOPTED CHILD INTO ONE'S HOME AND LOVE HIM
DONALD WINNICOTT (1896–1971)

IN CONTEXT

APPROACH
Psychoanalysis

BEFORE
1900s Sigmund Freud suggests that neurotic conflicts (and the superego) arise in the Oedipal period – between ages three and six.

1930s Melanie Klein claims that a primitive form of the superego develops during the first year of life, and that love and hate are inherently linked.

AFTER
1947 Psychologist and play therapist Virginia Axline develops her eight principles of play therapy, which include: "Accept the child as she or he is".

1979 Swiss psychoanalyst Alice Miller says in *The Drama of the Gifted Child* that we are encouraged to "develop the art of not experiencing feelings".

Many people believe that if a child has suffered an upbringing that was lacking in love and support, he or she will be able to settle and flourish with a new family that provides what is needed. However, while stability and acceptance help to give a foundation in which a child can grow and find a healthy state of being, these qualities make up only one part of what is required.

As the first paediatrician in England to train as a psychoanalyst, Donald Winnicott had a unique insight into the mother-infant relationship and the developmental process of children. He was strongly influenced by Sigmund Freud but also by the writings of Melanie Klein, particularly regarding the unconscious feelings of the mother or carer for the infant. Winnicott began his career by working with children displaced by World War II and he examined the difficulties faced by children who are trying to adapt to a new home.

As Winnicott notes in his paper, *Hate in the Countertransference*: "It is notoriously inadequate to take an adopted child into one's home and love him". In fact, the parents must be able to take the adopted child into their home and be able to tolerate hating him. Winnicott states that a child can believe he or she is loved only after being hated; he stresses that the role that "tolerance of hate" plays in healing cannot be underestimated.

Winnicott explains that when a child has been deprived of proper parental nurturing, and is then granted a chance of this in a healthy family environment, such as with an adoptive or foster family, the child begins to develop unconscious hope. But fear is associated with this hope. When a child has been so devastatingly disappointed in the past, with even basic emotional or physical needs unsatisfied, defences arise. These are unconscious forces that protect

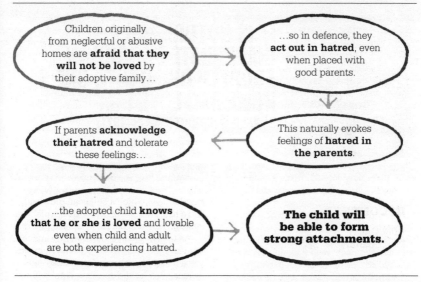

Children originally from neglectful or abusive homes are **afraid that they will not be loved** by their adoptive family…

…so in defence, they **act out in hatred**, even when placed with good parents.

This naturally evokes feelings of **hatred in the parents**.

If parents **acknowledge their hatred** and tolerate these feelings:…

…the adopted child **knows that he or she is loved** and lovable even when child and adult are both experiencing hatred.

The child will be able to form strong attachments.

the child against the hope that may lead to disappointment. The defences, maintains Winnicott, explain the presence of hatred. The child will "act out" in an outburst of anger against the new parental figure, expressing hatred and, in turn, invoking hatred from the carer. He termed the behaviour an "anti-social tendency".

According to Winnicott, for a child who has suffered, the need to hate and be hated is deeper even than the need for rebellion, and the importance of the carer tolerating the hate is an essential factor in the healing of the child. Winnicott says that the child must be allowed to express the hatred, and the parent must be able to tolerate both the child's and their own hatred as well.

The idea may be shocking, and people may struggle with the notion that they feel »

Donald Winnicott

The English paediatrician and psychoanalyst Donald Woods Winnicott was the youngest child and only son born to a prominent, prosperous family living in Plymouth, Devon, UK. His father, Sir John Frederick Winnicott, was an encouraging influence, although his mother suffered from depression. Winnicott first trained as a physician and paediatrician, completing psychoanalytic training later, in the 1930s.

Winnicott married twice, meeting his second wife Clare Britton, a psychiatric social worker, while working with disturbed children who had been evacuated during World War II. He continued to work as a paediatrician for more than 40 years and this gave his ideas a unique perspective. He twice served as president of the British Psychoanalytical Society, and sought to widen public knowledge through his many lectures and broadcasts.

Key works

1947 *Hate in the Countertransference*
1951 *Transitional Objects and Transitional Phenomena*
1960 *The Theory of the Parent–Infant Relationship*

> ❝ It seems that an adopted child can believe in being loved only after reaching being hated.
> **Donald Winnicott** ❞

hatred rising within them. They may feel guilty, because the child has been through such difficulties already. Yet the child is actively behaving hatefully towards the parent, projecting past experiences of being neglected and ignored onto present-day reality.

The child of a broken home or without parents, Winnicott says, "spends his time unconsciously looking for his parents" and so feelings from past relationships are displaced onto another adult. The child has internalized the hate, and sees it even when it is no longer present. In his new situation, the child needs to see what happens when hatred is in the air. Winnicott explains: "What happens is that after a while a child so adopted gains hope, and then he starts to test out the environment he has found, and to seek proof of his guardian's ability to hate objectively."

There are many ways for a child to express hatred and prove that he or she is indeed not worthy of being loved. This worthlessness is the message that was imparted by earlier, negative parental experiences. From the child's point of view, he

is attempting to protect himself from the risk of ever having to feel love or to be loved because of the potential disappointment that accompanies that state of being.

Dealing with the hatred
The emotions that the child's hatred invokes in the parents, as well as in the child's teachers and other authority figures, are very real. Winnicott believes that it is essential that adults acknowledge these feelings, rather than deny them, which might seem easier. They also need to understand that the child's hatred is not personal; the child is expressing anxiety about his previous unhappy situation with the person who is now at hand.

What the authority figure does with their own hatred, of course, is of critical importance. The child's belief that he or she is "bad" and unworthy of being loved must not be reinforced by the response from the adult; the adult must simply tolerate the feelings of hatred and realize that these feelings are part of the relationship. This is the only way the child will feel secure and be able to form an attachment.

No matter how loving a new environment may be, it does not erase the past for the child; there will still be residual feelings as a result of their past experience. Winnicott sees no short cuts to a resolution. The child is expecting that the adult's feelings of hatred will lead to rejection, because that is what has happened before; when the hatred does not lead to rejection and is tolerated instead, it can begin to dissipate.

The "anti-social tendency" in children is a way they express anxieties about their world, testing out their caregivers who must continue to provide a supportive and caring home.

Despite feeling the unconscious and natural negative feelings provoked by the child, a parent must provide an environment that "holds" the child, making him or her feel secure.

Healthy hatred

Even in psychologically healthy families with children who have not been displaced, Winnicott believes unconscious hatred is a natural, essential part of the parenting experience and speaks of "hating appropriately". Melanie Klein had suggested that a baby feels hatred for its mother, but Winnicott proposes that this is preceded by the mother hating the baby – and that even before this, there is an extraordinary primitive or "ruthless" love. The baby's existence places huge demands on the mother psychologically and physically and these evoke feelings of hatred in the mother. Winnicott's list of 18 reasons why the mother hates the baby include: that the pregnancy and birth have endangered her life; that the baby is an interference with her private life; that the baby hurts her when nursing, even biting her; and that the baby "treats her as scum, an unpaid servant, a slave". Despite all of this she also loves him, "excretions and all", says Winnicott, with a hugely powerful, primitive love, and has to learn how to tolerate hating her baby without in any way acting on it. If she cannot hate appropriately, he claims, she turns the feelings of hatred towards herself, in a way that is masochistic and unhealthy.

Therapeutic relationship

Winnicott also used the relationship between the parent and child as an analogy for the therapeutic relationship between therapist and client. The feelings that arise in a therapist during analysis are part of a phenomenon known as "countertransference". Feelings that are aroused in the client during therapy – usually feelings about parents or siblings – are transferred onto the therapist. In his paper, Winnicott described how as part of the analysis, the therapist feels hate towards the client, though this hate was generated by the patient as a necessary part of testing that the therapist can bear it. The patient needs to know that the therapist is strong and reliable enough to withstand this onslaught.

A realistic approach

While some of Winnicott's ideas may appear shocking, he believes we should be realistic about bringing up children, avoiding sentimentality in favour of honesty. This enables us as children, and later as adults, to acknowledge and deal with natural, unavoidable negative feelings. Winnicott is a realist and pragmatist; he refuses to believe in the mythical idea of "the perfect family" or in a world where a few kind words wipe away all of the horrors that may have preceded it. He prefers to see the real environment and mental states of our experience, and asks us to do likewise, with courageous honesty. His ideas did not fit neatly into one school of thought, though they were hugely influential, and continue to impact on social work, education, developmental psychology, and psychoanalysis around the world. ∎

> ❝ Sentimentality in a mother is no good at all from the infant's point of view.
> **Donald Winnicott** ❞

THE UNCONCIOUS IS THE DISCOURSE OF THE OTHER

JACQUES LACAN (1901-1981)

IN CONTEXT

APPROACH
Psychoanalysis

BEFORE
1807 German philosopher Georg Hegel states that consciousness of self depends on the presence of the Other.

1818 German philosopher Arthur Schopenhauer claims that there can be no object without a subject to observe it, and that perception of the object is limited by personal vision and experience.

1890 William James in *The Principles of Psychology* distinguishes between the self as the knower, or "I", and the self as the known, or "me".

AFTER
1943 French philosopher Jean-Paul Sartre states that our perception of the world around us, or the Other, alters when another person appears; we absorb his or her concept of the Other into our own.

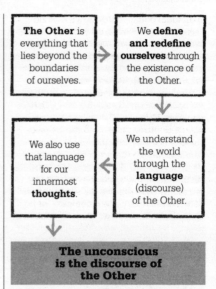

The **Other** is everything that lies beyond the boundaries of ourselves.

We **define and redefine ourselves** through the existence of the Other.

We understand the world through the **language** (discourse) of the Other.

We also use that language for our innermost **thoughts**.

The unconscious is the discourse of the Other

P sychoanalysts explain the unconscious as the place where all the memories that we wish to push aside are stored, and cannot be retrieved consciously. The unconscious sometimes speaks to the conscious self in limited ways: Carl Jung believed that the unconscious presents itself to the waking self through dreams, symbols, and in the language of archetypes, while Freud saw it as expressing itself through motivational behaviour and accidental "slips of the tongue". The one thing that the various psychoanalytical schools do agree on is that the unconscious holds a bigger picture than that retained by the conscious self. For French psychiatrist Jacques Lacan, however, the language of the unconscious is not that of the self, but of the "Other".

A sense of self

We easily take for granted the notion of the self – that each of us exists as a separate,

Our sense of self is shaped by our awareness of the "Other", or the world outside ourselves. However, Lacan stated, it is the language of the Other that forms our deepest thoughts.

individual being, who views the world through our own eyes, is familiar with the boundaries that separate us from others and from the world around us, and assumes a separateness in thinking and in the way we interact with our environment. But what if there was nothing out there that we could recognize as being separate from ourselves? We would then be unable to conceptualize our sense of self, because there would be no delineated being to think about. The only way we have of determining that as individuals we are distinct from the world all around us is our ability to recognize the separateness of ourselves from our environment, or from the Other, which allows us to become the

subject "I". Lacan therefore, concluded that each of us is a "self" only because we have a concept of the Other.

For Lacan, the Other is the absolute otherness that lies beyond the self; it is the environment into which we are born, and which we have to "translate" or make sense of, in order to survive and thrive. An infant must learn to assemble sensations into concepts and categories in order to function in the world, and he or she does this through gradually acquiring an awareness and understanding of a series of signifiers – signs or codes. But these signifiers can only come to us from the external world that lies beyond the self, therefore they must have been formed from the language – or what Lacan prefers to call the "discourse" – of the Other.

We are only able to think or to express our ideas and emotions through language, and the only language we have, according to Lacan, is that of the Other. The sensations and images that translate into the thoughts of our unconscious must therefore be constructed from this language of the Other, or, as Lacan stated, "the unconscious is the discourse of the Other". This idea has had a wide influence on the practice of psychoanalysis, leading to a more objective and open interpretation of the unconscious. ∎

Jacques Lacan

Jacques Marie Émile Lacan was born in Paris, where he was educated by Jesuits at the Collège Stanislas. He went on to study medicine,

qualifying in psychiatry. Lacan remained in occupied Paris during World War II, working at the Val-de-Grâce military hospital.

After the war, psychoanalysis became the key tool in Lacan's work. However, he was expelled by the International Psychoanalytical Association in 1953, after a row over his "deviant" use of shorter length therapy sessions. Lacan then set up La Société Françaisede Psychanalytique. Lacan's writings extend into philosophy, art,

literature, and linguistics, and he gave weekly seminars that were attended by eminent thinkers such as Roland Barthes, and Claude Lévi-Strauss. A keen Freudian, Lacan formed the École Freudienne de Paris in 1963, and the École de la Cause Freudienne in 1981.

Key works

1966 *Écrits*
1968 *The Language of the Self*
1954–80 *The Seminars* (27 volumes)

MAN'S MAIN TASK IS TO GIVE BIRTH TO HIMSELF
ERICH FROMM (1900–1980)

IN CONTEXT

APPROACH
Humanistic psychoanalysis

BEFORE
1258–61 The Sufi mystic Rumi says that the longing of the human soul comes from separation from its source.

1950s Rollo May says that the "true religion" consists of facing life's challenges with purpose and meaning, through accepting responsibility and making choices.

AFTER
1950 Karen Horney says that the neurotic self is split between an idealized and a real self.

1960s Abraham Maslow defines creativity and thinking of others as characteristics of self-actualized people.

1970s Fritz Perls says that we must find ourselves in order to achieve self-actualization.

The ability to find meaning in our lives is the defining characteristic of humankind. According to the German-American psychoanalyst Erich Fromm, it also determines whether we follow a path of joy and fulfilment or tread a road of dissatisfaction and strife. Fromm believed that although life is inherently painful, we can make it bearable by giving it meaning, through pursuing and constructing an authentic self. The ultimate aim of a human life is to develop what Fromm described as "the most precious quality man is endowed with – the love of life".

Life is inherently fraught with emotional frustration, according to Fromm, because man lives in a state of struggle. He is constantly trying to balance his individual nature – his existence as a separate being – with his need for connection. There is a part of man's inherent self that only knows how to exist in a united state with others; it lives at one with nature and at one with other people. Yet we see ourselves as separated from nature, and isolated from one another. Worse still, we have the unique capacity to ponder the fact of this separation

Life is fraught with anxiety and powerlessness because of our **separation from nature** and from one another.

→ These feelings can be overcome through…

→ …searching out and devoting ourselves to the **discovery of our own ideas and abilities**.

→ …embracing our **personal uniqueness**.

→ …developing our **capacity to love**.

and think about our isolation. Man, gifted with reason, is life being aware of itself.

Fromm suggests that our separation from nature originated with the growth of intellect, which has made us aware of our separateness. It is our ability to reason and relate that lets us transcend nature. It provides the capabilities for productive living and affords us intellectual superiority, but it also makes us realize that we exist alone in this world. Reason makes us aware of our own mortality and the mortality of our loved ones. This understanding creates a chronic source of tension and an unbearable loneliness that we are always seeking to overcome; man's inherent state of being is one of anxiety and hopelessness. But there is hope, Fromm insists, because man can overcome his sense of isolation and alienation through finding his purpose.

However, as we strive to become free, unique individuals, we still feel the need for unity with others, and in trying to balance these needs we may seek out the comfort of conforming to a group or an authority. This is a misguided approach, says Fromm; it is imperative to discover one's own independent sense of self, and one's own personal views and value systems, rather than adhering to conventional or authoritarian norms. If we try to hand responsibility for our choices to other people or institutions we become alienated from ourselves, when the very purpose of our lives is to define ourselves through embracing our personal uniqueness, discovering our own ideas and abilities, and embracing that which differentiates each of us from other people. Man's main task is to give birth to himself. In doing so, he frees himself from confusion, loneliness, and apathy.

Creativity and love

Paradoxically, Fromm believes that the only way we can find the sense of wholeness we seek is through the discovery of our individuality. We can achieve this by following our own ideas and passions, and through creative purpose, because "creativity requires the courage to let go of certainties".

One of the critical ways in which man delivers himself from isolation is through his

The creativity of artists encourages them to interpret the world around them in new ways. The world's most highly acclaimed artists have always essentially been non-conformist.

capacity to love. Fromm's concept of love is vastly different from popular understandings of the word. To Fromm, love is not an emotion, nor is it dependent on finding an object to love. It is an interpersonal creative capacity that one must actively develop as part of one's personality. He says "it is an attitude, an ordination of character which determines the relatedness of the person to the whole world".

In terms of personal love for another, Fromm says that the main tenets are care, responsibility, respect, and knowledge – an objective knowledge of what other people truly want and need. Love is only possible through respecting the separateness and uniqueness of ourselves and of another; paradoxically, this is how we develop the ability to create connectedness. Love demands a great amount of respect for the other person as an individual, and it is based on autonomy, not a blending of personalities. In our overwhelming desire to connect and unify, we try to love but our relationships often result in an unloving imbalance. We think we are loving, but in reality we may be seeking another form of conformity. We say "I love you" when really we mean "I see me in you", "I will become you", or "I will possess you". In loving, we try to lose our uniqueness, or steal it from the other person. Our yearning to exist "as one" makes us want to see ourselves reflected in other people, which in turn leads us to artificially impose our own traits onto someone else. »

The Four Nonproductive Personality Types

Receptive types have no choice but to accept their roles, and never fight for change or betterment.

Exploitative types are aggressive and self-centred, and typically engage in acts of coercion and plagiarism.

Hoarding types fight to retain what they have, and are always seeking to acquire more.

Marketing types "sell" everything, especially their own image.

The only way to love, says Fromm, is to love freely, granting the other person their full individuality; to respect the other person's differing opinions, preferences, and belief systems. Love is not found by fitting one person into another's mould, and it is not a question of finding the perfect "match". It is, he says, "union with somebody, or something, outside oneself, under the condition of retaining the separateness and integrity of one's own self".

Many people spend vast amounts of time and money attempting to cultivate the self that they feel is most worthy of acceptance, and most likely to result in being loved or desired. This is futile, because only a person who has a strong sense of self, and can stand firmly within their own understanding of the world, is able to give freely to others and love in an authentic way. Those who tend to orient themselves towards receiving love instead of being loving will fail; they will also seek to establish a receiving relationship in other ways, always wanting to be given things – material or immaterial – rather than to give. These people believe the source of all good things lies outside themselves, and they constantly feel the need to acquire, though this brings no relief.

Personality types

Fromm identified several personality types that he called "nonproductive", because they enable people to avoid assuming true responsibility for their actions and prevent productive, personal growth. Each of the four main nonproductive types – receptive, exploitative, hoarding, and marketing – have both positive and negative sides. A fifth type, necrophilous, is unremittingly negative, and a sixth type – the productive personality – is Fromm's ideal. In reality, our personalities are generally drawn from a mix of the four main types.

A person with a "receptive" orientation is said to live passively in the status quo, accepting the lot handed to them. These people follow rather than lead; they have things done to them. In extremes, this is the stance of the victim, but on the positive side, it is rich in devotion and acceptance. Fromm compares this type to the peasants and migrant workers of history.

The "exploitative" orientation thrives on taking from others; exploitative people take what they need instead of earning or creating. However, they show extreme

Hitler's fascination with death and destruction marks him out as an example of Fromm's necrophilous personality type, which is obsessed with control and the imposition of order.

self-confidence and strong initiative. This type is typified by historical aristocracies who took power and wealth from indigenous populations to line their own pockets.

"Hoarders" are always seeking friends in high places and rank even loved ones in terms of their value, seeing them as something owned. Power-hungry and ungenerous, at best they are pragmatic and economical. Historically, these are the middle classes, or bourgeoisie, that rise in great numbers during economic depressions.

The last of the main types is the "marketing" orientation. These people are obsessed with image and with how to successfully advertise and sell themselves. Every choice is evaluated in terms of reflected status, from the clothes, cars, and holidays they buy to marriage into the "right" family. At worst, they are opportunistic, tactless, and shallow; at best, they are highly motivated, purposeful, and energetic. This type is most representative of modern society, in its ever-growing acquisitiveness and self-consciousness.

The most negative personality type – necrophilous – seeks only to destroy. Deeply afraid of the disorderly and uncontrollable nature of life, necrophilous types love to talk about sickness and death, and are obsessed with the need to impose "law and order". They prefer mechanical objects to other people. In moderation, these people are pessimistic nay-sayers whose glasses are perpetually half empty, never half full.

Fromm's last personality type, the productive orientation, genuinely seeks and finds a legitimate solution to life through flexibility, learning, and sociability. Aiming to "become one" with the world and so escape the loneliness of separation, productive people respond to the world with rationality and an open mind, willing to change their beliefs in the light of new evidence. A productive person can truly love another for who they are, not as a trophy or safeguard against the world. Fromm calls this brave person "the man without a mask".

Fromm's work has a unique perspective, drawing on psychology, sociology, and political thinking, especially the writings of Karl Marx. His writing, aimed at a mainstream audience, influenced the general public more than academia – mainly because of his insistence on the freedom of ideas. He is nonetheless recognized as a leading contributor to humanistic psychology. ∎

Erich Fromm

Erich Fromm was the only child of his orthodox Jewish parents, and grew up in Frankfurt am Main, Germany. A thoughtful young man, he was initially influenced by his Talmudic studies, but later turned to Karl Marx and socialist theory, together with Freud's psychoanalysis. Driven by the need to understand the hostility he witnessed during World War I, he studied jurisprudence, then sociology (to PhD level), before training in psychoanalysis. After the Nazis took power in Germany in 1933, Fromm moved to Switzerland and then New York, where he established a psychoanalytic practice and taught at Columbia University.

Fromm married three times and had a well-documented affair with Karen Horney during the 1930s. In 1951, he left the USA to teach in Mexico, returning 11 years later to become professor of psychiatry at New York University. He died in Switzerland at the age of 79.

Key works

1941 *The Fear of Freedom*
1947 *Man for Himself*
1956 *The Art of Loving*

THE GOOD LIFE IS A PROCESS NOT A STATE OF BEING
CARL ROGERS (1902–1987)

IN CONTEXT

APPROACH
Person-centred therapy

BEFORE
1920s Austrian psychoanalyst Otto Rank proposes that separation from outdated thoughts, emotions, and behaviours is essential for psychological growth and development.

1950s Abraham Maslow says that people must not be viewed as a collection of symptoms but first and foremost as people.

AFTER
1960s Fritz Perls popularizes the concept of externalizing other people's expectations to find one's truest self.

2004 American humanistic psychologist Clark Moustakas explores the uniquely human components of life: hope, love, self, creativity, individuality, and becoming.

During the 19th and into the early 20th century, much of the approach to psychological treatment was based on the idea that mental illness was a fixed pathological malady that needed to be cured. Popular psychoanalytic theory, for example, defined people struggling with their mental health as "neurotic". Mental illness was seen in a negative light and most psychological practices and theories of the time offered strict definitions with structured explanations of the underlying causes of the mental illness, and fixed methods to cure it.

American psychologist Carl Rogers took a much more esoteric route to mental health, and in so doing expanded the approach of psychotherapy forever. He felt that the philosophies of the time were too structured and rigid to account for something as dynamic as the human experience, and that humanity is much too diverse to be fitted into delineated categories.

Achieving mental health
Rogers takes the view that it is absurd to view mental wellbeing as a specific fixed

The good life is a process, not a state of being.

In order to enjoy the good life, we need to…

…be fully **open to experience**.

…live in the **present moment**.

…**trust** ourselves.

…take **responsibility** for our choices.

…treat ourselves and others with **unconditional positive regard**.

Unlike a maze with only one route across, Rogers asserts that life is full of possibilities and offers multiple routes – but individuals are often unable or unwilling to see them. To experience "the good life" we need to stay flexible and open to what life brings, by experiencing it fully moment by moment.

state; good mental health is not something that is suddenly achieved at the end of a series of steps. Nor is it attained because an individual's previously neurotic state of tension has been reduced by the satisfaction of biological drives and impulses, as the psychoanalysts insisted. Neither is it cultivated by following a specific programme designed to develop and preserve a state of inner impermeable homeostasis, or balance, reducing the effect of the world's external chaos on the self, as the behaviourists recommended.

Rogers does not believe that anyone exists in a defective state that needs to be fixed in order to provide them with a better state, preferring to view human experience, and our minds and environment, as alive

and growing. He talks about the "ongoing process of organismic experience" – seeing life as instantaneous and ongoing; life exists in the experience of every moment.

For Rogers, a healthy self-concept is not a fixed identity but a fluid and changing entity, open to possibilities. Rogers embraces an authentic, unprescribed, free-flowing definition of healthy human experience, with limitless possibilities. Humans are not travelling a road where the destination is to become "adjusted" or "actualized", as fellow humanistic psychologist Abraham Maslow had suggested. Indeed, the purpose of existence is not about reaching any kind of destination, Rogers claims, because existence is less a journey towards an endpoint and more an ongoing process of growth and discovery that does not stop until we die.

Living "the good life"

Rogers uses the phrase living "the good life", to refer to the range of characteristics, attitudes, and behaviours displayed by people who have embraced the foundations of his approach – people who are "fully in the stream of life". One essential ingredient is the ability to stay wholly present in the moment. Since self and personality emerge out of experience, it is of the utmost importance to stay fully open to the possibilities offered by each moment, and to let experience shape the self. The individual lives in an environment of constant change, yet frequently and all too easily, people deny this fluidity and instead create constructs of how they think things should be. They then try to mould themselves and their idea of reality to fit the constructs they have made. This way »

> What I will be in the next moment, and what I will do, grows out of the moment, and cannot be predicted.
> **Carl Rogers**

Spending time working in a developing country can be a rewarding way to open up to new experiences, challenge fixed ideas about the world, and find out more about ourselves.

of being is the very opposite of the fluid, flowing, and changing organization of self that Rogers believes the nature of our existence requires.

Our preconceptions about how the world is, or should be, and our own role within it, define the limits of our world and reduce our ability to stay present and open to experience. In living the good life and remaining open to experience, Rogers believes we adopt a way of being that prevents us feeling trapped and stuck. The aim, as Rogers sees it, is for experience to be the starting point for the construction of our personalities, rather than trying to fit our experiences into a preconceived notion of our sense of self. If we hold on to our ideas of how things should be, rather than accepting how they really are, we are likely to perceive our needs as "incongruent" or mismatched to what is available.

When the world does not "do what we want", and we feel unable to change our ideas, conflict arises in the form of defensiveness. Rogers explains defensiveness as the tendency to unconsciously apply strategies to prevent a troubling stimulus from entering consciousness. We either deny (block out) or distort (reinterpret) what is really happening, essentially refusing to accept reality in order to stick with our preconceived ideas. In so doing, we deny

ourselves the full range of potential reactions, feelings, and ideas, and we dismiss a wide range of options as wrong or inappropriate. The defensive feelings and thoughts that rise up in us when reality conflicts with our preconceptions create a limited, artificial interpretation of experience. In order to really participate in what Rogers calls the "ongoing process of organismic experience", we need to be fully open to new experience, and be completely without defensiveness.

A full range of emotions
By tuning in to our full range of emotions, Rogers argues, we allow ourselves a deeper, richer experience in every part of our lives. We may think we can selectively block emotion, and dampen down disturbing or uncomfortable feelings, but when we repress some of our emotions, we inevitably turn down the volume of all our emotions, denying ourselves access to the whole of our nature. If on the other hand, we allow ourselves to be more comfortable with our emotions, including those we have deemed to be negative, the flow of positive feelings emerges more strongly; it is as if by permitting ourselves to feel pain, we allow for a more intense experience of joy.

By always remaining open to everything that occurs, Rogers says that we allow our fullest abilities to function, and in turn

A fixed view of the world often leads to unhappiness; we can feel like "a square peg in a round hole", constantly frustrated that our life is not how we expected it to be. Rogers urges us to abandon our preconceived ideas and see the world as it really is.

we can get the greatest satisfaction from our experiences. We have not raised our defences to shut off any part of the self, so we are able to experience everything fully. Once we escape from the rut of the preconceptions of the mind, we can allow ourselves to soar. Rather than organizing our experience to suit our idea of the world, we "discover structure *in* experience".

This openness is not for the faint-hearted, Rogers states; it requires a level of bravery on the part of the individual. We don't need to fear any type of feeling, he says – we need only to allow the full flow of cognition and experience. With true access to a fuller range of processing experience, each of us is more able to find the path that truly suits our authentic self – this is the fully functioning individual that Rogers urges us to become. We are always growing, and Rogers emphasizes that the direction in which people move – when there is freedom to move in any direction – is generally the direction they are best suited for, and that is best suited for them.

Unconditional acceptance

In contrast to the views of many of his predecessors in the field of psychotherapy, Rogers believed that people are, in their essence, healthy and good; and that mental and emotional wellbeing is the natural progression for human nature. These beliefs are the foundation of an approach that regards patients in an entirely positive light, one of absolute, unconditional acceptance. Rogers asked that his patients learn to do the same for themselves and for others. This perspective, grounded in compassion and the recognition of the potential of each and every individual, is famously termed "unconditional positive regard". Rogers believed that all people, not just his patients, needed to be able to view themselves in this way, as well as those around them and their environment.

Unconditional self-acceptance and unconditional acceptance of others are vital, and when these are lacking, people fail to remain open to experience. Rogers maintained that many of us have very strong, strident, specific conditions that must be met

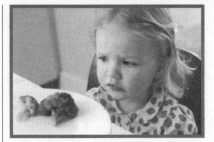

Love that is conditional on an action or situation – for example, on achieving A grades at school or eating the right foods – can leave children feeling unworthy and unaccepted.

before we will grant approval or acceptance. We also base self-worth and regard for others on achievements or appearance, rather than accepting people as they are.

Parents may inadvertently teach children that they are worthy of affection only if certain requirements are met, offering them rewards and praise when they eat their vegetables or get an A grade in physics, but fail to love them openly just for themselves. Rogers calls these requirements "conditions of worth", believing that the tendency of humankind to demand that people and things match our arbitrary expectations does all of us a great disservice.

Achievements are to be respected, he says, but they are both separate and secondary to acceptance, which is a basic human need, and does not have to be "earned" through deeds or action. Rogers says that the value of an individual is inherently granted merely by the miracle of existence. Acceptance must never be thought of as conditional; unconditional positive regard is key to how we might all live "the good life". »

> 66 No other person's ideas, and none of my own ideas, are as authoritative as my experience.
> **Carl Rogers** 99

> ❝ The subjective human being has an important value… that no matter how he may be labelled and evaluated he is a human person first of all. ❞
> **Carl Rogers**

As people become more accepting of themselves, they also become more patient with themselves. Acceptance alleviates the pressure to do, see, and acquire, which builds when we live with the mistaken idea that these activities define our worth. We can begin to realize that each of us is a continual work-in-progress; that we are each of us in a process of change, as Rogers says in his seminal work, *On Becoming A Person* – we are all in a constant "state of becoming". The irony is that with greater self-acceptance, and with less unhealthy pressure and constant criticism, we can actually become much more productive.

Trusting oneself

To live "the good life", as Rogers sees it, is to learn to trust ourselves. As an individual moves towards openness, he finds that he simultaneously makes progress in his ability to trust himself and his instincts, and begins to rely more comfortably on his decision-making capabilities. With no need to repress any part of himself, he has a greater ability to tune in to all the parts of himself. This gives him access to a variety of perspectives and feelings, and in turn he is better able to evaluate choices that will truly realize his potential. He is able to see more clearly what direction his authentic self wishes to take, and can make choices that are truly in congruence with his needs. No longer at the mercy of what he thinks he should be doing, nor of what society or parents may have conditioned him to think he wants, he can much more easily simply exist in the moment and be truly aware of what he actually wants. And now he can trust himself, "not because he is infallible, but because he can be fully open to the consequences of each of his actions and correct them if they prove to be less than satisfying", Rogers explains.

In living "the good life" we also have a sense of owning our lives and taking responsibility for ourselves – this is another tenet of Rogers' philosophy and comes from an existential viewpoint. What we choose to think or do is down to us; there can be no residual resentments when we have truly identified for ourselves what we want and

Carl Rogers

Carl Rogers was born in Oak Park, Illinois, USA, to a strictly Protestant family, and apparently had few friends outside the family before going to college. Initially, Rogers majored in agriculture, but after marrying his childhood sweetheart, Helen Elliott, in 1924, he enrolled at a theological seminary, before withdrawing to pursue a course in psychology. Rogers worked at the universities of Ohio, Chicago, and Wisconsin, developing his client-centred therapy based on humanistic psychology. He also spent time with the United Service Organizations (USO), offering therapy to returning army personnel during World War II. In 1964, he was awarded "Humanist of the Year" by the American Humanist Association, and devoted the last ten years of his life to working for world peace. He was nominated for a Nobel Peace Prize in 1987.

Key works

1942 *Counseling and Psychotherapy*
1951 *Client-centered Therapy*
1961 *On Becoming a Person*

need, and taken the steps to create it. At the same time, there is greater accountability and an increased tendency to truly invest in our lives. It is not uncommon to hear about a doctor who hates medicine but practises because his parents said that being a doctor was the way to earn respect and approval – both from them and from society. In direct contrast, the rates of students who drop out or fail university courses are strikingly low among those who have received little support but worked to pay for their own tuition.

The ways in which people can influence our desires and how we define ourselves can be intensely complex. Resentment can be buried deep within us when we act in accordance with someone else's wishes rather than our own. If our actions are free of external influences, we feel more authentic, more solidly in control of creating our own destiny, and more satisfied with the results.

Person-centred approach

Rogers' philosophy became the cornerstone of a new approach called humanistic psychology, which he founded in the 1950s with Abraham Maslow and Rollo May. It was based on a positive view of humanity as basically healthy and capable of growing and realizing its potential. This approach was in contrast to the other main psychological therapies of the time – psychoanalysis and behaviourism – both of which focus on the pathology of the individual and how to fix it.

Rogers initially called his approach "client-centred", and then changed it to "person-centred", and it has since been hugely influential in education, parenting, business, and other areas a well as clinical work. In person-centred therapy, which Rogers described as "non-directive therapy", the therapist takes the role of a facilitator who helps the client find his own answers, based on the belief that the client knows himself best. In person-centred therapy, the client identifies his problems and what direction the therapy should take. For example, the client may not wish to focus on his childhood but rather deal with issues he is facing at work and the therapist may help him find what

Teaching a child to ride a bicycle requires encouragement and support but ultimately the child must be brave and trust himself. Rogers likened his person-centred therapy to this process.

sort of role he would really like to take. Rogers describes the process as "supportive, not reconstructive"; the client must not come to rely on the therapist for support, but instead needs to learn how to become sufficiently self-aware and self-trusting to be independent and able to live "the good life".

Rogers' legacy

Rogers was one of the most influential psychotherapists of the 20th century, and his new client-centred, non-directive therapy marked a turning point in the development of psychotherapy. He was instrumental in the encounter-group philosophy of the 1960s, which encouraged open communication between individuals. He was responsible for the spread of professional counselling into areas such as education and social work, and was a pioneer in attempting to resolve international conflict through more effective communication. ∎

> 66 The process of the good life… means launching oneself fully into the stream of life.
> **Carl Rogers** 99

WHAT A MAN CAN BE, HE MUST BE

ABRAHAM MASLOW (1908–1970)

IN CONTEXT

APPROACH
Humanistic psychology

BEFORE
1920s Alfred Adler claims there is only one motivating force behind all our behaviour and experience: the striving for perfection.

1935 Henry Murray develops the Thematic Apperception Test, which measures personality and motivation.

AFTER
1950s Kurt Goldstein defines self-actualization as the tendency to actualize, as much as possible, the organism's individual capacities, and proclaims that the drive to self-actualize is the only drive that determines the life of an individual.

1974 Fritz Perls says that every living thing "has only one inborn goal – to actualize itself as it is".

Throughout recorded history, questions have been posed about why we are here, and what the purpose is of our lives. Underlying these questions is a need to identify what will make us truly satisfied, and a confusion about how to find it. Psychoanalysts would claim that the fulfilment of innate biological drives leads towards satisfaction, and behaviourists would describe the importance of meeting physiological needs with food, sleep, and sex, but the new wave of psychotherapeutic thought in the early to mid-20th century believed that the path to inner fulfilment was much more complex.

One of the main proponents of this new approach to the problem was Abraham Maslow, a psychotherapist who is considered one of the founders of the humanist movement in psychology. He examined human experience by looking at the things that are most important to us: love, hope, faith, spirituality, individuality, and existence. One of the most crucial aspects of his theories was that in order to reach the most highly developed state of consciousness and realize the greatest potential, an individual must discover his true purpose in life and pursue it. Maslow refers to this ultimate state of being as self-actualization.

Towards self-actualization
Maslow created a highly structured plan to explain the path of human motivation, defining the steps that humans need to follow as they move towards self-actualization. His famous Hierarchy of Needs, which is often drawn as a pyramid, positions the most basic needs at the base and each of the other essential requirements for a fulfilled life in groups on top.

Maslow's hierarchy is split into two distinct sections: at the beginning are the four stages that make up the "deficiency needs" and all of these must be met before a person is able to reach for greater intellectual satisfaction through the "growth needs". The deficiency needs are simple and basic; they

The Hierarchy of Needs

Maslow's hierarchy of needs lists the qualities he observed in successful individuals who aimed high but kept their feet on the ground.

Growth needs

Self-transcendence
Connecting with something outside ourselves

Self-actualization
Fulfilling personal potential

Aesthetic
Order, beauty, symmetry

Cognitive
Knowing, understanding

Self-esteem
Achievement, recognition, respect, competence

Love and Belongingness
Acceptance, friendship, intimacy, relationships

Safety
Security, stability, health, shelter, money, employment

Physiological
Air, food, drink, sleep, warmth, exercise

Deficiency needs

include physiological necessities (such as food, water, and sleep), the need for safety (to be safe and out of danger), love and belongingness needs (our need to be close to and accepted by others), and self-esteem requirements (our need to achieve in our lives and be recognized).

The "nature–nurture debate" continues to this day. Some people have favoured Galton's theories, including his notion – now known as eugenics – that people could be "bred" like horses to promote certain characteristics. Others have preferred to believe that every baby is a tabula rasa, or "blank slate", and we are all born equal. Most psychologists today recognize that nature and nurture are both crucially important in human development, and interact in complex ways. ∎

Abraham Maslow

Abraham Maslow was born the eldest of seven children in Brooklyn, New York. His parents were Jewish immigrants who had left Russia for the USA to escape the tumultuous political situation there. They had high expectations of Maslow, and forced him to study law – a parental dominance that continued until 1928 when Maslow decided to take control of his life and pursue psychology instead. In the same year he disobeyed his parents by marrying his cousin, Bertha Goodman, with whom he had two children.

Maslow moved to the University of Wisconsin and worked under Harry Harlow, the behavioural psychologist famous for his work with primates. Later, at Columbia University, Maslow found a mentor in psychoanalyst and former colleague of Freud's, Alfred Adler.

Key works

1943 *A Theory of Human Motivation*
1954 *Motivation and Personality*
1962 *Toward a Psychology of Being*

RATIONAL BELIEFS CREATE HEALTHY EMOTIONAL CONSEQUENCES
ALBERT ELLIS (1913–2007)

IN CONTEXT

APPROACH
Rational Emotive Behaviour Therapy

BEFORE
1927 Alfred Adler says that a person's behaviour springs from his or her ideas.

1940s The role of perception in creating reality is popularized by the Gestalt Therapy movement.

1950 Karen Horney suggests we escape from the "tyranny of the shoulds".

AFTER
1960s Aaron Beck says that depression is a result of unrealistic negative views about the world.

1980 American psychiatrist David Burns gives labels to cognitive distortions such as: Jumping to Conclusions, All or Nothing Thinking, Always Being Right, Over Generalizing, and Catastrophizing.

Epictetus, an ancient Greek philosopher, proclaimed in 80 CE, that "men are disturbed not by events, but by the views which they take of them". This principle is the foundation of Rational Emotive Behaviour Therapy (REBT), devised by Dr Albert Ellis in 1955, which asserts that experiences do not cause any specific emotional reaction; instead it is the individual's belief system that produces the reaction.

Practising as a psychoanalyst in the 1940s and 50s, Ellis began to realize that while many of his patients gained an insight into themselves and their childhood, their symptoms unfortunately remained. It seemed that when one problem was resolved, the patient would put another in its place. The issue, Ellis decided, lay in the way the person was thinking (their cognition), and it required more than insight to change it.

Irrational thinking
Ellis began to describe his way of working as Rational Therapy because he believed that the majority of long-standing emotional problems are almost always due to irrational thinking. One of the most common ways in which irrationality occurs, he says, is the tendency to draw extreme conclusions, especially negative ones, about events. For example, if a man who is an irrational thinker loses his job, to him it is not merely unfortunate, but *awful*. He believes that he is worthless because he was fired, and that he will never find another job. Ellis describes irrational beliefs as illogical, extreme, damaging, and self-sabotaging because they cause unhealthy emotional consequences.

Rational thinking creates the opposite effect. Ellis defines rational thinking as helpful to the self. It is based on tolerance and the ability to bear distress without

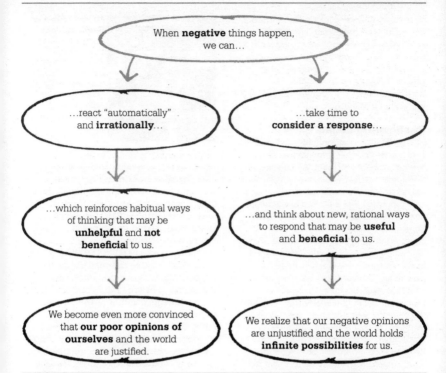

When **negative** things happen, we can...

...react "automatically" and **irrationally**...

...take time to **consider a response**...

...which reinforces habitual ways of thinking that may be **unhelpful** and **not beneficia**l to us.

...and think about new, rational ways to respond that may be **useful** and **beneficial** to us.

We become even more convinced that **our poor opinions of ourselves** and the world are justified.

We realize that our negative opinions are unjustified and the world holds **infinite possibilities** for us.

assuming catastrophic negative conclusions, and is rooted in a belief in positive human potential. This is not to say one turns a blind eye to negative factors in favour of naïve, positive beliefs – rational thinking does acknowledge reasonable feelings of sorrow, guilt, and frustration. The rational thinker may lose her job; it may have even been her fault that she lost the job, but she knows she is not worthless. She may be upset with herself, but she knows that rationally there is the possibility of another job. Rational thinking is balanced and always allows room for optimism and possibilities; it creates healthy emotional consequences.

Ellis's notion of irrational thinking is influenced by Karen Horney's idea of the "tyranny of the shoulds" – a preoccupation with the idea that something should (magically) be different from how it is. The struggle to reconcile these thoughts with reality is a painful and unending one.

Rational thinking, on the other hand, focuses on acceptance; it maintains the balanced sense that sometimes things happen that we would prefer not to, but they are a part of life.

Conditioned response

We become so used to our responses to people and events that they appear to be almost automatic; our reaction becomes inextricably linked to the event itself. However, Ellis aimed to teach people to recognize how an event may contribute to a feeling, but it does not directly cause that feeling. Our emotional response depends on the meaning we put on what took place, which in turn is governed by rational or irrational thinking.

As the name implies, Rational Emotive Behaviour Therapy examines both the emotional response (a cognitive process) and the behaviour. The links between these two flow in both directions: it is » possible to change your thinking through changing your behaviour, and to change your behaviour through changing your thinking. Ellis suggests that the way to change one's thinking involves being able to recognize and then dispute irrational beliefs, challenging them with rational thoughts.

Challenging beliefs

During REBT, an individual is asked to consider whether they have several overriding beliefs about themselves and their position in life as these contribute to irrational responses. This process is known as "disputing". For instance, some people hold the belief that "I am the only really dependable person I know" or "I am destined to be always alone in this world". In therapy, the individual is encouraged to search their personal history to find rationalizations for these belief systems. Someone who has been through the break-up of several relationships may have the delusion that it is their "destiny to be alone" or that they are somehow "unlovable". REBT encourages people to allow for the pain of loss or loneliness, and to logically evaluate factors that led to the loss; but discourages the practice of believing that one or two instances mean that something will always happen, and therefore being happy is impossible.

If someone has been unlucky in love they may feel sad and rejected however, there is a difference between feeling these emotions and allowing them to become a belief system.

One of the difficulties inherent in irrational thinking is that it tends to perpetuate itself, because in thinking, for instance, "nothing good ever happens to me", there is little or no motivation to seek opportunities where good things might happen. The irrational thinker sees the possibilities of having a good experience as so unlikely that he gives up searching for them. It also makes him blind to the good things that do happen. Many people express the self-perpetuating belief: "Yes, I have tried, and *I know* that good things never happen", which rationalizes and reinforces their belief system.

Irrational thinking is "black and white"; it stops an individual from recognizing the full spectrum of possible experiences. If a faulty belief system leads us to always interpret situations negatively, then it prevents the possibility of alternate positive experiences. Though it often appears that "seeing is

Albert Ellis

Albert Ellis was born in Pittsburgh, Pennsylvania, USA. His father was often away on business and his mother suffered from bipolar disease; Ellis frequently took care of his three younger siblings. Ellis began a career in business and then became an author, before his writing on sexuality led him to start studying clinical psychology at Columbia University in 1942. Initially Ellis practised psychoanalysis and was influenced by Sigmund Freud, Albert Adler, and Erich Fromm. However, his Rational Therapy broke away from psychoanalytic theory and is considered to have led the shift towards cognitive behavioural therapy. He is recognized as one of the most influential psychologists in the USA. He wrote more than 70 books, continuing to write and teach until his death at the age of 93.

Key works

1957 *How to Live with a Neurotic*
1961 *A Guide to Rational Living*
1962 *Reason and Emotion in Psychotherapy*
1998 *Optimal Aging*

believing", the reality is that what we believe is what we see.

Constructivist theory

REBT is a constructivist theory, suggesting that although our preferences are influenced by our upbringing and culture, we construct our own beliefs and reality. As a therapy, it attempts to reveal people's inflexible and absolutist thoughts, feelings, and actions; and helps them see how they are choosing to "disturb themselves", as Ellis puts it. It suggests how to think of and choose healthier pathways; and how to internalize and habituate new, more beneficial beliefs. In so doing, the therapist becomes obsolete – once the client grasps the idea of becoming self-aware in decision-making, and choosing deliberately (and often differently), the therapist is no longer needed.

An active therapy

Albert Ellis's theories challenged the slow-moving methodology of psychoanalysis and created the first form of cognitive behavioural therapy, an approach that is

> The best years of your life are the ones in which you decide your problems are your own... You realize that you control your own destiny.
> **Albert Ellis**

popular today. He was an active and directive therapist and in place of long-term, passive psychoanalysis, he put the work and power squarely in the hands of the client – an approach that prefigured Carl Rogers. He also emphasized that theorizing was not enough – "you have to back it up with action, action, action", he said. REBT became one of the most popular therapies of the 1970s and 80s, and was highly influential on the work of Aaron Beck, who described Ellis as an "explorer, revolutionary, therapist, theorist, and teacher". ∎

REBT identifies the patterns of irrational thinking that lead to unhealthy and entrenched beliefs, and describes how to challenge them.

Adversity: An event that may cause mental distress.

I've lost my job!

Beliefs: The initial (irrational) thoughts about the event.

Consequences: The feelings caused by these beliefs.

I'm worthless. I'll never get another job!

I'm depressed and anxious.

Disputation: Taking a rational look at beliefs.

Effect: Revised and rational beliefs about the event.

Hang on, I'm looking at this all wrong!

I'll be able to get another job – it's not that bad.

THE FAMILY IS THE "FACTORY" WHERE PEOPLE ARE MADE
VIRGINIA SATIR (1916–1988)

IN CONTEXT

APPROACH
Family therapy

BEFORE
1942 Carl Rogers publishes
Counseling and Psychotherapy,
emphasizing the role of respect and
a non-judgmental approach in mental
health treatment.

AFTER
1953 US psychiatrist Harry
Stack Sullivan publishes *The
Interpersonal Theory of Psychiatry*,
which states that people are
products of their environment.

1965 Argentinian-born psychiatrist
Salvador Minuchin brings family
therapy to prominence at the
Philadelphia Child Guidance Clinic.

1980 Italian psychiatrist Mara
Selvini Palazzoli and her colleagues
publish articles about their "Milan
systems" approach to family therapy.

We **learn to react** in certain ways
to the members of our family.

⬇

These reactions **shape
a role** that we adopt,
especially when under stress.

⬇

This role may **overwhelm our
authentic self** and be taken with
us into adulthood.

⬇

**The family is the
"factory" where
people are made.**

The role that a person assumes in their
"family of origin" (the family they
grew up in) tends to be the seed
from which the adult will grow. American
psychologist Virginia Satir recognized the
importance that the original family plays in
shaping personality, and looked at differences
between a healthy, functioning family and
one that was dysfunctional. She was
especially interested in the roles that people
tend to adopt in order to compensate when
healthy dynamics are lacking between
family members.

A healthy family life involves open and
reciprocated displays of affection, and
expressions of positive regard and love
for one another. More than any previous
therapist, Satir emphasized the power that
compassionate, nurturing relationships have
in developing well-adjusted psyches.

Role playing

When family members lack the ability to
openly express emotion and affection, Satir
suggested that personality "roles" tend to

The Five Family Roles

| Distractor | Computer | Leveller | Blamer | Placator |

Five distinct personality roles, according to Satir, are commonly played out by individual family members in order to cover up difficult emotional issues.

emerge in place of authentic identities. She noted five commonly played roles that individual family members are likely to adopt, especially in times of stress. These are: the family member who constantly finds fault and criticizes ("the blamer"); the non-affectionate intellectual ("the computer"); the person who stirs things up in order to shift the focus away from emotional issues ("the distractor"); the apologetic people-pleaser ("the placator"); and the open, honest, and direct communicator ("the leveller").

Only levellers maintain a healthy, congruent position, with their inner feelings matching their communications with the rest of the family. Others adopt their various roles because low self-esteem makes them afraid to show or share their true feelings. Placators are afraid of disapproval; blamers attack others to hide feelings of unworthiness; computers rely on their intellect to stop them acknowledging their feelings; and distracters – often the youngest in the family – believe they will only be loved if they are seen as cute and harmless.

These adopted roles may allow the family to function, but they can overwhelm each individual's ability to be his or her authentic self. Satir believed that in order to cast aside these false identities, whether as children or as adults, we must accept self-worth as a birthright. Only then will it be possible to start moving towards a truly fulfilling existence. This begins with a commitment to straightforward, open, and honest communication.

The need for basic, positive, emotional connections lies at the root of Satir's pioneering work. She believed that love and acceptance are the most potent healing forces for any dysfunctional family. By fostering close, compassionate relationships with her patients, she mimicked the dynamic she was encouraging them to adopt. ∎

Virginia Satir

Virginia Satir was born on a farm in Wisconsin, USA, and is said to have decided she wanted to be a "detective of people's parents" at the age of six. Losing her hearing for two years due to an illness helped to make her acutely observant of non-verbal communication, and gave her a sensitive insight into human behaviour. Her father was an alcoholic, and she was well aware of the dynamics of caretaking, blaming, and pleasing that went on around her during her own childhood.

Satir trained as a teacher, but her interest in problems of self-esteem in children led her to take a master's degree in social work. She set up the first formal family therapy training programme in the USA and the "Satir Model" is still hugely influential in personal and organizational psychology.

Key works

1964 *Conjoint Family Therapy*
1972 *Peoplemaking*

MADNESS NEED NOT BE ALL BREAKDOWN IT MAY ALSO BE BREAK-THROUGH

R.D. LAING (1927–1989)

IN CONTEXT

APPROACH
Anti-psychiatry

BEFORE
1908 Swiss psychiatrist Eugen Bleuler coins the term "schizophrenia" to refer to the splitting of mental functions.

1911 Sigmund Freud proposes that schizophrenia is purely psychological, though it cannot be treated with psychoanalysis.

1943 French philosopher Jean-Paul Sartre introduces the distinction between the true self and the false self.

1956 Gregory Bateson, British social scientist, defines a "double bind" as an emotionally distressing dilemma in which all the potential resolutions lead to negative consequences.

AFTER
1978 CT brain scans reveal physical differences between chronic schizophrenics and non-schizophrenics.

Mental illness is **not biological**; it is developed through **difficult social interactions**.

Psychosis is a valid and understandable **expression of distress**.

Mental illness should be valued as a **cathartic and transformative** experience.

Psychiatry wrongly **stigmatizes** mental illness because it **does not conform** to social norms.

Madness need not be all breakdown. It may also be break-through.

A t the end of the 19th century, the notion that mental illness was different in degree – rather than in kind – from the psychological suffering of normal people began to gain acceptance. Sigmund Freud suggested that neurosis and normality are part of the same scale, and that anyone is capable of succumbing to mental

disturbance in dire circumstances. It was from this context that R.D. Laing emerged as the pre-eminent icon of a new cultural trend.

Biology and behaviour

Like Freud, Laing challenged the fundamental values of psychiatry, rejecting its focus on mental illness as a biological phenomenon and highlighting the significance of the social, cultural, and familial influences that shape personal experience. Although he never denied the grim reality of mental illness, his views were in stark contrast to the accepted medical basis and practice of psychiatry.

Laing's work calls into question the validity of psychiatric diagnosis on the grounds that the accepted process of diagnosing mental disorders does not follow the traditional medical model. Doctors perform examinations and tests to diagnose physical illness, whereas psychiatric diagnosis is based on behaviour. According to Laing, there is also an inherent problem in diagnosing mental illness based on conduct, but treating it biologically with drugs. If a diagnosis is based on behaviour, then so too should be the treatment. He argues that drugs also hinder the ability to think, and as a result interfere with the natural process of true recovery.

Approach to schizophrenia

Laing's main work centres on the understanding and treatment of schizophrenia – a serious mental disorder characterized by severe disruptions in psychological functioning – and on explaining it to ordinary people. Schizophrenia, he says, is not inherited, but is an understandable reaction to unlivable situations. He applies social scientist Gregory Bateson's theory of the "double bind", in which a person is put into situations where he or she faces conflicting expectations, and every action leads to negative consequences, resulting in extreme mental distress.

Illness as break-through

Laing was revolutionary in viewing the abnormal behaviour and confused speech of schizophrenics as valid expressions of distress. For him, psychotic episodes represent attempts to communicate concerns, and should be seen as cathartic and transformative experiences that could lead to important personal insights. Laing accepts that these expressions are difficult to comprehend, but he explains that this is merely because they are wrapped in the language of personal symbolism, which is only meaningful from within. Laing's drug-free psychotherapy tries to make sense of a patient's symbolism by listening in an attentive and empathetic

spirit. This is based on the belief that people are healthy in their natural state, and that so-called mental illness is an attempt to return to it. ∎

Shakespeare's King Lear is an iconic example of a man driven mad by difficult circumstances. In Laing's view, Lear's madness is an attempt to return to his natural, healthy, state.

R.D. Laing

Ronald David Laing was born in Glasgow, Scotland. After studying medicine at Glasgow University, he became a psychiatrist in the British Army, developing an interest in working with the mentally distressed. He later trained at the Tavistock Clinic, London, England. In 1965, Laing and a group of colleagues created the Philadelphia Association and started a radical psychiatric project at Kingsley Hall, London, where patients and therapists lived together.

Laing's erratic behaviour and spiritual preoccupations in later life led to a decline in his reputation. As he was unable to develop a workable alternative to conventional medical treatment, his ideas are not generally accepted by the psychiatric establishment. Yet his contributions to the anti-psychiatry movement, particularly in family therapy, have had a lasting impact. He died of a heart attack in 1989.

Key works

1960 *The Divided Self*
1961 *The Self and Others*
1964 *Sanity, Madness and the Family*
1967 *The Politics of Experience*

COGNITIVE PSYCHOLO

THE CALCULATING BRAIN

The first half of the 20th century was dominated by two strands of thinking in psychology: behaviourism (which concentrated on learning theory) and psychoanalysis (which focused on the unconscious and development in early childhood). The mental processes that had preoccupied psychologists in the previous century, such as perception, consciousness, and memory, were largely neglected.

There were inevitably some exceptions. Psychologists Frederic Bartlett of the UK and Bluma Zeigarnik of Russia were both studying the process of memory in the 1920s and 30s, anticipating the work of later cognitive psychologists. In Germany, Wolfgang Köhler's work on problem-solving and decision-making drew on Gestalt psychology – a German school of thought that concentrated on perception and perceptual organization – and was also a precursor of cognitive psychology.

The cognitive revolution

What eventually swung the balance from interest in behaviour to the study of mental processes came from outside psychology. Improvements in communications and computer technology, and possibilities opened up by artificial intelligence – then a growing field thanks to advances made during World War II – led to a new way of thinking about the brain: as an information processor. The mental processes, referred to as "cognitive processes" or "cognition", which behaviourism would not or could not examine, now had a model for psychologists to work from. At the same time, advances in neuroscience led to a greater understanding of the functions of the brain and nervous system. This allowed psychologists, notably Donald Hebb, to examine mental processes directly, rather than merely inferring them from observations of behaviour.

One of the first to apply the information-processing analogy to psychology was a student of Frederic Bartlett's at Cambridge, Donald Broadbent, who had been inspired by the work of computer scientist Alan Turing and communications expert Colin Cherry in the 1940s and 50s. But the turning point came in the USA, where behaviourism began to be criticized for its limitations, leading to a so-called "cognitive revolution" in the late 1950s. In the vanguard of this dramatic shift of approach were the Americans George

GY

Armitage Miller and Jerome Bruner, who in 1960 co-founded the Center for Cognitive Studies at Harvard University.

A new direction

Miller and Bruner's ground-breaking work led to a fundamental change of direction in psychology. Areas that had been neglected by behaviourists, such as memory, perception, and emotions, became the central focus. While Bruner incorporated the concepts of cognition into existing theories of learning and developmental psychology, Miller's application of the information-processing model to memory opened up the field, making memory an important area of study for cognitive psychologists, including Endel Tulving, Elizabeth Loftus, Daniel Schacter, and Gordon H. Bower. There was also a reappraisal of Gestalt psychology: Roger Shepard re-examined ideas of perception, and Wolfgang Köhler's work on problem-solving and decision-making resurfaced in the theories of Daniel Kahneman and Amos Tversky. And, perhaps for the first time, cognitive psychologists, including Bower and Paul Ekman, made a scientific study of emotion.

But it wasn't only the theories of behaviourists that were overturned; Freud's psychoanalytic theory and its followers were also criticized for being unscientific. Aaron Beck found that cognitive psychology could provide a more effective therapy – and that it was more amenable to objective scrutiny. The cognitive therapy he advocated, later incorporating elements of behavioural therapy and meditation techniques, soon became standard treatment for disorders such as depression and anxiety, and led to a movement of positive psychology advocating mental wellbeing rather than just treating mental illness.

At the beginning of the 21st century, cognitive psychology is still the dominant approach to the subject, and has had an effect on neuroscience, education, and economics. It has even influenced the nature/nurture debate; in the light of recent discoveries in genetics and neuroscience, evolutionary psychologists such as Steven Pinker have argued that our thoughts and actions are determined by the make-up of our brains, and that they are like other inherited characteristics: subject to the laws of natural selection. ■

INSTINCT IS A DYNAMIC PATTERN

WOLFGANG KOHLER (1887–1967)

IN CONTEXT

APPROACH
Gestalt psychology

BEFORE
1890 Austrian philosopher Christian von Ehrenfels introduces the concept of Gestalt in his book, *On the Qualities of Form*.

1912 Max Wertheimer publishes *Experimental Studies of the Perception of Movement*, a landmark in Gestalt psychology.

AFTER
1920s Edward Tolman brings together ideas from Gestalt and behaviourist psychology in his purposive behaviourism (now cognitive behaviourism).

1935 *Psychology of Productive Thinking* by Karl Duncker – a German Gestalt psychologist – describes experiments in problem-solving and mental restructuring.

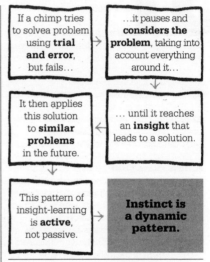

If a chimp tries to solve a problem using **trial and error**, but fails… → …it pauses and **considers the problem**, taking into account everything around it…

It then applies this solution to **similar problems** in the future. ← … until it reaches an **insight** that leads to a solution.

This pattern of insight-learning is **active**, not passive. → **Instinct is a dynamic pattern.**

I n the late 19th century, a group of German psychologists who disagreed with the prevailing schools of thought developed a new, scientific, and distinctly holistic approach, which they called Gestalt. Wolfgang Köhler, who founded the new movement along with Max Wertheimer and Kurt Koffka, explained that the word means both "pattern" and, when applied to their theory, "organized whole". Gestalt psychology (not to be confused with Gestalt therapy, a much later development) took as its starting point the idea that concepts such as perception, learning, and cognition should be considered as wholes, not studied by investigating their various parts.

Köhler thought the dominant branch of psychology, behaviourism, was too simplistic and overlooked the dynamic nature of perception. Pavlov and Thorndike claimed that animals learn by trial and error through simple stimulus–response conditioning, but Köhler believed they were capable of insight and intelligence. He was able to put this to the test when he

Köhler studied chimpanzees solving task-related problems. He realized they could actively perceive several possible solutions before finding the answer through a moment of insight.

Wolfgang Köhler

Wolfgang Köhler was born in Estonia, but his family returned to their native Germany soon after his birth. He studied at various colleges before completing a PhD in Berlin. In 1909, he and Kurt Koffka worked with Max Wertheimer at the Frankfurt Academy on his perception experiments; these formed the basis of Gestalt psychology.

In 1913, Köhler became director of the Prussian Academy of Sciences research station in Tenerife, where he became stranded at the start of World War I, remaining there until 1920. On his return to Berlin, he served as director of the Psychological Institute until 1935, when he emigrated to the USA to escape the Nazi regime. He taught at several US colleges, and was elected president of the American Psychological Association for 1959. Ulric Neisser described him as "a genuinely creative thinker as well as a person of great dignity and honor".

Key works

1917 *The Mentality of Apes*
1929 *Gestalt Psychology*
1938 *The Place of Values in a World of Facts*

became director of an anthropoid research centre on Tenerife from 1913–20, where he studied chimpanzees tackling a number of problem-solving tasks.

Insightful learning

What Köhler observed confirmed his belief, and also demonstrated that problem-solving and learning could be explained in terms of Gestalt. When faced with a problem, such as reaching food in an inaccessible place, the chimpanzees were frustrated in their initial attempts, but would then pause and apparently take stock of the situation before attempting some kind of solution. This often involved using tools – such as sticks or crates that were lying around in their play area – to reach the food. When subsequently faced with the same problem, they instantly applied the same solution. Köhler concluded that the chimps' behaviour showed a cognitive trial-and-error process rather than an actual one; they were solving the problem in their minds first, and only after an insight (the "aha" moment) tried out their solution. This is contrary to the behaviourist view that learning is conditioned by response to a stimulus, and reinforced by reward. The chimps learned by perceiving the problem, not by receiving rewards.

This was a demonstration of Köhler's dynamic model of behaviour, involving organization within perception, rather than passive learning through response to rewards. The pattern (Gestalt) of learning by insight – failure, pause, perception, insight, and attempt – is an active one; but this is not necessarily apparent to someone watching the chimp's separate attempts to solve the problem, mainly because it is not possible to see the organization of perception in the chimp's mind. What we call instinct, the apparently automatic response to solving a problem, is affected by this process of insight learning, and is itself an active, dynamic pattern. ∎

KNOWING IS A PROCESS NOT A PRODUCT

JEROME BRUNER (1915–2016)

IN CONTEXT

APPROACH
Cognitive development

BEFORE
1920s Lev Vygotsky develops his theory that cognitive development is both a social and a cultural process.

1952 Jean Piaget publishes his developmental theories in his book, *The Origins of Intelligence in Children*.

AFTER
1960s The teaching programme "Man: A Course of Study (MACOS)", based on Bruner's theories, is adopted in schools in the USA, the UK, and Australia.

1977 Albert Bandura publishes *Social Learning Theory*, which looks at development through a mixture of behavioural and cognitive aspects.

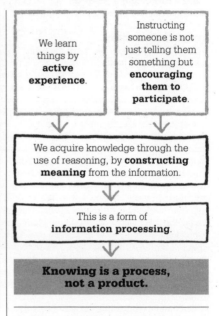

We learn things by **active experience**.

Instructing someone is not just telling them something but **encouraging them to participate**.

We acquire knowledge through the use of reasoning, by **constructing meaning** from the information.

This is a form of **information processing**.

Knowing is a process, not a product.

The field of developmental psychology was dominated throughout much of the 20th century by Jean Piaget, who explained how a child's thinking develops and matures in stages, as a result of a natural curiosity to explore the environment. Lev Vygotsky's theory, which appeared in English shortly after Piaget's, also claimed that a child finds meaning through experience, but widened the meaning of the word "experience" to encompass cultural and social experience. Children, he said, learn mainly through interaction with other people.

At this point in the 1960s, the "cognitive revolution" was gaining momentum; mental processes were increasingly being explained by the analogy of the brain as an "information processor". Jerome Bruner was a key figure in this new approach, having previously studied the ways that our needs and motivations influence perception – and concluding that we see what we need to see. He became interested

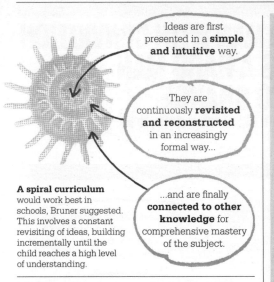

Ideas are first presented in a **simple and intuitive** way.

They are continuously **revisited and reconstructed** in an increasingly formal way...

A spiral curriculum would work best in schools, Bruner suggested. This involves a constant revisiting of ideas, building incrementally until the child reaches a high level of understanding.

...and are finally **connected to other knowledge** for comprehensive mastery of the subject.

Jerome Bruner

The son of Polish immigrants in New York City, Jerome Seymour Bruner was born blind, but regained his sight after cataract operations at the age of two. His father died of cancer when Bruner was 12, and his grief-stricken mother frequently moved the family during his subsequent school years. He studied psychology at Duke University, North Carolina, then at Harvard, where he attained a PhD in 1941 in the company of Gordon Allport and Karl Lashley.

Bruner served in the US army's Office for Strategic Studies (an intelligence unit) during World War II, then returned to Harvard, where he collaborated with Leo Postman and George Armitage Miller. In 1960, he co-founded the Center for Cognitive Studies with Miller at Harvard, remaining until it closed in 1972. He spent the next ten years teaching in Oxford, before returning to the USA. Bruner continued to teach into his nineties.

Key works

1960 *The Process of Education*
1966 *Studies in Cognitive Growth*
1990 *Acts of Meaning*

in how cognition develops, and so began to study cognitive processes in children.

The mind as processor
Bruner began his investigations by applying cognitive models to Piaget and Vygotsky's ideas, shifting the emphasis in the study of cognitive development from the construction of meaning to the processing of information: the means by which we acquire and store knowledge. Like Piaget, he believed that acquiring knowledge is an experiential process; but like Vygotsky, sees this as a social occupation, not a solitary one. He maintained that learning cannot be conducted unassisted: some form of instruction is essential to a child's development, but "to instruct someone... is not a matter of getting him to commit results to mind. Rather, it is to teach him to participate in the process". When we acquire knowledge, we need to actively participate and reason, rather than passively absorb information, because this is what gives knowledge meaning. In terms of cognitive psychology, reasoning is seen as "processing information", so the acquisition of knowledge should be seen as a process, not a product or end result. We need encouragement and guidance in that process, and for Bruner, that is the role of a teacher.

In *The Process of Education* (1960), Bruner presented the idea that children should be active participants in the process of education. The book became a landmark text, altering educational policy in the USA at governmental and school-teacher level. ∎

A MAN WITH CONVICTION IS A HARD MAN TO CHANGE

LEON FESTINGER (1919–1989)

IN CONTEXT

APPROACH
Learning theory

BEFORE
1933 Gestalt psychologist Kurt Lewin leaves the Berlin School of Experimental Psychology and emigrates to the USA.

AFTER
1963 Stanley Milgram publishes his experiments on willingness to obey authority figures, even when orders conflict with one's conscience.

1971 Philip Zimbardo's Stanford prison study shows how people adapt to the roles they are assigned.

1972 US social psychologist Daryl Bem proposes the alternative self-perception theory of attitude change.

1980s Elliot Aronson defends Festinger's theory, conducting experiments into initiation rites.

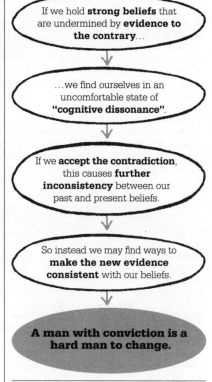

If we hold **strong beliefs** that are undermined by **evidence to the contrary**…

…we find ourselves in an uncomfortable state of **"cognitive dissonance"**.

If we **accept the contradiction**, this causes **further inconsistency** between our past and present beliefs.

So instead we may find ways to **make the new evidence consistent** with our beliefs.

A man with conviction is a hard man to change.

By the end of World War II, social psychology had become an important field of research, spearheaded in the USA by Kurt Lewin, the founder of the Research Center for Group Dynamics at the Massachusetts Institute of Technology in 1945.

On the staff at the centre was one of Lewin's former students, Leon Festinger.

Originally attracted by Lewin's work in Gestalt psychology, he later took an interest in social psychology. In the course of his research, Festinger observed that people continually seek to bring order to their world, and a key part of that order is consistency. To achieve this, they develop routines and habits, such as establishing regular mealtimes and choosing favourite seats on their daily commute to work. When these routines are disrupted, people feel very uneasy. The same is true, he found, of habitual thought patterns or beliefs. If a very strong opinion is met with contradictory evidence, it creates an uncomfortable internal inconsistency; Festinger called this "cognitive dissonance". He reasoned that the only way to overcome this discomfort is to somehow make the belief and the evidence consistent.

Unshakeable conviction

After reading a report in a local newspaper in 1954, Festinger saw an opportunity to study the reaction to just such a cognitive dissonance. A cult claimed to have received messages from aliens warning of a flood that would end the world on 21 December; only true believers would be rescued by flying saucers. Festinger and some of his colleagues at the University of Minnesota gained access to the group, interviewing them before the designated apocalyptic date and again afterwards, when the events had failed to transpire. The now-famous Oak Park study of this

group, written up by Festinger, Henry Riecken, and Stanley Schachter in *When Prophecy Fails*, describes the reaction of the cult members. Where common sense might lead us to expect that the failure of their prediction and consequent cognitive dissonance would cause cult members to abandon their beliefs, the opposite occurred. As the day of reckoning drew near, another "message" came through, declaring that, due to the group's dedication, the world was to be spared. Cult members became even more fervent believers. Festinger had anticipated this; to accept the contradictory evidence would set up an even greater dissonance between past belief and present denial, he argued. This effect was compounded if a great deal (reputation, jobs, and money) had been invested in the original belief.

Festinger concluded that cognitive dissonance, or at least the avoidance of it, makes a man of strong conviction unlikely to change his opinion in the face of contradiction; he is immune to evidence and rational argument. As Festinger explains: "Tell him you disagree and he turns away. Show him facts or figures and he questions your sources. Appeal to logic and he fails to see your point." ∎

Leon Festinger

Leon Festinger was born in Brooklyn, New York, to a Russian immigrant family. He graduated from City College of New York in 1939, then studied at the University of Iowa under Kurt Lewin, finishing his PhD in Child Psychology in 1942. After spending the later years of World War II in military training, he rejoined Lewin in 1945 at the Research Center for Group Dynamics at the Massachusetts Institute of Technology (MIT).

It was during his appointment as professor at the University of Minnesota that Festinger made his famous Oak Park study of a cult predicting the end of the world. He moved to Stanford University in 1955, continuing his work in social psychology, but in the 1960s he turned to research into perception. He later focused on history and archaeology at the New School for Social Research in New York. He died of liver cancer, aged 69.

Key works

1956 *When Prophecy Fails*
1957 *A Theory of Cognitive Dissonance*
1983 *The Human Legacy*

THE MAGICAL NUMBER 7 PLUS OR MINUS 2
GEORGE ARMITAGE MILLER (1920–2012)

IN CONTEXT

APPROACH
Memory studies

BEFORE
1885 Hermann Ebbinghaus publishes his pioneering book Memory: *A Contribution to Experimental Psychology.*

1890 William James makes the distinction between primary (short-term) and secondary (long-term) memory in *The Principles of Psychology.*

1950 Mathematician Alan Turing's test suggests that a computer can be considered a thinking machine.

AFTER
1972 Endel Tulving makes the distinction between semantic and episodic memory.

2001 Daniel Schacter proposes a list of the different ways we misremember in *The Seven Sins of Memory.*

Before information is stored in long-term memory, it is processed by **working memory**.

⬇

Working memory has a **limited capacity** – about seven (plus or minus two) elements.

⬇

If individual "bits" of information are **organized into "chunks"** (meaningful patterns) of information they are easier to store.

⬇

Working memory can then hold **seven (plus or minus two)** of these larger chunks of information.

George Armitage Miller once famously complained: "My problem is that I have been persecuted by an integer. For seven years this number has followed me around". So begins his now famous article *The Magical Number Seven, Plus or Minus Two: Some Limits on our Capacity for Processing Information.* He goes on: "There is… some pattern governing its appearances. Either there really is something unusual about the number or I am suffering from delusions of persecution". Despite the whimsical nature of his title and introduction, Miller had a serious intent, and the article was to become a landmark of cognitive psychology and the study of working memory (the ability to remember and use pieces of information for a limited amount of time).

Miller's paper was published in *The Psychological Review* in 1956, when behaviourism was being superseded by the new cognitive psychology. This fresh approach – which Miller wholeheartedly embraced – focused on the study of mental processes, such as memory and attention. At the same time, advances in computer science had brought the idea of artificial intelligence closer to reality, and while mathematicians, such as Alan Turing, were comparing computer processing with the human brain, cognitive psychologists were engaged in the converse: they looked to the computer as a possible model for explaining the workings of the human brain. Mental processes were being described in terms of information processing. Miller's main interest was in the field of psycholinguistics, stemming from his work during World War II on speech perception, which formed the basis for his doctoral thesis. This led him to take an interest in the growing field of communications, which in turn introduced him to information theory. He was particularly inspired by Claude Shannon, a leading figure in communications, who was investigating effective ways of turning messages into electronic signals. Shannon's communication model, which involved translating ideas into codes made up of "bits", underpins all digital communication. Miller was inspired to look at mental processes in a similar way, and to establish the ground rules for the modern field of psycholinguistics in his 1951 book, *Language and Communication*.

Seven categories

Miller took Shannon's method of measuring information and his idea of "channel capacity" (the amount of information that can be processed by a system) and applied it to the model of short-term memory as an information processor. This was when he began to be "persecuted" by the recurrence and possible significance of the number seven; "sometimes a little larger and sometimes a little smaller than usual, but never changing so much as to be unrecognizable".

The first instance of the "magical" number came from experiments to determine the span of absolute judgment

– how accurately we can distinguish a number of different stimuli. In one experiment cited in Miller's paper, the physicist and acoustic specialist Irwin Pollack played a number of different musical tones to participants, who were then asked to assign a number to each tone. When up to around seven different tones were played, the subjects had no difficulty in accurately assigning numbers to each of them, but above seven (give or take one or two), the results deteriorated dramatically.

In another experiment, by Kaufman, Lord, *et al,* in 1949, researchers flashed varying numbers of coloured dots on to a screen in front of participants. When there were fewer than seven dots, participants could accurately number them; when there were more than seven, participants were only able to estimate the number of dots. This suggests that the span of attention is limited to around six, and caused Miller to wonder whether the same basic process might be involved in both the span of absolute judgment and the span of attention.

The tones and dots in these experiments are what Miller calls "unidimensional stimuli" (objects that differ from one another in only one respect); but what interested Miller is the amount of information in speech and language we can effectively process, and items such as words are "multidimensional stimuli". He looks to »

An experiment into the span of attention presented participants with random patterns of dots flashed on a screen for a fraction of a second. Participants instantly recognized the number if there were fewer than seven.

later studies by Pollack in which the simple tones were replaced by tones that varied in six ways (such as pitch, duration, volume, and location). Surprisingly, despite the apparently larger amount of information, the results still pointed to a differential limit of seven, plus or minus two. The difference is that as more variables are added, accuracy slightly decreases. Miller claims this allows us to make "relatively crude judgments of several things simultaneously". It may explain how we are able to recognize and distinguish such complex things as spoken words and people's faces, without having to process the individual sounds or features.

Miller sees the human mind as a communication system: as the input information increases, the amount transmitted to the brain also increases initially, before levelling off at an individual's "channel capacity". Miller then took this idea of channel capacity a stage further, applying it to the model of short-term memory. William James first proposed the notion of short-term memory, and it had long been an accepted part of the model of the brain as an information processor, coming between the sensory input of information and long-term memory. Hermann Ebbinghaus and Wilhelm Wundt had even suggested that short-term memory had a capacity limited to around seven items (seven, again). Miller believed that what he called working memory had a capacity that corresponded to the limits of absolute judgment and span of attention.

Bits and chunks

In terms of our ability to process information, if working memory is limited to about seven elements, there is a potential bottleneck restricting the amount that can be put into long-term memory. But Miller suggested that there was more to the correspondence than just the number seven, no matter how magical it appeared. The multidimensional stimuli of previous experiments could be seen as composed of several "bits" of related information, but treated as a single item. Miller believed that by the same principle, working memory organizes "bits" of information into "chunks", to overcome the informational bottleneck caused by our limited spans of absolute judgment and short-term memory. A chunk is not, however, just an arbitrary grouping, but an encoding of bits into a meaningful unit; for example, a string of 21 letters represents 21 bits of information, but if this can be broken down into a sequence of three-letter words, it becomes seven chunks. Chunking is dependent on our ability to find patterns and relationships in the bits of information. To someone who does not speak the same language, the seven words might be meaningless, and would not constitute seven chunks, but 21 bits.

Miller's theory was backed up by earlier experiments by other psychologists. In 1954, Sidney Smith conducted experiments in memorizing a sequence of binary digits – a meaningless string of ones and zeroes to anyone unfamiliar with the binary

Miller's theory of chunking says that by building up or breaking down long streams of numbers or letters into memorable chunks, we increase the amount of information we can hold in working memory.

Binary code is a way of recoding information into ever-more tightly packed parcels (through multi-base arithmetic). Miller claims our chunking process operates in a similar way.

system. Smith broke the series down into chunks, at first into pairs of digits, and then into groups of three, four, and five, and then "recoded" them by translating the binary chunks into decimal numbers: 01 became 1, 10 became 2, and so on. He found that by using this system it was possible to memorize and accurately reproduce a string of 40 digits or more, as long as the number of chunks was limited to the span of working memory.

As an aid to memorizing large amounts of information, chunking and recoding is an obvious boon, but it is more than a mnemonic trick. Miller pointed out that this form of recoding is an "extremely powerful weapon for increasing the amount of information we can deal with". It effectively stretches the informational bottleneck.

The study of memory
Miller himself moved away from the subject of memory in his later research, but his theory prompted others to examine it in more detail. Donald Broadbent argued that the real figure for working memory is probably less than seven, and this was later confirmed in experiments by Nelson Cowan, who found it to be around four chunks, depending on the length and complexity of the chunks, and the age of the subject.

In the conclusion to his paper, Miller is dismissive of the significance of the number that originally prompted it. He concludes by saying: "Perhaps there is something deep and profound behind all these sevens… but I suspect that it is only a pernicious, Pythagorean coincidence". ∎

George Armitage Miller

George Armitage Miller, born in West Virginia, USA, graduated from the University of Alabama in 1941 with an MA in speech pathology, and went to Harvard to study for a PhD in psychology in Stanley Smith Stevens' Psychoacoustic Laboratory, with Jerome Bruner and Gordon Allport. World War II was then at its height, and the laboratory was called upon to help with military tasks such as radio jamming.

In 1951, Miller left Harvard for Massachusetts Institute of Technology (MIT), then returned to Harvard in 1955, where he worked closely with Noam Chomsky. In 1960, he co-founded the Harvard Center for Cognitive Studies. He later worked as a professor of psychology at Rockefeller University, New York, and Princeton University. In 1991, he was awarded the National Medal of Science.

Key works

1951 *Language and Communication*
1956 *The Magical Number Seven, Plus or Minus Two*
1960 *Plans and the Structure of Behavior* (with Eugene Galanter and Karl Pribram)

THERE'S MORE TO THE SURFACE THAN MEETS THE EYE

AARON BECK (1921–)

IN CONTEXT

APPROACH
Cognitive therapy

BEFORE
1890s Sigmund Freud proposes an analytic approach to psychotherapy.

1940s and 1950s Fritz Perls, with Laura Perls and Paul Goodman, develops Gestalt therapy – a cognitive approach to psychotherapy.

1955 Albert Ellis introduces Rational Emotive Behaviour Therapy (REBT), breaking with the tradition of analysis.

AFTER
1975 Martin Seligman defines "learned helplessness" in *Helplessness: On Depression, Development, and Death.*

1980s A blend of Beck's ideas and the behaviour therapies of Joseph Wolpe give rise to new cognitive behavioural therapies.

After psychology had become established as a distinct field of study in its own right, around the turn of the 20th century, two main schools of thought emerged: behaviourism, originating from Ivan Pavlov's experiments – and which was enthusiastically championed in the USA – dominated the field of experimental psychology; and the psychoanalytical approach of Sigmund Freud and his followers, which was the basis for the field of clinical psychology. The two had little in common. Behaviourists rejected the introspective, philosophical approach of earlier psychologists, and strove to put the subject on a more scientific, evidence-based footing. The psychoanalysts explored those very introspections, with theories, rather than proof, to support their case.

Cognitive revolution
By the mid-20th century, both approaches to psychology were being critically examined. But although behaviourism was being overtaken by cognitive psychology in experimental work, the clinical sphere was offering no alternative to the psychoanalytical model. Psychotherapy had evolved into many forms, but the basic idea of psychoanalysis and exploration of the unconscious was common to all of them. Some psychologists were beginning to question the validity of this kind of therapy, and Aaron Beck was among them.

When Beck qualified as a psychiatrist in 1953, experimental psychology was focused on the study of mental processes – it was the dawn of the "cognitive revolution". However, the practical approach of cognitive psychologists remained much the same as that of the behaviourists. If anything, they were frequently even more rigorous in establishing evidence for their theories. Beck was no exception to this. He had trained in and practised psychoanalysis,

Psychoanalytic therapy places an emphasis on delving into the patient's **unconscious** to solve current disorders.

Cognitive therapy places an emphasis on examining people's **perceptions** of their experiences.

The evidence for the success of psychoanalytic therapy is based on **personal accounts** rather than facts or research.

There is **strong empirical evidence** for the success of cognitive therapy.

The key to **effective treatment** lies not in the unconscious, but in the examination of **how a disorder manifests itself** in a patient's perceptions.

There's more to the surface than meets the eye.

but grew sceptical of its effectiveness as a therapy. He could find no reliable studies of the success rates of psychoanalysis – only anecdotal evidence of case reports. In his experience, only a minority of patients showed improvement under analysis, and the general consensus among therapists was that some got better, some got worse, and some stayed about the same, in almost equal numbers.

Of particular concern was the resistance of many psychoanalysts to objective scientific examination. Compared with experimental psychology, or with medicine, psychoanalysis seemed largely faith-based, with widely different results between individual practitioners. Reputation was frequently based solely on the charisma of a particular analyst. Beck concluded that "the psychoanalytic mystique was overwhelming... It was a little bit like the evangelical movement". Many psychoanalysts regarded criticism of their theories as a personal attack, and Beck soon discovered that any questioning of the validity of psychoanalysis was likely to be countered with personal denouncement. At one time, he was turned down for membership »

Aaron Beck

Born in Providence, Rhode Island, Aaron Temkin Beck was the son of Russian-Jewish immigrants. Athletic and outgoing as a young child, he became far more studious and introspective after suffering a serious illness at the age of eight. He also acquired a fear of all things medical and, determined to overcome this, decided to train as a doctor, graduating from Yale in 1946. Beck then worked at Rhode Island Hospital, before qualifying as a psychiatrist in 1953. Disillusioned with the psychoanalytical approach to clinical psychology, he instigated cognitive therapy and later established the Beck Institute for Cognitive Therapy and Research in Philadelphia, now run by his daughter, Dr Judith Beck.

Key works

1972 *Depression: Causes and Treatment*
1975 *Cognitive Therapy and the Emotional Disorders*
1980 *Depression: Clinical, Experimental, and Theoretical*
1999 *Prisoners of Hate: The Cognitive Basis of Anger, Hostility, and Violence*

of the American Psychoanalytic Institute on the grounds that his "desire to conduct scientific studies signalled that he'd been improperly analysed". Those who found fault with the idea of analysis did so, some analysts argued, because of insufficient analysis of themselves.

Beck was suspicious of both the circularity of these arguments, and the link with the therapist's own personality. Coupled with his personal experience as a practising psychoanalyst, this led him to examine thoroughly every aspect of therapy, looking for ways in which it could be improved. He carried out a series of experiments designed to evaluate the basis and treatment of depression, one of the most common reasons for seeking psychotherapy, and found that far from confirming the idea that this condition could be treated by examination of unconscious emotions and drives, his results pointed to a very different interpretation.

Changing perceptions

In describing their depression, Beck's patients often expressed negative ideas about themselves, their future, and society in general, which came to them involuntarily. These "automatic thoughts", as Beck called them, led him to conclude that the way the patients perceived their experiences – their cognition of them – was not just a symptom of their depression, but also the key to finding an effective therapy. This idea, which came to him in the 1960s, chimed with concurrent developments in experimental psychology, which had established the dominance of cognitive psychology by studying mental processes such as perception.

When Beck applied a cognitive model to treatment, he found that helping his patients to recognize and evaluate how realistic or distorted their perceptions were was the first step in overcoming depression. This flew in the face of conventional psychoanalysis, which sought and examined underlying drives, emotions, and repressions. Beck's "cognitive therapy" saw this as unnecessary or even counterproductive.

The patient's perception could be taken at face value because, as he was fond of putting it, "there's more to the surface than meets the eye".

What Beck meant by this was that the immediate manifestations of depression – the negative "automatic thoughts" – provide all the information needed for therapy. If these thoughts are examined and compared with an objective, rational view of the same situation, the patient can recognize how his perception is distorted. For example, a patient who has been offered a promotion at work might express negative thoughts such as "I'll find the new job too difficult, and fail", a perception of the situation that leads to anxiety and unhappiness. A more rational way of looking at the promotion would be to see it as a reward, or even a challenge. It is not the situation that is causing the depression, but the patient's perception of it. Cognitive therapy could help him to recognize how biased it is, and find a more realistic or broader way of thinking about the situation.

A distorting mirror creates a view of the world that can 'seem' terrifying and ugly. Similarly, depression tends to cast a negative perspective on life, making sufferers feel more helpless.

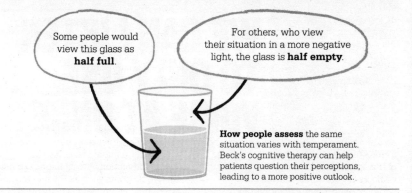

Some people would view this glass as **half full**.

For others, who view their situation in a more negative light, the glass is **half empty**.

How people assess the same situation varies with temperament. Beck's cognitive therapy can help patients question their perceptions, leading to a more positive outlook.

Empirical evidence

Beck's cognitive therapy worked. for a large number of his patients. What is more, he was able to demonstrate that it worked, as he applied scientific methods to ensure that he had empirical evidence for his findings. He designed special assessments for his patients, so that he could monitor their progress closely. The results showed that cognitive therapy was making his patients feel better, and feel better more quickly, than was the case under traditional psychoanalysis. Beck's insistence on providing evidence for any claims he made for his therapy opened it up to objective scrutiny. Above all, he was most anxious to avoid acquiring the guru-like status of many successful psychoanalysts, and was at great pains to demonstrate that it was the therapy that was successful, and not the therapist.

Beck was not the only, or even the first, psychologist to find traditional psychoanalysis unsatisfactory, but his use of a cognitive model was innovatory. He had been influenced in his reaction against psychoanalysis by the work of Albert Ellis, who had developed Rational Emotive Behaviour Therapy (REBT) in the mid-1950s, and he was no doubt aware of the work of behaviourists elsewhere in the world, including the South Africans Joseph Wolpe and Arnold A. Lazarus. Although different in approach, their therapies shared with Beck's a thoroughly scientific methodology and a rejection of the importance of unconscious causes of mental and emotional disorders.

❝ Don't trust me, test me.
Aaron Beck ❞

Once the success of cognitive therapy had been established, it was used increasingly for treating depression, and later Beck found that it could also be helpful for other conditions, such as personality disorders and even schizophrenia. Always open to new ideas – as long as it could be shown that they were effective – Beck also incorporated elements of behaviour therapy into his treatments, as did many other psychotherapists in the 1980s. This has resulted in the varied forms of cognitive behavioural therapy that are used by psychologists today.

Beck's pioneering work marked a turning point for psychotherapy, and his influence is considerable. As well as bringing a cognitive approach into clinical psychology, Beck subjected it to scientific scrutiny, exposing the weaknesses of psychoanalysis. In the process, he introduced several methods for assessing the nature and severity of depression that are still used: the Beck Depression Inventory (BDI), the Beck Hopelessness Scale, the Beck Scale for Suicidal Ideation (BSS), and the Beck Anxiety Inventory (BAI). ■

WE CAN LISTEN TO ONLY ONE VOICE AT ONCE
DONALD BROADBENT (1926–1993)

IN CONTEXT

APPROACH
Attention theory

BEFORE
1640s René Descartes says the human body is a kind of machine with a mind, or soul.

1940s British psychologist and APU director Kenneth Craik prepares flow diagrams comparing human and artificial information processing.

AFTER
1959 George Armitage Miller's studies suggest that short-term memory can hold a maximum of seven bits of information.

1964 British psychologist Anne Treisman suggests that less important information is not eliminated at the filter stage but attenuated (like turning down the volume) so it can still be "shadowed" by the mind.

I n Britain prior to World War II, psychology as an academic discipline lagged behind Europe and the USA. Britain's psychologists had tended to follow in the footsteps of the behaviourist and psychotherapeutic schools of thought that had evolved elsewhere. In the few university psychology departments that existed, the approach followed that of the natural sciences: the emphasis was on practical applications rather than theoretical speculations.

It was in this unpromising academic environment that Donald Broadbent, who went on to become one of the most influential of the early cognitive psychologists, found himself when he left the Royal Air Force after the war and decided to study psychology. However, the practical approach proved ideal for Broadbent, who was able to make perfect use of his wartime experience as an aeronautical engineer and pilot.

Practical psychology
Broadbent had enlisted in the RAF when he was 17, and he was sent to the USA as

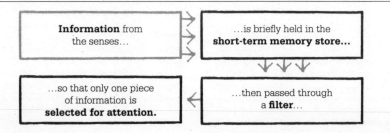

Information from the senses… …is briefly held in the **short-term memory store…** …then passed through a **filter**… …so that only one piece of information is **selected for attention.**

part of his training. Here he first became aware of psychology and the kind of problems it addresses, which led him to look at some of the problems encountered by pilots in a different way. He thought these problems might have psychological causes and answers, rather than simply mechanical ones, so after leaving the RAF, he went to Cambridge University to study psychology.

Broadbent's mentor at Cambridge, Frederic Bartlett, was a kindred spirit: a thoroughgoing scientist, and England's first professor of experimental psychology. Bartlett believed that the most important theoretical discoveries are often made while attempting to find solutions to practical problems. This idea appealed to Broadbent, and prompted him to continue working under Bartlett at the new Applied Psychology Unit (APU) after it opened in 1944. It was during his time there that Broadbent was to do his most ground-breaking work. He chose to ignore the then-dominant behaviourist approach to psychology and to concentrate on the practical problems he had come across in his time in the RAF. For example, pilots sometimes confused similar-looking controls; in some planes, the lever for pulling up the wheels was identical to the one for pulling up the flaps, and the two were situated together under the seat; this led to frequent accidents. Broadbent thought these incidents could be avoided if the capacities and limitations of the pilots were taken into consideration during the design process, rather than surfacing at the point of use.

Broadbent was interested in using psychology to reach a better understanding of what affected the pilots' capabilities. They clearly had to cope with large amounts of incoming information, and then »

Donald Broadbent

Born in Birmingham, England, Donald Broadbent considered himself to be Welsh, as he spent his teenage years in Wales after his parents' divorce. He won a scholarship to the prestigious Winchester College, then joined the Royal Air Force aged 17, where he trained as a pilot and studied aeronautical engineering.

After leaving the RAF in 1947, he studied psychology under Frederic Bartlett at Cambridge, then joined the newly founded Applied Psychology Unit (APU), becoming its director in 1958. Married twice, he was a shy, famously generous man whose "puritanical streak" led him to believe that his work was a privilege and should always be of real use. In 1974, he was awarded the CBE and appointed a fellow of Wolfson College, Oxford, where he remained until his retirement in 1991. He died two years later of a heart attack, aged 66.

Key works

1958 *Perception and Communication*
1971 *Decision and Stress*
1993 *The Simulation of Human Intelligence*

A World War II plane incorporates a dazzling display of informational data; Broadbent was interested in discovering how pilots prioritized information and what design changes would aid this.

had to select the relevant data they needed to make good decisions. It seemed to Broadbent that mistakes were often made when there were too many sources of incoming information.

Broadbent was influenced in his thinking about how we process information by another product of wartime research: the development of computers and the idea of "artificial intelligence". The first director of the APU, Kenneth Craik, had left the unit important manuscripts and flow diagrams comparing human and artificial information processing, which Broadbent clearly studied.

At the same time, code breakers such as the mathematician Alan Turing had been tackling the notion of information processing, and in the postwar period he applied this to the idea of a "thinking machine". The comparison of a machine to the workings of the brain was a powerful analogy, but it was Broadbent who turned the idea around, considering the human brain as a kind of information-processing machine. This, in essence, is what distinguishes cognitive psychology from behaviourism: it is the study of mental processes, rather than their manifestation in behaviour.

To study how our attention works, Broadbent needed to design experiments that would back up his hunches. His background in engineering meant that he would not be satisfied until he had evidence on which to base a theory, and he also wanted that research to have

Air traffic controllers have to deal with a multitude of simultaneous signals. By re-creating this problem in listening experiments, Broadbent was able to identify attention processes.

a practical application. The APU was dedicated to applied psychology, which for Broadbent referred not only to therapeutic applications, but also to applications that benefited society as a whole; he was always very conscious that his research was publicly funded.

One voice at a time

One of Broadbent's most important experiments was suggested by his experience with air traffic control. Ground crew often had to deal with several streams of incoming information simultaneously, sent from planes arriving and departing, which was relayed to the operators by radio and received through headphones. The air traffic controllers then had to make quick decisions based on that information, and Broadbent had noticed that they could only effectively deal with one message at a time. What interested him was the mental process that must take place in order for them to select the most important message from the various sources of incoming information. He felt that there must be some kind of mechanism in the brain that processes the information and makes that selection.

The experiment that Broadbent devised, now known as the dichotic listening experiment, was one of the first in the field of selective attention – the process our brains use to "filter out" the irrelevant information from the masses of data we receive through our senses all the time. Following the air traffic control model, he chose to present aural (sound-based) information through headphones to the subjects of his experiment. The system was set up so that he could relay two different streams of information at the same time – one to the left ear and one to the right – and then test the subjects on their retention of that information.

As Broadbent had suspected, the subjects were unable to reproduce all the information from both channels of input. His feeling that we can only listen to one voice at once had been confirmed, but still the question remained as to exactly how the subject had chosen to retain some of the incoming information and effectively disregard the rest.

Thinking back to his initial training as an engineer, Broadbent suggested a mechanical model to explain what he felt was happening in the brain. He believed that when there are multiple sources of input, they may reach a "bottleneck" if the brain is unable to continue to process all the incoming information; at this point, there must be some kind of "filter" that lets through only one channel of input. The analogy he uses to explain this is typically practical: he describes a Y-shaped tube, into which two flows of ping pong balls are channelled. At the junction of the two branches of the tube, there is a flap that acts to block one flow of balls or the other; this allows balls from the unblocked channel into the stem of the tube.

A question still remained, however: at what stage does this filter come into operation? In a series of experiments that were variations on his original dichotic listening tasks, Broadbent established that information is received by the senses and then passed on in its entirety to some kind of store, which he called the short-term memory store. It is at this stage, he believes, that the filtering occurs. His description of how and when information is selected for attention is known as the "Broadbent Filter Model", and it demonstrated a completely new approach to experimental psychology, not only in combining the theoretical with the practical, but also in considering the workings of the brain as a form of information processing.

The cocktail party problem

Broadbent was not the only person to address the problem of selective attention.

> **❝** One of the two voices is selected for response without reference to its correctness, and the other is ignored.
> **Donald Broadbent ❞**

Our short-term memories are like a **Y-shaped tube**.

Information from all the senses is fed in...

...which creates a **"bottleneck"** where information must be filtered...

...so that only **one stream of information** is processed.

Another British scientist, Colin Cherry, also investigated the subject during the 1950s. Working in communication rather than psychology, Cherry posed what he called the "cocktail party problem": how, at a party where lots of people are talking, do we select which of many conversations to give our attention to, and which to ignore? And how is it possible to be distracted from our focused attention on conversation "A" by conversations "B" or "C"?

To help answer these questions, Broadbent turned his attention to the nature of the filter in his model. Precisely what information does it filter out, and what does it allow through? Following another process of rigorous experimenting, he found that the selection is made not on the content of the information (what is being said), but on the physical characteristics of any message, such as clarity or tone of voice. This suggests that even though information is stored, albeit very briefly, in short-term memory, it is only after filtering that it is processed for meaning and actually understood. This finding had important implications when applied to air traffic control, for example, where decisions could be made on » possibly irrelevant or inaccurate information, rather than being prioritized according to meaning and importance.

Broadbent and Cherry worked together on many dichotic listening experiments to test the filtering process. They realized that filtering is also affected by expectation. In one experiment, participants were asked to listen to different sets of numbers presented simultaneously to each ear. In some cases they were instructed which ear (the information channel) they would be asked about first; in others no instructions were given. The results showed that when people know which ear is receiving the stream of information they will be asked for first, they switch attention to that ear, and the information that enters the other ear is not always accurately retrieved from memory. In all cases the information that people chose or were asked to remember first seemed to be processed more accurately than the later material; it was thought this might be due to parts of the information being lost from the short-term memory store before the participant tried to retrieve it. In 1957, Broadbent wrote: "We can listen to only one voice at once, and the first words we hear are the best recalled".

Modifying the model

In 1958, Broadbent published the results of his research in a book, *Perception* and *Communication*, which effectively outlined a framework for studying attention, comprehension, and memory. The timing was significant, as it coincided with a divergence of opinion about the importance of behaviourism in the USA, and the book slowly became known as one of the landmarks in the development of the new cognitive psychology. As a result, Broadbent was recognized, by his peers if not the public, as the first major psychologist Britain had produced, and was rewarded the same year by being appointed director of the APU to succeed Bartlett.

Not one to rest on his laurels, however, Broadbent saw his new appointment as an opportunity to continue his work on attention, widening the scope of his research and refining the theory. From the starting point of his filter model, he returned to the cocktail party problem, and in particular one phenomenon Cherry had identified concerning the nature of information that is selected for attention. When an overheard conversation includes

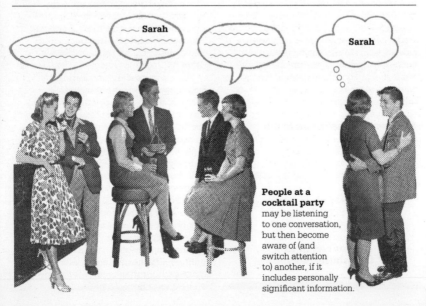

People at a cocktail party may be listening to one conversation, but then become aware of (and switch attention to) another, if it includes personally significant information.

information that has some kind of special significance for a person – such as a personal name – the attention is switched towards that conversation, and away from the one previously attended to.

Further dichotic listening experiments at the APU bore out Cherry's findings: attention is filtered by physical characteristics but also by meaning, using feedback from memory stores, prior experience, and expectations. The sound of a siren, for instance, would divert attention on to that stream of sound. This suggests that information is in some way understood before being selected for attention.

Broadbent realized that his filter model needed modification, but was pleased rather than dismayed to have to make the changes. As a scientist, he felt that all scientific theories are temporary, derived from the evidence available at the time, and so susceptible to change in the light of new evidence; this is how science progresses.

The work of the APU centred around Broadbent's research into attention, but this allowed for a constantly widening range of applications. Broadbent worked tirelessly to ensure that his work was practically useful, examining the effects of noise, heat, and stress on attention in work environments, and he constantly reviewed his ideas as he worked. In the process, he gained government support for his ideas, and the respect of many industries whose practices were improved by his work. This led to yet more research into areas such as differences of attention between individuals, and lapses of attention and their causes. In each

Complex industrial processes could be transformed in efficiency, Broadbent thought, through the application of psychology. He was committed to producing genuinely useful research.

case the results of his experiments led to refinements of his theories. In 1971, he published a second book, *Decision and Stress*, which detailed an extended version of his filter theory. Like its predecessor, this book became a classic textbook of cognitive psychology.

The cognitive approach

Broadbent's books did not reach the general public, but were widely read by scientists from other disciplines. His comparison of the workings of the human brain with electronic machines became more and more relevant as interest in computing increased. His model of the various stages of human information processing – acquisition, storage, retrieval, and use – echoed the work on artificial intelligence at that time.

Broadbent was instrumental in setting up a Joint Council Initiative on Cognitive Science and Human-Computer Interaction, which helped shape the development of cognitive science. His work also established applied psychology as an important approach for problem-solving, increasing its impact well beyond the confines of the laboratory. A key figure in the founding of cognitive psychology, his research into attention laid the groundwork for a new field of enquiry that continues to yield rich results today. ∎

> ❝ His psychology was intended for society and its problems, not merely for the dwellers in ivory towers.
> **Fergus Craik and Alan Baddely** ❞

TIME'S ARROW IS BENT INTO A LOOP
ENDEL TULVING (1927–)

Episodic memory is made up of events and experiences that are stored in long-term memory.

It is distinct from **semantic memory**, which is our long-term memory store for facts and knowledge.

Memories of our experiences are **associated with particular times and places** and can be triggered by these cues.

Associated **sensory cues** such as a particular song or scent can also help us recall seemingly complete memories of past events.

Only humans can **"travel back in time"** to reflect on their experiences in this way...

...as if time's arrow is bent into a loop.

M emory was one of the first fields of study for psychologists in the 19th century, as it was closely connected with the concept of consciousness, which had formed the bridge between philosophy and psychology. Hermann Ebbinghaus in particular devoted much of his research to the scientific study of memory and learning, but the next generation of psychologists turned their attention to a behaviourist study of learning, and "conditioning" replaced memory as the focus of research. Apart from a few isolated studies, notably by Bluma Zeigarnik and Frederic Bartlett in the 1920s and 30s, memory was largely ignored as a topic until the "cognitive revolution" took place following World War II. Cognitive psychologists began to explore the idea of the brain as an information processor, and this provided a model for the storage of memory: it was seen as a process, where by some items passed from short-term or working memory into long-term memory.

By the time Endel Tulving finished his doctorate in 1957, memory was once more a central area of study. Forced to abandon the study of visual perception due to a lack of facilities, Tulving turned his attention to memory. The funding deficit also shaped his approach to the subject, designing experiments that used no more than a pen, some paper, and a supply of index cards.

The free-recall method

Learning about the subject as he went along, Tulving worked in a rather unorthodox way, which occasionally earned him criticism from his peers, and was to make publishing his results difficult. His maverick instincts did, however, lead to some truly innovative research. One hurriedly designed, *ad hoc* demonstration to a class of students in the early 1960s was to provide him with the model for many later experiments. He read out a random list of 20 everyday words to the students, and then asked them to write down as many as they could recall, in any order. As he expected, most of them managed to remember around half of the list. He then asked them about the words that they had not remembered, giving hints such as "Wasn't there a colour on the list?", after which the student could often provide the correct answer.

Tulving developed a series of experiments on this "free recall" method, during which he noticed that people tend to group words together into meaningful categories; the better they organize the information, the better they are able to remember it. His subjects were also able to recall a word when given a cue in the form of the category (such as "animals") in which they had mentally filed that word. Tulving concluded that although all the words memorized from the list were actually available for remembering, the ones that were organized by subject were more readily accessible to memory, especially when the appropriate cue was given.

Memory types

Where previous psychologists had concentrated on the process of storing information, and the failings of that process, Tulving made a distinction »

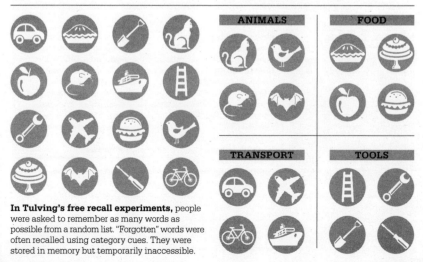

In Tulving's free recall experiments, people were asked to remember as many words as possible from a random list. "Forgotten" words were often recalled using category cues. They were stored in memory but temporarily inaccessible.

ANIMALS   FOOD

TRANSPORT   TOOLS

between two different processes – storage and retrieval of information – and showed how the two were linked.

In the course of his research, Tulving was struck by the fact that there seemed to be different kinds of memory. The distinction between long-term memory and short-term memory had already been established, but Tulving felt there was more than one kind of long-term memory. He saw a difference between memories that are knowledge-based (facts and data), and those that are experience-based (events and conversations). He proposed a division of long-term memory into two distinct types: semantic memory, the store of facts; and episodic memory, the repository of our personal history and events.

Tulving's experiments had demonstrated that organization of semantic information, such as lists of words, helps efficient recollection, and the same appeared to be true of episodic memory. But where semantic memories are organized into meaningful categories of subject matter, episodic memories are organized by relation to the specific time or circumstances in which they were originally stored. For example, a particular conversation may have taken place during a birthday dinner, and the memory of what was said would be stored in association with that occasion. Just as the category of "city" might provide a retrieval cue for the semantic memory "Beijing", the mention of "40th birthday" might act as a cue for the retrieval of what had been said over that dinner. The more strongly these autobiographical memories are associated with the time and circumstances of their occurrence, the greater their accessibility is likely to be. "Flashbulb memories", which are stored when a highly memorable event – such as the 9/11 terrorist attacks – occurs, are an extreme example of this.

Tulving described recollection from episodic memory as "mental time travel", involving us in a revisiting of the past to access the memory. In his later work he pointed out that episodic memory is unique in featuring a subjective sense of time. Specific to humans, it involves not merely awareness of what has been, but also of what may come about. This unique ability allows us to reflect on our lives, worry about future events, and make plans. It is what enables humankind to "take full advantage of its awareness of its continued existence in time" and has allowed us to transform the natural world into one of numerous civilizations and cultures. Through this facility, "time's arrow is bent into a loop".

Encoding information

Tulving realized that organization is the key to efficient recall for both semantic and episodic memory, and that the brain

Endel Tulving

Born the son of a judge in Tartu, Estonia, Endel Tulving was educated at a private school for boys, and although a model student, he was more interested in sports than academic subjects. When Russia invaded in 1944, he and his brother escaped to Germany to finish their studies and did not see their parents again until after the death of Stalin 9 years later. After World War II, Tulving worked as a translator for the American army and briefly attended medical school before emigrating to Canada in 1949. He was accepted as a student at the University of Toronto, where he graduated in psychology in 1953, and took his MA degree in 1954. He then moved to Harvard where he gained a PhD for his thesis on visual perception. In 1956, Tulving returned to the University of Toronto, where he continues to teach to this day.

Key works

1972 *Organization of Memory*
1983 *Elements of Episodic Memory*
1999 *Memory, Consciousness, and the Brain*

somehow organizes information so that specific facts and events are "pigeonholed" with related items. Recalling that specific information is then made easier by direction to the appropriate pigeonhole – the brain "knows where to look" for the memory it wants and can narrow down the search. The implication, he believed, is that the brain encodes each memory for storage in long-term memory, so that specific memories can be located for recollection by a more general retrieval cue. The cues that prompt episodic memory are usually sensory. A specific sound, such as a piece of music, or a scent can trigger a complete memory.

Tulvings's theory of the "encoding specificity principle" was especially applicable to episodic memory. Memories of specific past events are encoded according to the time of their occurrence, along with other memories of the same time. He found that the most effective cue for retrieving any specific episodic memory is the one which overlaps with it most, as this is stored together with the memory to be retrieved. Retrieval cues are necessary to access episodic memory, but not always sufficient, because sometimes the relationship is not close enough to allow recollection, even though the information is stored and available in long-term memory.

Unlike previous theories of memory, Tulving's encoding principle made a distinction between memory that is available and that which is accessible. When someone is unable to recall a piece of information, it does not mean that it is "forgotten" in the sense that it has faded or simply disappeared from long-term memory; it may still be stored, and therefore be available – the problem is one of retrieval.

Scanning for memory

Tulving's research into the storage and retrieval of memory opened up a whole new area for psychological study. The publication of his findings in the 1970s coincided with a new determination by many cognitive psychologists to find confirmation of their theories in neuroscience, using brain-imaging

Semantic memory stores facts and knowledge.

Episodic memory stores events and recollections.

Procedural memory stores methods and techniques.

Different types of memory are physically distinct, according to Tulving, because each behaves and functions in a significantly different way.

techniques that had just become available. In conjunction with neuroscientists, Tulving was able to map the areas of the brain that are active during encoding and retrieval of memory, and establish that episodic memory is associated with the medial temporal lobe and, specifically, the hippocampus.

Partly due to his unorthodox and untutored approach, Tulving made innovative insights that proved inspirational to other psychologists, including some of his former students such as Daniel Schacter. Tulving's focus on storage and retrieval provided a new way of thinking about memory, but it was perhaps his distinction between semantic and episodic memory that was his breakthrough contribution. It allowed subsequent psychologists to increase the complexity of the model to include such concepts as procedural memory (remembering how to do something), and the difference between explicit memory (of which we are consciously aware) and implicit memory (of which we have no conscious awareness, but which nonetheless continues to affect us). These topics remain of great interest to cognitive psychologists today. ■

EVENTS AND EMOTION ARE STORED IN MEMORY TOGETHER
GORDON H. BOWER (1932–)

IN CONTEXT

APPROACH
Memory studies

BEFORE
1927 Bluma Zeigarnik describes the "Zeigarnik effect" of interrupted tasks being better remembered than uninterrupted ones.

1956 George Armitage Miller's *The Magical Number Seven, Plus or Minus Two* provides a cognitive model for storage in short-term memory.

1972 Endel Tulving makes a distinction between semantic and episodic memory.

AFTER
1977 Roger Brown coins the term "flashbulb memory" for autobiographical memory connected with highly emotional events.

2001 Daniel Schacter publishes *The Seven Sins of Memory*, which categorizes the ways that memory can fail.

When we are in a **happy mood**, we tend to store in memory the **positive things** that happen...

When we are in an **unhappy mood**, we tend to store in memory the **negative things** that happen...

...because we **pay more attention** to the information that **agrees with our mood**.

Events and emotion are stored in memory together.

When we are **happy,** we find it easier to recall memories from a **happy time**.

When we are **unhappy,** we find it easier to recall memories from an **unhappy time**.

The 1950s saw a revival of interest in the study of memory. Increasingly sophisticated models of short-term and long-term memory were developed, in order to explain how information is selected, organized, stored, and retrieved. The ways in which memories could be forgotten or distorted were also identified.

Memory and mood

By the 1970s, the focus in learning theory and memory had moved to investigating why some memories are better stored or more easily retrieved than others. One of the foremost psychologists in the field, Gordon H. Bower, had noticed that emotion appeared to impact on memory. Bower carried out studies in which people learned lists of words while in different moods, and later had to recall them, again when in varying emotional states. He uncovered what he called "mood-dependent retrieval": whatever a person has learned when unhappy is easier to recall when they are again unhappy. Bower concluded that we form an association between our emotional state and what is going on around us, and the emotion and the information are stored in memory together. It is then easier to recall facts that we learned when we were in the same mood as we are when recollecting them.

Bower also discovered that emotion plays a part in the type of information that the brain stores. When we are happy, he observed that we tend to notice – and therefore remember – positive things; when we are sad, negative things attract our attention and are committed to memory more easily. For example, Bower found that unhappy people recalled details of a sad story better than those who were happy when they read it. He called this "mood-congruent processing", and concluded that episodic memory – of events, not just words or facts – is especially linked to emotions. The events and emotions are stored together, and we remember best the events that match our mood, both when they occurred, and when recalling them.

Bower's findings led him to study people in various emotional states, retrospectively observing their videotaped interactions with others. Memory and judgement of past behaviour varied with current mood. This research helped Bower to refine his ideas about emotion and memory, and inspired further psychological examination of the role emotions play in our lives. ∎

An idyllic holiday, according to Bower, is more easily recalled when we are in a happy mood. Bad memories of the holiday are likely to be forgotten, or only remembered when we are unhappy.

Gordon H. Bower

Gordon H. Bower was brought up in Scio, Ohio, USA. At high school, he was more interested in baseball and playing jazz than studying, until a teacher introduced him to the works of Sigmund Freud. He went on to graduate in psychology at Case Western Reserve University, Cleveland, switching to Yale for his PhD in learning theory, which he completed in 1959.

From Yale, Bower moved on to the internationally acclaimed psychology department of Stanford University, California, where he taught until his retirement in 2005. His research there helped to develop the field of cognitive science, and in 2005 Bower was awarded the US National Medal of Science for his contributions to cognitive and mathematical psychology.

Key works

1966, 1975 *Theories of Learning* (with Ernest Hilgard)
1981 *Mood and Memory*
1991 *Psychology of Learning and Motivation* (Volume 27)

HAPPY PEOPLE ARE EXTREMELY SOCIAL
MARTIN SELIGMAN (1942–)

IN CONTEXT

APPROACH
Positive psychology

BEFORE
1950s Carl Rogers develops the
concept and practice of "client-
centred" therapy.

1954 Abraham Maslow uses the term
"positive psychology" for the first time,
in his book *Motivation and Personality*.

1960s Aaron Beck exposes the
weaknesses of traditional
psychoanalytical therapy, and
proposes cognitive therapy.

AFTER
1990 Mihály Csíkszentmihályi
publishes *Flow: The Psychology of
Optimal Experience*, based on his
research into the links between
meaningful, engaging activity
and happiness.

1994 Jon Kabat-Zinn's *Wherever You
Go, There You Are* introduces the idea
of "mindfulness meditation" to cope
with stress, anxiety, pain, and illness.

While experimental psychology
after World War II became
deeply concerned with the
cognitive processes of the brain, clinical
psychology continued to examine ways
to treat disorders such as depression and
anxiety. The new cognitive therapies still
focused largely on alleviating unhappy
conditions rather than on creating and
promoting happier ones. Martin Seligman,
whose theory of "learned helplessness"
(the spiral of acquiring pessimistic
attitudes in illnesses such as depression)
had led to more successful treatments in
the 1980s, believed that what psychology
offered was good, but it could offer more.
He felt that therapy should be "as concerned
with strength as with weakness; as
interested in building the best things
in life as repairing the worst". Having
studied philosophy, he likened the task
of his "positive psychology" to that of
Aristotle seeking *eudaemonia* – "the
happy life". Like his philosophical
forebears, Seligman found this was not
a matter of relieving or removing things
that make us unhappy, but of encouraging
those things that might make us happy –
and first he had to discover what they were.

"Happy" lives

Seligman noticed that extremely happy,
fulfilled people tend to get on with others,
and enjoy company. They seemed to lead
what he called "the pleasant life", one of
the three distinct types of "happy" life
that he identified, the others being "the
good life" and "the meaningful life". The
pleasant life, or seeking as much pleasure
as possible, appeared to bring happiness,
though Seligman found this was often
short-lived. Less obviously, the good
life, or being successfully engaged in
relationships, work, and play, gave a
deeper, more lasting happiness.

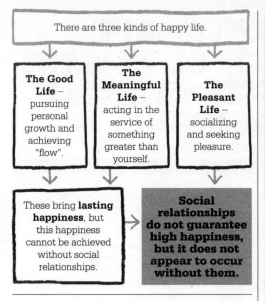

There are three kinds of happy life.

The Good Life – pursuing personal growth and achieving "flow".

The Meaningful Life – acting in the service of something greater than yourself.

The Pleasant Life – socializing and seeking pleasure.

These bring **lasting happiness**, but this happiness cannot be achieved without social relationships.

Social relationships do not guarantee high happiness, but it does not appear to occur without them.

Similarly, the meaningful life, or acting in the service of others or something bigger than oneself, led to great satisfaction and fulfilment.

Seligman also observed that good and meaningful lifestyles both involve activities that his colleague Mihály Csíkszentmihályi had described as generating "flow", or deep mental engagement. The pleasant life clearly does not involve "flow", but Seligman did find that all the "extremely happy people" he studied were also very sociable, and in a relationship. He concluded that "social relationships do not guarantee high happiness, but it does not appear to occur without them". A good and meaningful life may bring *eudaemonia*, but having a pleasant life as well will intensify whatever happiness you achieve. ∎

Martin Seligman

Born in Albany, New York, Martin Seligman took his first degree in philosophy at Princeton University in 1964. He then turned his attention to psychology, gaining a doctorate from the University of Pennsylvania in 1967. He taught at Cornell University, New York, for three years, before returning in 1970 to Pennsylvania, where he has been Professor of Psychology since 1976.

Seligman's research into depression during the 1970s led to a theory of "learned helplessness", and a method of countering the pervasive pessimism associated with it. But after an incident with his daughter that highlighted his own innate negativity, he was persuaded that focusing on positive strengths, rather than negative weaknesses, was key to happiness. Regarded as one of the founding fathers of modern positive psychology, Seligman instigated the Positive Psychology Center at the University of Pennsylvania.

Key works

1975 *Helplessness*
1991 *Learned Optimism*
2002 *Authentic Happiness*

Enjoying social events and the company of others may not offer deep intellectual or emotional satisfaction, but Seligman observed that it was an essential part of being truly happy.

WHAT WE BELIEVE WITH ALL OUR HEARTS IS NOT NECESSARILY THE TRUTH

ELIZABETH LOFTUS (1944–)

IN CONTEXT

APPROACH
Memory studies

BEFORE
1896 Sigmund Freud proposes the notion of repressed memory.

1932 Frederic Bartlett claims that memory is subject to elaboration, omission, and distortion in *Remembering*.

1947 Gordon Allport and Leo Postman conduct experiments that demonstrate various types of non-deliberate misreporting.

AFTER
1988 The self-help book for sexual abuse survivors, *The Courage to Heal*, by Ellen Bass and Laura Davis, is influential in popularizing recovered memory therapy in the 1990s.

2001 In *The Seven Sins of Memory*, Daniel Schacter describes the seven different ways in which our memories can malfunction.

T owards the end of the 19th century, Sigmund Freud claimed that the mind has a way of defending itself against unacceptable or painful thoughts and impulses, by using an unconscious mechanism that he called "repression" to keep them hidden from awareness. Freud later modified his thinking to a more general theory of repressed desires and emotions. However, the idea that the memory of a traumatic event could be repressed and stored beyond conscious recall became accepted by many psychologists.

The rise of various forms of psychotherapy in the 20th century focused attention on repression, and the possibility of retrieving repressed memories became associated with psychoanalysis so strongly that even Hollywood dramas began to explore the link. Memory in general was a popular subject among experimental psychologists too, particularly as behaviourism began to wane after World War II, and the "cognitive revolution" was suggesting new models for how the brain processed information into memory. By the time Elizabeth Loftus began her studies, long-term memory in particular was an attractive area for research, and repressed and recovered memory was about to become a hot topic, as a number of high-profile child abuse cases reached the courts in the 1980s.

Suggestible memory

During the course of her research, Loftus grew sceptical about the idea of recovering repressed memories. Previous research by Frederic Bartlett, Gordon Allport, and Leo Postman had already shown that even in the normal working of the human brain, our ability to retrieve information from memory can be unreliable; Loftus believed that this must also be true of the recollection of events that are so traumatic that they

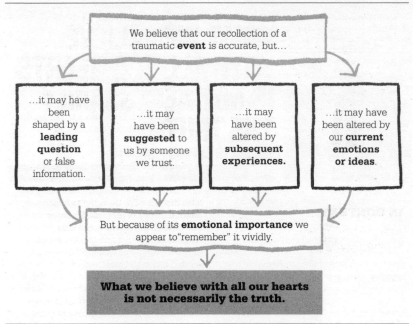

We believe that our recollection of a traumatic **event** is accurate, but...

...it may have been shaped by a **leading question** or false information.

...it may have been **suggested** to us by someone we trust.

...it may have been altered by **subsequent experiences.**

...it may have been altered by our **current emotions or ideas**.

But because of its **emotional importance** we appear to "remember" it vividly.

What we believe with all our hearts is not necessarily the truth.

are repressed – perhaps even more so, given the emotive nature of the events.

Loftus began her research into the fallibility of recollection in the early 1970s, with a series of simple experiments designed to test the veracity of eyewitness testimony. Participants were shown film clips of traffic accidents and then asked questions about what they had seen. Loftus found that the phrasing of questions had a significant influence on how people reported events. For example, when asked to estimate the speed of the cars involved, the answers varied widely, depending on whether the questioner had used the words "bumped", "collided", or "smashed" to describe the collision. They were also asked if there was any broken glass after the accident, and the answers again correlated to the wording of the question of speed. In later versions of the experiment, participants were verbally given false information about some details of the accident (such as road signs around the scene), and these appeared as recollections in many of the participants' reports.

Legal implications

It became clear to Loftus that recollection can be distorted by suggestions and leading questions, made after the event in question. Misinformation can be "planted" into the recollection of an observer. The title of her 1979 book describing her experiments, *Eyewitness Testimony*, shows that Loftus was well aware of the implications of this "misinformation effect", not only for the psychological theory of memory, but also for the legal process. Anticipating the controversy that was to follow, she wrote that "the unreliability of eyewitness identification evidence poses one of the most serious problems in the administration of criminal justice and civil litigation".

False memory syndrome

Loftus was soon to be increasingly involved in forensic psychology, as an expert witness in the spate of child abuse cases of the 1980s. What she realized then was that memories could not only be distorted by subsequent suggestion and incorrect details introduced by »

In a 1974 experiment, Loftus showed a group of people a film of cars colliding, then asked them how fast the cars "bumped", "collided", or "smashed" into each other. Her choice of verb determined their estimate of car speeds.

misinformation, but may even be totally false. Among the many cases in which she was involved, that of George Franklin perfectly illustrates the different aspects of what came to be known as "false memory syndrome". Franklin was convicted in 1990 for the murder of a child who was best friends with his daughter, Eileen. Her eyewitness testimony, 20 years after the murder, was crucial to the conviction. Loftus found numerous discrepancies in Eileen's evidence, and proved her memories to be incorrect and unreliable in several respects, but the jury nonetheless found Franklin guilty.

In 1995, the conviction was overturned because the court had been deprived of "crucial evidence": the fact that Eileen had "recovered" the memory during hypnotherapy. Loftus believed that Eileen's memory of seeing her father commit the murder was sincerely believed, but false, and had evolved because Eileen had witnessed her father commit other cruel actions, and "one brutal image overlapped another". Loftus successfully argued in court that a combination of suggestion during hypnosis, existing frightening memories, and Eileen's rage and grief had created a completely false "repressed memory". The case of Paul Ingram (which Loftus was not involved in) also pointed towards the possibility of implanting false memories. Arrested in 1988 for sexually abusing his daughters, Ingram initially denied the

charges, but after several months of questioning confessed to them along with a number of other cases of rape and even murder. A psychologist involved in the case, Richard Ofshe, grew suspicious and suggested to Ingram he was guilty of another sexual offence – but this time, one that was provably fabricated. Ingram again initially denied the allegation, but later made a detailed confession.

Lost in the mall

The evidence for the implantation of false memories was still anecdotal, however, and far from conclusive; Loftus suffered harsh criticism for what were then considered to be controversial opinions. So she decided to collect irrefutable evidence through an experiment that aimed to deliberately implant false memories. This was her 1995 "Lost in the Mall" experiment. Loftus presented each of the participants with four stories from their own childhood that had apparently been remembered and supplied by members of the participant's family. In fact, only three of the four stories were true; the fourth, about getting lost in a shopping mall, was concocted for the experiment. Plausible details, such as a description of the mall, were worked out in collaboration with the relatives. Interviewed about these stories one week later and then again two weeks later, the participants were asked to rate how well they remembered the events in the four stories. At both interviews, 25% of the participants claimed to have some memory of the mall incident. After the experiment, participants were debriefed and told that one of the stories was false – did they know which it was? Of the 24 participants, 19 correctly chose the mall as the false memory; but five participants had grown to sincerely believe in a false memory of a mildly traumatic event.

Loftus had provided an insight into how false memories might form in real, everyday settings. For ethical reasons Loftus could not devise an experiment to test whether a truly traumatic false memory (such as child abuse) would be even more vividly recalled and sincerely believed, but she suggested that it would, in the same way that a more disturbing dream is more vividly recalled and even mistaken for reality. It was this idea that prompted her to say, "what we believe with all our hearts is not necessarily the truth".

However, in 1986, psychologists John Yuille and Judith Cutshall did manage to conduct a study of memory following a traumatic situation. They found that witnesses to an actual incident of gun shooting had remarkably accurate memories, even six months after the event, and resisted attempts by the researchers to distort their memories though misleading questions.

Questionable therapy

Loftus points out that her findings do not deny that crimes such as abuse may have taken place, nor can she prove that repressed memories do not exist; she merely stresses the unreliability of recovered memory, and insists that courts must seek evidence beyond this. Her work has also called into question the validity of the various methods used to recover memory, including psychotherapeutic techniques such as regression, dream work, and hypnosis. Consequently, it raised the possibility that false memories can be implanted during the therapeutic process by suggestion, and in the 1990s several US patients who claimed they were victims of "false memory syndrome" successfully

sued their therapists. Unsurprisingly, this apparent attack on the very idea of repressed memory earned an adverse reaction from some psychotherapists, and split opinion among psychologists working in the field of memory. Reaction from the legal world was also divided, but after the hysteria surrounding a series of child abuse scandals in the 1990s had died down, guidelines incorporating Loftus's theories on the reliability of eyewitness testimony were adopted by many legal systems.

Today, Loftus is acknowledged as an authority on the subject of false memory. Her theories have become accepted by mainstream psychology and have inspired further research into the fallibility of memory in general, notably by Daniel Schacter in his book *The Seven Sins of Memory*. ∎

Despite the unreliability of eyewitness testimony, Loftus found that jurors tend to give more weight to it than any other form of evidence when reaching a verdict.

Elizabeth Loftus

Born Elizabeth Fishman in Los Angeles, USA in 1944, Loftus took her first degree at the University of California with the intention of becoming a high school maths teacher. While at UCLA, however, she started classes in psychology, and in 1970 received a PhD in psychology at Stanford University. It was here that she first became interested in the subject of long-term memory, and met and married fellow psychology student Geoffrey Loftus, whom she later divorced. She taught at the University of Washington, Seattle, for 29 years, becoming professor of psychology and adjunct professor of law. She was appointed distinguished professor at the University of California in 2002, and was the highest-ranked woman in a scientifically quantified ranking of the 20th century's most important psychologists.

Key works

1979 *Eyewitness Testimony*
1991 *Witness for the Defense* (with Katherine Ketcham)
1994 *The Myth of Repressed Memory* (with Katherine Ketcham)

COMPULSIVE BEHAVIOUR RITUALS ARE ATTEMPTS TO CONTROL INTRUSIVE THOUGHTS
PAUL SALKOVSKIS (1950s–)

IN CONTEXT

APPROACH
Cognitive behavioural therapy

BEFORE
1950s Joseph Wolpe applies behaviourist ideas to clinical psychology in techniques such as systematic desensitization.

1952 Behaviour and personality theorist Hans J. Eysenck causes controversy with claims that psychotherapy has no beneficial effect.

1955 Albert Ellis offers an alternative to traditional psychotherapy with his Rational Emotive Behaviour Therapy (REBT).

1960s Aaron Beck questions whether psychoanalytical therapy is effective; he goes on to develop cognitive therapy.

AFTER
2000s Cognitive behavioural therapy becomes a standard treatment for anxiety, panic attacks, and other disorders.

T he second half of the 20th century saw a profound change in clinical psychology. Psychoanalysis was seen by many psychologists as less than scientific, and by the 1960s it was replaced as the treatment for some disorders by behaviourist therapies, or the newer cognitive therapy developed by Aaron Beck. Combinations of these approaches, under the umbrella term cognitive behavioural therapy (CBT), evolved in the 1980s, pioneered in Britain by Paul Salkovskis. CBT, he found, was especially successful in treating obsessive-compulsive disorder (OCD); where psychoanalysis had failed to find a root cause for the disorder in repression or past trauma, Salkovskis explained the problem in terms of cognitive psychology, and offered a cognitive and behavioural treatment.

Obsessive thoughts

Salkovskis suggests that obsessive-compulsive disorder has its basis in the sort of unwelcome and intrusive thoughts that we all have from time to time – the idea that something terrible is about to happen, or that we will suffer or cause some awful misfortune. Most of the time, we can put these thoughts out of our minds and carry on with life, but sometimes they are more difficult to shake off. At the extreme end of the scale, the thoughts

Compulsive activities such as repeated hand washing may be an attempt to control intrusive thoughts. Shakespeare's Lady Macbeth is driven by guilt to continually wash her hands.

We all have unwelcome **intrusive thoughts**.

⬇

But some people have trouble shaking them off, and the thoughts become **over-important and obsessional**.

⬇

They overestimate the **threat** posed by these thoughts.

They feel **responsible** for any harm implied by these intrusive thoughts.

⬇

They therefore feel compelled to take action to counter the threats and control the thoughts.

⬇

Compulsive behaviour rituals are attempts to control intrusive thoughts.

Paul Salkovskis

A graduate of the Institute of Psychiatry, London in 1979, Paul Salkovskis took up a post at the University of Oxford in 1985 to research panic disorders. His interest in the application of cognitive theory to anxiety disorders led to his appointment as a Senior Fellow and later as Professor of Cognitive Psychology.

While at Oxford, the emphasis of his work moved to the treatment of obsessive-compulsive disorder using cognitive behavioural therapy. In 2000, he became Professor of Clinical Psychology and Applied Science at the Institute of Psychiatry, and Clinical Director in the Centre for Anxiety Disorders and Trauma. Since 2010, Salkovskis has been based at the University of Bath, where he is establishing a specialist CBT research and treatment centre.

Key works

1998 *Panic Disorder*
1999 *Understanding and Treating Obsessive-Compulsive Disorder*
2000 *Causing Harm and Allowing Harm* (with A. Wroe)

become obsessive and bring with them a feeling of dread and responsibility. People predisposed to these kinds of obsessive thoughts find it difficult to make a rational appraisal of their importance, and overestimate not only any risk of harm, but also the amount of control they have to prevent it. Obsessive thoughts of catching and passing on a deadly disease, for example, may result in compulsive cleaning or hand washing. There is also a feeling of a responsibility to act, even if the action is out of proportion to the risk. The resulting compulsive actions can become ritual behaviour patterns, carried out repeatedly in an attempt to gain control over a perceived threat.

Cognitive behavioural therapy combines cognitive and behavioural techniques to address both the cause and the symptoms of OCD to great effect. First, the patient is helped through cognitive therapy to recognize the obsessional thoughts for what they are, making a more rational appraisal of the risk and, crucially, of how much responsibility he or she has for taking preventative action. This cognitive approach helps reduce the distress. Alongside this, behavioural therapy techniques, such as desensitization (gradual exposure to the perceived threat) help the patient to control his or her compulsive behaviour. Salkovskis uses CBT techniques to successfully treat anxiety, panic attacks, and phobias. ■

SOCIAL PSYCHOLO

BEING IN A WORLD OF OTHERS

As psychology became established as a scientific discipline, its scope was at first limited to the examination of the mind and its workings, before broadening to include the study of behaviour. For much of the first half of the 20th century, this meant the emphasis was very much on a study of the mind and behaviour of individuals and their responses to their environment, though it became increasing clear to some psychologists that "the environment" includes other people.

The field of social psychology emerged in the 1930s, when psychologists began to explore the interactions of individuals within groups and society as a whole. They examined the effect of social organizations on the individual, and the way that social structures are influenced by the psychology of their individual members. Social psychologists, as they were called, also studied the relationships between individuals within these groups and between different groups. This introduced a new set of topics to psychology, including group dynamics, attitudes, and prejudice, as well as social conflict, conformity, obedience, and social change.

Social environment

Among the first to make a systematic study of the psychology of social groups was German–American Kurt Lewin, considered the "father of social psychology". Lewin took a fresh look at the dominant behaviourist approach, examining how behaviour results from the interaction between the individual and his environment, as well as the nature of that environment. In his studies of small groups, he laid the foundations for later examinations of group dynamics and how groups and their members bring about change.

Behaviourism fell out of favour after World War II, and Lewin's ideas about the effect of the social environment provided an alternative that was enthusiastically taken up by the next generation. The concept of "attribution" – the way we see and interpret the behaviour of others – became an area of specific research, and from that came theories of conformity and cultural norms such as those of Solomon Asch. Erving Goffman's best-known theory – that we act out certain behaviours to suit the impression we want to give to others – also came out of this new emphasis on the importance of social interaction.

Research in the 1960s shed light on the darker aspects of behaviour; Melvin Lerner showed how victims are sometimes blamed for what happens to them, and Elliot Aronson explained that apparently aberrant behaviour could be the result of circumstances rather than insanity. More controversially, especially at a time when the atrocities of World War II were still fresh in people's minds, experiments by Stanley Milgram and Philip Zimbardo showed just how far the need to obey and conform affects our behaviour.

Applying psychology

The advent of cognitive psychology brought a new influence on social psychology. The effects of cognitive processes such as memory and emotion were highlighted by Roger Brown and Robert Zajonc, and these findings were exploited widely by the mass media and advertising, which began to play an increasingly important role in modern society. Mass media and advertising in turn had a growing effect on social structures, prompting theories of social constructivism by psychologists such as Serge Moscovici.

As a result, social psychology has rapidly become more applicable to many different situations. It has influenced other areas of psychology – in particular psychotherapy, through William Glasser's "reality therapy". It has also impacted on other disciplines, including sociology, anthropology, and even politics and economics. The 1960s saw the rise of the civil rights movement and feminism, both of which challenged the status quo. Issues surrounding prejudice, cultural norms, and beliefs came to the fore, and the work of social psychologists such as Janet Taylor Spence did much to alter attitudes towards women, while others used Lewin's process of social transformation to bring about organizational changes. Theories and models pioneered by social psychologists are now used by business, industry, and all kinds of social organizations, and more recently have been adopted as a means of achieving social and political reform in societies suffering from oppression, most notably in the "Liberation Psychology" espoused by Ignacio Martín-Baró.■

YOU CANNOT UNDERSTAND A SYSTEM UNTIL YOU TRY TO CHANGE IT

KURT LEWIN (1890–1947)

IN CONTEXT

APPROACH
Field theory

BEFORE
Early 1900s Sigmund Freud and other psychotherapists argue that human behaviour is a result of past experience.

1910s Wolfgang Köhler, among other Gestalt psychologists, argues that people must be understood holistically, according to all of their elements and their interactions with the surrounding environment.

AFTER
1958 In *The Dynamics of Planned Change*, Ronald Lippitt, Jeanne Watson, and Bruce Westley create a seven-step change theory that focuses on the role of the change agent rather than on the evolution of change itself.

In order for a change of behaviour to take place, details about both the **individual and the environment** must be taken into account.

As a change occurs, more **key qualities and values** of a system are revealed.

Therefore, the **change process itself** offers important information about a system.

You cannot understand a system until you try to change it.

---

he behaviourists believed that behaviour is dictated by the environment alone, but in the 1920s Kurt Lewin made the claim that behaviour is a result of both the individual and the environment. His revolutionary ideas developed and evolved into the study of group dynamics that is invaluable to organizations today.

In his investigation of human behaviour, Lewin developed field theory, which explores the forces and factors that influence any given situation. Lewin's "field" refers to the psychological environment of the individual or the collective group at a particular point in time, and he identified two opposing forces present in any given field: helpful forces, which drive people towards achieving their goals, and hindering forces, which inhibit movement towards these goals.

Lewin's change model

Field theory provided the basis for Lewin's model of change, which offers an invaluable guide for successful transformation, both for individuals and organizations. The model shows that in order to carry out the process of change successfully, a person or organization leader must take into account the various influences at play both within the minds of individuals and within their environment.

In explaining his change model, Lewin emphasizes that the entire situation, including all the relevant personal and environmental details, must be taken into account, as focusing on isolated facts can lead to a skewed perception of the circumstances. Not only must you have a thorough and holistic understanding of a situation in order to change it, but that understanding actually deepens throughout the change process, and therefore "you cannot understand a system until you try to change it".

Lewin's model describes a three-step process for achieving personal or organizational transformation. The first stage – which he called "unfreezing" – involves preparing by recognizing that change is necessary, and dismantling old beliefs and practices. Change occurs in the second stage, and is often accompanied by confusion and distress as the old mindset or system breaks down. The third and final stage, "freezing", occurs when a new mindset is crystallized and there is an accompanying sense of comfort and stability within the new framework. The process is difficult because it involves painful unlearning, difficult relearning, and the restructuring of thoughts, feelings, attitudes, and perceptions.

Unfreezing beliefs

The unfreezing stage is perhaps the most complex stage of the process, as people are naturally inclined to resist changes to their established mindsets and routines. It requires careful preparation; many change efforts within organizations fail simply because employees are not adequately prepared, making them more resistant to change and less likely to function effectively under the new system. Preparation might include creating an exciting vision for change that employees can rally around, communicating it effectively, developing a sense of urgency and necessity for change, providing employees with support, and allowing them to participate actively in the process.

Successful organizational change is engendered by making a unique diagnosis of the people and situational forces involved, and understanding the interplay between them.

On an individual level, people may react to this stage defensively, not wanting to leave their comfort zone and undergo the challenge of learning new skills or accepting a new set of beliefs. This natural resistance can be overcome if the individual is helped to accept that the change is necessary, valid, and will lead to the best outcome, and if support is given to engender a feeling of psychological safety.

Lewin demonstrated the positive effect of creating an environment of psychological safety during the unfreezing stage (and of allowing active participation in the change process) in his efforts to convince American housewives to serve animal organs as food at home during World War II. Historically, offal had only been eaten by low-income families, but the American government wanted to ensure that nutritious food was not going to waste during a time of food shortages, especially as kidneys, livers, and hearts are all high-protein foods. The US Department of Agriculture called upon Lewin to help convince housewives to include these meats in their family meals. During interviews with housewives, Lewin realized that there were both helpful and hindering forces at play. The helpful forces, or incentives, towards changing the housewives' view of organ meat was its high nutritional value. The hindering forces, or barriers, to change centred around the women's view that the meat »

Learning to use new technologies in place of old ones is made easier by an increase in driving forces – such as the ability to contact friends and family worldwide, instantly and inexpensively.

was inappropriate for them and their families, and to a lesser degree, that it would not taste good.

Lewin set up a study using two groups of housewives to explore the best ways of initiating change. The first group was told repeatedly that eating offal was beneficial for them, while the other group took part in a small group discussion focusing on how the food shortage problem could be eased if women like themselves could be convinced to take part in a programme of using secondary cuts of meat such as livers, kidneys, and hearts. When around one-third of the women who had participated in the discussion group later served offal for dinner, Lewin concluded that increasing the level of people's involvement also increases the likelihood of changing their attitudes and behaviours. Lecturing to the first group had proved ineffective, but in the discussion group he had created an environment in which women felt psychologically safe enough to express their concerns and opinions. Through exploring their beliefs as well as the realities of the food shortages, he helped them change their opinions about which meats were edible and guided them towards a new belief: that offal is acceptable to buy and serve at home.

Making the change
During Lewin's second stage – the actual change process – people are confronted with the daunting and confusing task of implementing a new system. They must give up familiar routines and practices and master new skills (which itself can arouse feelings of uncertainty or a fear of failure). In an organization, the new system will be defined by the leadership, and often relates to technology, structure, procedures, or culture. It is important at this stage to provide sufficient support for employees and ensure the elimination of obstacles.

At the level of personal change, people cannot be given a new belief system, but must find and accept one for themselves. When an old belief has been proven wrong or ineffective, we are naturally inclined to replace the old value system with a new one, filling the uncomfortable void left by the unfreezing process. We do this in a combination of ways: relying on our instinctive feelings, studying role models, and looking more generally to the vast array of information available. We hope in this way to expose ourselves to a new piece of information that will solve the problem. Once this insight is achieved, we have accepted and established a new mindset.

In the case of the American housewives during World War II, Lewin provided the women with new information by educating them about the good taste and nutritional value of offal (thereby replacing their old belief that it was an inferior meat), and convincing them that given the reality of wartime food shortages, there was absolutely no shame in serving it to their families (thereby replacing their pre-wartime belief that they would be viewed as social inferiors for eating it).

The freezing stage
After change has been implemented within an organization, it must become part of the company's culture (or "frozen") in order for it to be successful in the long term. The new thought processes, practices, and behaviours adopted during the transition must become routine. Management can help to ensure changes become more firmly established by publicizing the ways in which change has benefited the company, and by nurturing positive feelings towards the change among employees, perhaps by delivering rewards for implementing the new skills or

processes. For example, in the 1990s, Continental Airlines was forced to file for bankruptcy. In order to stay in business, the management implemented a major change: they shifted the company focus from saving costs to putting out a quality product that met high customer standards. They decided to reward employees for adopting the new policies and practices (to ensure compliance to the new priorities) by offering them a $65 bonus if the US Department of Transportation rated the company among the top five airlines. The use of Lewin's change model marked Continental's evolution from being the poorest-performing airline to being named Airline of the Year.

At the individual level, the freezing stage marks a time when new beliefs and practices are tested through trial and error; this either reinforces the changes or starts a new change cycle. For example, after a week of serving offal to her family, a wartime housewife might assess whether her family seems to enjoy the meat, whether they seem healthy, and whether other families seem to be judging her positively or negatively based on her meal choices. If the answers to these questions are positive, she will continue to serve offal at dinnertime. If, however, her children do not appear to be as healthy as they were

During World War II, housewives were encouraged to change many of their beliefs, from the types of food and clothing that were acceptable to their capability to do "men's jobs".

when eating chicken or steak, or if other women are criticizing her choice of meat, she may decide to abandon offal and look for other ways to feed her family, starting the unfreezing and change processes all over again.

Lewin's pioneering experimental work into social systems has led him to be widely recognized as the founder of social psychology. He was the first psychologist to study "group dynamics" and organizational development in a methodical way. He applied rigorous social science to effect useful social transformation, and his work has been influential across the fields of experimental and social psychology. ∎

Kurt Lewin

German-American psychologist Kurt Lewin was born in 1890 into a middle-class Jewish family in Mogilno, Poland (then Prussia). In 1905, his family moved to Berlin, where he studied medicine at the University of Freiburg before transferring to the University of Munich to study biology. During World War I, he served in the German army, but returned to Berlin to complete his PhD after being injured. He worked at the Psychological Institute, Berlin, from 1921 to 1933, when restrictions on the Jewish population compelled him to resign and seek refuge in the USA. He began working at Cornell University, then moved to the University of Iowa where he became a professor. In 1944, he became director of the Center for Group Dynamics at the Massachusetts Institute of Technology, but died of a heart attack just three years later.

Key works

1935 *A Dynamic Theory of Personality*
1948 *Resolving Social Conflicts*
1951 *Field Theory in Social Science*

HOW STRONG IS THE URGE TOWARDS SOCIAL CONFORMITY?

SOLOMON ASCH (1907-1996)

IN CONTEXT

APPROACH
Conformism

BEFORE
1880s Hippolyte Bernheim, a French physician, uses hypnosis to demonstrate the concept of "suggestibility".

1935 Muzafer Sherif's conformism experiment leads Asch to develop the Asch Paradigm.

AFTER
1963 Stanley Milgram's obedience experiments show that people conform for an authority figure despite experiencing a moral conflict.

1976 Serge Moscovici argues that a consistent minority can be influential.

1979 Knud S. Larsen, a Danish psychologist, shows that conformity may be tied to cultural climate.

Social psychologist Solomon Asch challenged our idea of ourselves as autonomous beings when he devised an experiment to demonstrate our urge to conform. His famous experiment showed that when people are confronted with a majority opinion, the tendency to conform may be stronger than their commitment to what they perceive to be true. He detailed his findings in his 1955 paper *Opinions and Social Pressure*, which also discusses the social influences that shape a person's beliefs, judgments, and practices. Asch wanted to investigate the effects of group pressure on individual decision-making, and how and to what extent people's attitudes were influenced by social forces around them.

Turkish psychologist Muzafer Sherif set out to answer similar questions in 1935, using a visual illusion called the autokinetic effect, whereby a stationary spot of light seen in a dark room appears to move. He told the subjects of his study that he was going to move the light and asked them how far they thought it had shifted. Tested in groups, the participants' estimates converged into a group norm, revealing that they used others' estimates as a frame of reference in an ambiguous situation. Although Sherif believed that he had demonstrated the principles of conformity, Asch contended that – because there was no right or wrong answer to the task – no definitive conclusions could be drawn. Conformity, he believed, could only be measured in terms of an individual's tendency to agree with group members who unanimously give the wrong answer on a task that has an unambiguous solution. The simple perceptual task that became known as the Asch Paradigm was designed to offer this.

The Asch Paradigm

The experiment was conducted with 123 male subjects, each of whom was put individually into a group of five to seven "confederates" (people who were aware of

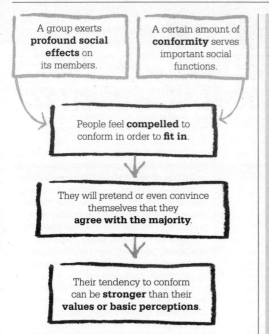

A group exerts **profound social effects** on its members.

A certain amount of **conformity** serves important social functions.

People feel **compelled** to conform in order to **fit in**.

They will pretend or even convince themselves that they **agree with the majority**.

Their tendency to conform can be **stronger** than their **values or basic perceptions**.

Solomon Asch

Solomon Elliott Asch was a pioneer in the field of social psychology. He was born into a Jewish family in Warsaw (then part of the Russian Empire) in 1907. At the age of 13 he emigrated to the US and studied psychology. He received a PhD in 1932 from Columbia University, where he was influenced by Max Wertheimer.

Asch became a professor at Swarthmore College in 1947, and worked closely with Wolfgang Köhler. He held visiting posts at Massachussets Institute of Technology (MIT) and Harvard, where he supervised Stanley Milgram's PhD, before moving to the University of Pennsylvania. His many awards include the Distinguished Scientific Contribution Award from the American Psychological Association. He died aged 88.

Key works

1951 *Effects of Group Pressure Upon the Modification and Distortion of Judgment*
1952 *Social Psychology*
1955 *Opinions and Social Pressure*
1956 *Studies of Independence and Conformity*

the real aims of the experiment but were introduced as fellow participants). The group was shown one card with a line on it, followed by another card with three lines labelled A, B, and C, and asked which one of those three lines was the same length as the line on the first card.

The room was always organized so that the subject would give either the last or the penultimate answer. Over the course of 18 trials, confederates were instructed to provide the correct answers for the first six, but then to give identical but incorrect answers for another 12. This was to test whether or not the subject would answer correctly or whether he would match his response to that of the confederates when all gave the same – incorrect – answer. Initially, Asch thought that only a few of the subjects would comply with the confederates' answers. After all, the task was simple and the answers obvious; during the pilot study in which there was no pressure to yield to an erroneous group, only three errors were made out of 720 total trials. The results of the actual study were surprising. When surrounded by a group of people all giving the same incorrect answer, subjects gave incorrect answers on almost a third (32 per cent) of the questions; 75 per cent of them provided an incorrect response for at least one » question. One person complied with the group giving a wrong answer on 11 out of 12 trials. Because the task was both simple and unambiguous, these figures indicate a high degree of conformity by the subjects. However, not a single participant conformed on all critical trials, and 13 of the 50 participants (26 per cent) never conformed.

The results proved that the subjects themselves were highly consistent. Those who broke away from the group opinion and provided an independent answer did not succumb to the majority even over many trials, while those who chose to comply with the majority seemed unable to break this pattern.

Explanations

To get a deeper understanding of his results, Asch interviewed his subjects to find out why they offered incorrect answers. Some said they wanted to go along with what they believed to be the experimenter's wishes and avoid upsetting the overall experiment. A few actually wondered if they were perhaps suffering from eye strain or were seated at a misleading angle. Some denied that they were aware of having given incorrect answers. Eventually, some admitted to knowing their answers were incorrect, adding that they did not want to stand out or appear different and foolish: they wanted to fit in. Asch also spoke to the subjects who had maintained correct and independent responses, and found that they had not been unresponsive to the majority, but had been able to recover from the doubt that they felt in order to give an honest account of what they saw. Asch performed variations on the experiment to test what difference the size of the majority group made to levels of conformity. He found that just one confederate had virtually no influence on the subject's conformity, two had only a small influence, but three or more encouraged a relatively stable tendency to conform. Unanimity in the confederates' responses was a more powerful factor; but even if only one confederate offered an alternative answer, the subjects were much more likely to provide an independent (and correct)

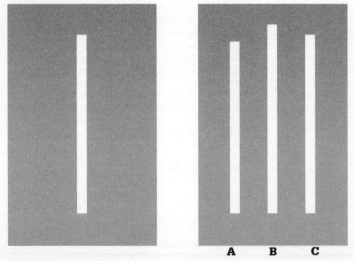

In the Asch Paradigm experiment, participants were given a visual test. They had to decide which of the three lines on the second card was the same length as the one on the first card. Each question was called a "trial" and there were 18 trials in all.

A   B   C

response. This finding highlights the power of even a very small dissenting minority. Furthermore, Asch discovered that if he allowed the participants to give their answers privately, by writing them down on a piece of paper, conformity noticeably decreased, and this held true even if the confederates were still giving their answers aloud.

Cultural norms

Some psychologists hypothesized that Asch's findings reflected the cultural climate of 1950s America during McCarthyism, when dissent was seen as anti-American and people were imprisoned for their opinions. Later studies found variations in levels of conformity. For instance, a study conducted in the early 1970s (a time of liberal, progressive thinking in the US) found far lower rates of conformity. However, a study in the late 1970s showed a return to higher rates.

Conformity rates for cultures worldwide also differ. Researchers found that individualist cultures such as the US, the UK, and other Western European countries, where personal choice and individual achievements are valued highly, show lower levels of conformity than collectivist cultures such as Japan, Fiji, and African countries, where group belonging is valued highly.

US Senator Joseph McCarthy launched a Communist witch hunt during the 1950s, generating an environment of fear and high levels of political and social conformity.

> ❝ A member of a tribe of cannibals accepts cannibalism as altogether fitting and proper.
> **Solomon Asch** ❞

Psychologists have criticized Asch's methods on the grounds that he focused on a stripped-down version of group behaviour that does not feature much interaction between participants, or that he was more focused on the individuals within a group than on the group dynamic. Others wonder if he overstated the power of the majority to influence the minority. Serge Moscovici, in particular, disagreed with Asch's analysis and argued that an active minority could influence the majority and bring about change. Moscovici was inspired to develop his own studies to demonstrate how a consistent minority can affect the thinking of the majority.

Although Asch acknowledges that social life requires some consensus, he also emphasizes that this is most productive when each individual contributes his independent insight and experience. Consensus should not come out of fear or conformity; the fact that he found the tendency to conform was strong even among intelligent people raised questions about societal values and the quality of education.

Asch's conclusions note the power (and danger) of social influence to shape a person's beliefs and behaviour. If something becomes normal for a group, social pressure will ensure conformity. Inspired by Asch's theory, Stanley Milgram's experiment on obedience showed that ordinary people are capable of cruelty when under pressure to conform.

However, the majority of participants in Asch's study, even those who had conformed, stated that they valued independence of mind, leaving him optimistic about humanity. ∎

THE MORE YOU SEE IT THE MORE YOU LIKE IT

ROBERT ZAJONC (1923–2008)

IN CONTEXT

APPROACH
Familiarity

BEFORE
1876 German experimental psychologist Gustav Fechner suggests familiarity increases positive feeling towards art objects, but "supersaturation" leads to aversion.

1910 Edward B. Titchener documents the mere exposure effect, describing it as a "glow of warmth" that people experience in the presence of familiar things.

AFTER
1971 Psychologists T.T. Faw and D. Pien find that adults and children prefer unfamiliar line drawings and patterns to familiar ones.

1989 Robert Bornstein finds that the mere exposure effect is strongest when unfamiliar stimuli are presented briefly.

Until the middle of the 20th century, social scientists tended to base their explanations of human behaviour on environmental factors. However, the Polish-born psychologist Robert Zajonc believed that to develop a more complete understanding, it is necessary to take into account the functions of the mind as well. Zajonc's main interest was in the relationship between feeling and thought – the intersection of emotion and cognition – and he devoted much of his career towards exploring which of these factors has a stronger influence on behaviour. To this end, he performed a seminal experiment in 1968 that led to his discovery of the "mere exposure effect", which is arguably his best-known contribution to the field of social psychology.

Familiarity experiments

Mere exposure, Zajonc explained, simply refers to a condition in which the given stimulus is accessible to the subject's perception, either consciously or subconsciously. The effects of mere exposure had been documented previously by the psychologist Edward B. Titchener who, in 1910, described the "glow of warmth" and feeling of intimacy that a person experiences in the presence of something familiar. However, Titchener's hypothesis was rejected at the time, and the idea faded into relative obscurity.

Zajonc's interest in the effect was aroused by a newspaper article that described a curious experiment that took place at Oregon State University in 1967. The article stated that a "mysterious student" had been attending class for two months, enveloped in a black bag. The professor, Charles Goetzinger, knew the identity of the person inside, but none of the class had any idea who it might be. Goetzinger then observed the class to gauge their reactions over time. Initially, the students treated the black bag with

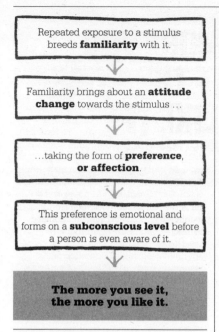

Repeated exposure to a stimulus breeds **familiarity** with it.

Familiarity brings about an **attitude change** towards the stimulus …

…taking the form of **preference, or affection**.

This preference is emotional and forms on a **subconscious level** before a person is even aware of it.

The more you see it, the more you like it.

hostility, but this softened in time and they were eventually friendly and even protective towards the person in the bag. Goetzinger noted that the students' attitude gradually "changed from hostility towards the black bag to curiosity and finally to friendship".

Zajonc's ground-breaking paper, *Attitudinal Effects of Mere Exposure,* was published in *The Journal of Personality and Social Psychology* in 1968. Zajonc's paper describes a series of experiments in which he showed participants a sequence of random images – geometric shapes, Chinese symbols, paintings, and pictures of faces –that were flashed in front of them so rapidly that they were unable to discern which were shown

repeatedly. When subjects were later asked which images they preferred, they consistently chose the ones to which they had been most frequently exposed, although they were not consciously aware of this fact. What Zajonc seemed to have discovered was that familiarity brings about an attitude change, breeding affection or some form of preference for the familiar stimulus. This increases with exposure: the greater your number of exposures to something, the more affection you will feel towards it. To put it simply, "the more you see it, the more you like it".

Researchers into the mere exposure phenomenon since Zajonc's experiment have found that it is even possible to re-create this effect using sound rather than images. In 1974, the social psychologist D.W. Rajecki used fertile chicken eggs as test subjects, playing tones of different frequencies to different groups of eggs before they hatched, and then playing these tones to both groups of chicks again after hatching. Without exception, the chicks preferred the tones that had been played to them prenatally.

Preferences are not rational

Zajonc's findings indicate that this preference for familiar things is based purely on the history of exposure to it, and is not affected by a person's expressed personal beliefs or attitudes. This holds true even when exposures take place only on the subliminal level, when subjects are completely unaware that they are being presented with a stimulus. This discovery led to Zajonc's claim that "preferences need no inferences", meaning that affectionate feeling is not based on reasoned judgement. This is contrary to what most of us might imagine to be the case. »

Zajonc's 1968 experiment tested the mere exposure effect by showing people slides of symbols with uneven rates of repetition; the more frequently someone saw a symbol, the more they claimed to like it.

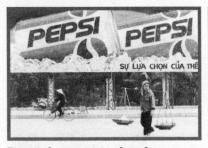

Repeated exposure to a brand can create a liking for it, even when it is presented without any factual information and requires no decision-making from the person viewing it.

In a paper called *Feeling and Thinking*, written in 1980, Zajonc argued that feelings and thoughts are actually very independent of one another. Feelings not only precede thoughts during a person's complex response to a stimulus, but are actually the most powerful determinants of a person's attitudes and decisions. This paper was widely debated, and it helped to bring the study of emotion back to the forefront of Western psychology, in part because the theory bears important implications for the study of decision-making processes. It suggests that, contrary to what we may believe, it is not reason and logic that guide our decisions; in fact, we make fast, instinctive, emotion-based decisions before we have even had a chance to consider the choice cognitively – we make judgments without information. If this is true, it follows that our logical reasoning merely justifies and rationalizes the decisions we have already made, rather than actually serving to inform the choice in the first place.

Zajonc concludes that "affect is always present as a companion to thought, whereas the converse is not true for cognition". We can never think about something without a feeling attached; as Zajonc says, we do not just see "a house", we see "a handsome house" or "a pretentious house". Every perception we have contains some affect, or feeling. The primacy of affect over cognition is also apparent in memory, he says, as Frederick Bartlett noted in his book, *Remembering:* "When a subject is being asked to remember, very often the first thing that emerges is something of the nature of attitude".

Interpersonal attraction

The impact of the mere exposure effect extends beyond the confines of the laboratory, and out into the area of interpersonal attraction. In this context, the phenomenon is referred to as the "propinquity effect", the way we tend to form friendships or romantic relationships with people we see regularly. One explanation for this focuses on evolution: when animals are exposed to something for the first time, they often respond with fear and aggression, but repeated exposures – during which the animal realizes the perceived threat does not materialize – lead to a reduction in negative responses. Zajonc explored this notion further with human subjects, discovering that people form very negative attitudes towards an imaginary group of unfamiliar people, attributing unpleasant qualities to them for no apparent reason other than the fact that they are complete strangers. However, as with shapes and symbols, repeated exposure is shown to increase trust and affection.

Another explanation for the propinquity effect focuses on the many factors involved in interpersonal attraction, which include familiarity, similarity of attitudes, physical attraction, and reciprocal affection. Frequent interactions between people may not only increase the level of familiarity, but also provide an increasing impression of similarity, thereby breeding positive feelings and ultimately attraction.

Exposure and advertising

Advertising is another arena in which the mere exposure effect plays a crucial role, although the picture here is less clear. Research seems to suggest that repeated exposure to a brand or corporate name would boost sales, but this assumption is evidently overly simplistic, as it doesn't take into account other possible effects of frequent exposure.

One study used banner ads to test the mere exposure effect on college-aged students. Subjects were presented with an article to read on a computer screen while banner ads flashed along the top of the screen. The results indicated that those who had been exposed more frequently to the banner ads did indeed rate the ads more favourably than those who had seen it less frequently or not at all. However, another study found that familiarity with a brand name can create an ambivalent attitude. This may be because people have both good and bad associations with familiar companies, and all of these associations are brought to mind with frequent exposure, leading to greater ambivalence. As a result, it is unclear whether mere familiarity, created through repeated advertising, is good for sales.

Familiar faces

Zajonc found that not only does exposure influence how a person feels about someone, but it can even change the way a person looks over time. With a group of colleagues, he conducted a study to find out whether the faces of spouses appear more similar after 25 years together. They compared photographs of couples taken during their first year of marriage with those taken 25 years later, and found that couples looked more alike after many years of being together. After ruling out several other potential explanations, the researchers decided that empathy was the most likely cause. Time had increased the couple's empathy for each other, and since human emotion is communicated through facial expressions, they may have begun to mimic each others' expressions in the process of empathizing, resulting in similar wrinkle patterns over time.

Known for the breadth of his work on the basic processes of social behaviour, Zajonc helped to create the modern field of social psychology. He used his work on thought and feeling to explore issues such as racism, genocide, and terrorism, hoping that research could ultimately help to prevent war and human suffering. ■

Couples grow to resemble each other over time because they express empathy through reflecting each other's facial expressions; this leads to the formation of similar facial lines.

Robert Zajonc

Robert Zajonc was born in Lodz, Poland. When he was 16 his family fled to Warsaw during the Nazi invasion of Poland. Two weeks later, their building was bombed and both of his parents were killed. Zajonc spent six months recuperating in a hospital, after which he was arrested by Nazi soldiers and sent to a German labour camp. He escaped along with two other prisoners and walked 320km (200 miles) to France only to be recaptured and imprisoned again. He broke out for a final time and made his way to the UK.

After World War II, Zajonc moved to the USA, where he established himself as an eminent psychologist, gaining psychology degrees to PhD level at the University of Michigan. He worked there until his retirement in 1994, when he became an emeritus professor at Stanford University. Zajonc died of pancreatic cancer at the age of 85.

Key works

1968 *Attitudinal Effects of Mere Exposure*
1975 *Birth Order and Intellectual Development*
1980 *Feeling and Thinking*

PEOPLE DO WHAT THEY ARE TOLD TO DO
STANLEY MILGRAM (1933–1984)

IN CONTEXT

APPROACH
Conformism

BEFORE
1939–45 During World War II, approximately six million Jews are systematically killed on the orders of Nazi Germany.

1950 Solomon Asch demonstrates the power of social pressure to make people conform in his line-task experiments.

1961 Nazi war criminal Adolf Eichmann is tried, and claims he was just "following orders".

AFTER
1971 Philip Zimbardo conducts his prison experiment, which demonstrates that in certain situations, otherwise good people can perform evil deeds.

1989 American psychologists Herbert Kelman and V.L. Hamilton state that members of a group obey authority when they accept its legitimacy.

Humans are **socialized to be obedient** from an early age.

↓

We feel **compelled to comply** with the commands of authority figures...

↓

...even when this **conflicts** with our own **moral values**.

↓

People do what they are told to do.

S ocial psychologist Stanley Milgram dramatically changed our understanding of human obedience when he published *Behavioral Study of Obedience* in 1963. This paper contained results of an experiment that seemed to suggest that the majority of people are capable of causing extreme harm to others when told to do so by a figure of authority. It also caused people to question the ethical limits of psychological experimentation.

Milgram became particularly interested in studying obedience during the trial of German Nazi war criminal Adolf Eichmann. The prevailing view was that there was something inherently different about the 20th-century Germans; in the 1950s, psychologists such as Theodor Adorno had suggested that the Germans had certain personality characteristics that made them specifically susceptible to committing the atrocities of the Holocaust. Eichmann, however, claimed he had just been "following orders", so Milgram set out to investigate if this could be true – would an ordinary person lay aside what he knew to be right or wrong merely because he was ordered to do so? His study went on to demonstrate important aspects of the relationship between authority and obedience, and it remains one of the most controversial experiments in the history of psychology.

The power of the group

Milgram believed that it was the situation of World War II and the compulsion to obey – rather than the dispositions of the Germans – that had enabled Nazi cruelty. He maintained that the behaviour was a direct result of the situation, and any of us might have behaved identically in that very same context. In the late 1950s, Milgram had worked extensively with Solomon Asch on his conformity studies and had witnessed people agreeing with the decisions of a group, even when they knew these decisions to be wrong. The experiments showed that people are prepared to do or say things that conflict with their own sense of reality. Would they also allow their moral judgments to be affected by the authority of a group or even a single figure?

The Milgram experiment

Milgram set out to test whether normally kind, likeable people could be made to act against their own moral values in a setting where some kind of authority held sway. He devised an investigation of how obedient a selection of "ordinary" men would be when they were told by an authority figure to administer electric shocks to another person. The experiment took place in a laboratory at Yale University in 1961, where Milgram was a professor of psychology. The participants were recruited through a newspaper advertisement, and a total of 40 men were selected from a wide range of occupations, including teachers, postal workers, engineers, labourers, and salesmen. They were each paid $4.50 for their participation; the money was given to them as soon as they arrived at the laboratory, and they were told that the payment was theirs to keep regardless of what happened during the experiment.

In the laboratory, Milgram had created a phony (but very impressive and realistic-looking) electric shock generator. This had 30 switches marked in 15-volt increments with labels that indicated the intensity of different ranges of shock levels, from "slight shock" at one end, to "extreme intensity shock", "danger: severe shock", and finally, one marked simply "XXX", at the other.

The role of the experimenter or "scientist" was played by a biology teacher who introduced himself to the participants as Jack Williams. In order to give the impression of authority, he was dressed in a grey »

Stanley Milgram

Stanley Milgram was born in 1933 to a Jewish family in New York City. His Hungarian parents ran a bakery in the Bronx, and he attended James Monroe High School with Philip Zimbardo.

A high academic achiever and a leader among his peers, Milgram initially studied political science, but went on to receive a PhD in psychology from Harvard in 1960 under Gordon Allport. After working with Solomon Asch on conformity studies at Harvard, he became assistant professor at Yale, where he carried out his obedience experiments. In 1961, he married Alexandra Menkin, with whom he had two children. In 1963, he returned to Harvard, but was denied tenure because of the controversy surrounding his experiment, so he moved to the City University of New York, where he taught until his death at the age of 51.

Key works

1963 *Behavioral Study of Obedience*
1967 *The Small World Problem*
1974 *Obedience to Authority: An Experimental View*

Milgram's shock generator
produced totally unexpected results.
A team of 40 psychiatrists predicted
that fewer than 5 per cent of participants
would administer shocks as high as
300 volts; in fact, every participant
went to this level.

100% of the participants applied shocks up to 300 volts; the point at which the learner began to shout in apparent pain.

35% of the participants applied shocks of between 300 and 375 volts, but then refused to apply any more.

65% of the participants continued the experiment to the end, applying the maximum shock of 450 volts as many times as requested.

Slight shock
Moderate shock
Strong shock
Very strong shock
Intense shock
Extreme intensity shock
Danger: severe shock
X X X

0V — 450V

laboratory technician's coat and maintained a stern and emotionless demeanour throughout each of the experiments.

The participants were told that the study intended to investigate the effects of punishment on learning. They were told that of two volunteers, one would be the learner and the other the teacher. In fact, one of the two "volunteers" in each case was not a participant but a stooge: he was a likeable accountant called Mr Wallace, who had been trained to play the role of the victim. When Mr Wallace and the genuine participant drew paper from a hat to determine which role they would play, the draw was always rigged so that Mr Wallace took on the role of "learner" in every instance. In full view of the participant, the "learner" (Mr Wallace) was strapped into an "electric chair" with an electrode attached to his wrist; the participant was told that

Convincingly wired up, Mr Wallace pretended to be an innocent volunteer. His screams failed to prevent 65 per cent of participants from administering the highest level of fake electric shock.

this electrode was attached to the shock generator located in an adjacent room. The participant heard the "scientist" tell the "learner" (Mr Wallace) that "although the shocks can be extremely painful, they cause no permanent damage". To make the situation appear more authentic, the scientist then wired up the participant and gave him a sample shock of 45 volts – which was in fact the only shock strength that the generator could produce.

At this point, the participant was moved to the room containing the shock generator and asked to assume the role of "teacher". He was asked to read a series of word pairs (such as "blue-girl", "nice-day") aloud for the learner to memorize. After this he was to read out a series of single words; the learner's task was to recall the pairing word in each case and to indicate his answer by pressing a switch that illuminated a light on the shock generator. If the learner's answer was correct, the questions continued; if the answer was incorrect, the participant was instructed to tell the learner the correct answer, announce the level of shock he was about to receive, and press a switch to administer the shock. Participants were instructed to increase the shock level by 15 volts (in other words, to keep moving up the shock scale on the machine) with every wrong answer.

Applying the shocks

As part of the experiment, the learner (Mr Wallace) had been briefed to answer incorrectly to around one question in every four, to ensure that the participant would be required to start applying electric shocks. During the experiment, the learner would pound the wall once the voltage had reached 300, and shout: "I absolutely refuse to answer any more! Get me out of here! You can't hold me here! Get me out!" As the shock level increased, the learner would shout more frantically, and then eventually cease making any noise at all; questions would be met with nothing but an eerie silence. The participant was told to treat any unanswered question as an incorrectly answered question and apply the next level of shock voltage. If he expressed misgivings about continuing the experiment, he received a verbal prod from the "scientist" to encourage him, from a simple request to continue, to finally being told that he had no choice but to go on. If he refused to obey after the last prod, the experiment was terminated.

In advance of the experiment, Milgram had asked several different groups of people, including ordinary members of the public as well as psychologists and psychiatrists, how far they thought participants would go when asked to administer the electric shocks. Most people thought participants would stop at a level that caused pain, and the psychiatrists predicted that, at most, one in 1,000 would continue to the highest level of shock. Astonishingly, when the experiment took place, Milgram found that all 40 of the participants obeyed commands to administer shocks up to 300 volts. Only five people refused to continue at this point; 65 per cent of the participants obeyed the instructions of the "scientist" right to the end, obeying commands to administer shocks to the top level of 450 volts.

Their discomfort at doing so was often evident: many showed signs of severe distress, tension, and nervousness over the course of the experiment. They stuttered, trembled, sweated, groaned, broke out into nervous laughing fits, and three people had full-blown seizures. In every instance of the experiment, the participant stopped and

questioned it at some point; some even offered to refund the money they were paid at the beginning. Interviews after the experiments confirmed that, with only a few exceptions, participants had been completely convinced that the "learning experiment" was real.

All participants were fully debriefed so they understood what had actually taken place, and they were asked a series of questions to test that they were not emotionally harmed by the experience. The participants were also reunited with the "learner" (Mr Wallace) so that they could see that no actual shocks had been administered.

Feeling obliged to obey

Milgram noted several features of the experiment that may have contributed to such high levels of obedience; for example, the fact that it took place at the prestigious Yale University gave it credibility. In addition, participants believed that the study was designed to advance knowledge, and they had been assured that the shocks were painful but not dangerous. Being paid may have increased their sense of obligation, as did the fact they had volunteered to take part. To test these explanations, Milgram ran many variations on the study, but changing the context had only minor effects on the results.

Milgram wanted to see if the inclination to obey authority figures can become the major factor in determining behaviour, even in extreme circumstances. It is clear from the reactions and responses of the »

By the 1960s, Yale University was known to the general public as being highly prestigious; its authority may have seemed literally unquestionable to the participants of Milgram's study.

participants that obeying the "scientist" was violating their own sense of morality and negatively affecting them both physically and emotionally, but the pressure to comply was simply too powerful to defy in most cases.

This sense of obedience, Milgram felt, comes from the fact that people are socialized from a very young age (by parents and teachers) to be obedient and to follow orders – especially the rules set forth by authority figures. As Milgram says, "obedience is as basic an element in the structure of social life as one can point to... it serves numerous productive functions". But equally, the inhumane policies of the death camps in World War II "could only be carried out on a massive scale if a very large number of persons obeyed orders". His experiments clearly demonstrated that normally harmless people become capable of committing cruel acts when a situation pressures them to do so.

In describing his results, Milgram also turned to the theory of conformism, which states that when a person has neither the ability nor expertise to make a decision, he will look to the group to decide how to behave. Conformity can limit and distort an individual's response to a situation, and seems to result in a diffusion of responsibility – which Milgram felt was crucial to comprehending the atrocities carried out by the Nazis. However, the conflict between a person's conscience and external authority exerts a huge internal pressure, and Milgram felt that this accounted for the extreme distress experienced by the participants in his study.

Ethical concerns

There were many ethical concerns associated with Milgram's study. When it was first published, the ensuing controversy was so great that the American Psychological Association revoked his membership for a full year. However, it was eventually reinstated, and Milgram's 1974 book *Obedience to Authority* received the annual Social Psychology Award.

The major concern was that the participants in the experiment were explicitly deceived, both about the nature of the study and about the reality of the electric shocks. Milgram's defence was that he could not have obtained realistic results without employing deception, and all of the participants were debriefed after the experiment. Self-knowledge, he argued, is a valuable asset, despite the discomfort that the participants may have felt when forced to confront the fact that they behaved in a previously unthinkable way.

However, many psychologists remained uneasy, and the study was ultimately crucial in the development of ethical standards of psychological experimentation. It helped to define important principles such as the avoidance of intentional deceit of participants, and the need to protect experimental participants from emotional suffering.

Cross-cultural validity

Another criticism of Milgram's study was that he used an unrepresentative sample: American men do not necessarily reflect the general population. Even so, Milgram was able to conclude that obedience was

The behaviour of Nazis during World War II had been attributed to a prevalence of the "authoritarian personality" in the population; this was questioned by Milgram's experiments.

American soldiers in Vietnam reported that their behaviour became unacceptable by degrees – as with the shock generator – until they found themselves murdering innocents.

screen. Those with only text contact with the learner had little trouble administering the shocks, but when the virtual learner was visible participants acted exactly as they had in Milgram's original experiment.

Society demands obedience

The notion of a society rests on an understanding that individuals are prepared to relinquish some personal autonomy and look to others of higher authority and social status to make decisions on a larger scale or from a higher, broader perspective. Even the most democratic of societies requires the rulings of a recognized, legitimate authority to take precedence over individual self-regulation, in pursuit of the greater collective good. In order for any society to function, its populace must agree to obey its rules. Legitimacy is, of course, the key, and there are countless historical examples of people using their authority to persuade others to commit crimes against humanity.

not a particular feature found in the minds of 20th-century Germans, but something more universal. A number of cross-cultural replications of the original experiment have demonstrated remarkably high consistency in results within societies, but slight differences between one country and another. For example, in most of North America and Europe, results are very similar to those found in Milgram's original experiment, with very high percentages of obedience. Asian studies, however, show even greater levels of obedience (in East Asian and Muslim countries in particular), while aboriginal African and Latin American populations, as well as the Inuit peoples of Canada, show far less obedience.

Virtual torture

In 2006, the psychologist Mel Slater set out to see what the effect would be if participants were made explicitly aware that the situation was not real. His replication used a computer simulation of the learner and shock process, so participants administering the shocks were fully aware that the learner was computer-generated. The experiment was run twice: first with the virtual learner communicating only by text, and then with the computer-generated model visible on

Equally importantly, Milgram showed that it is "not so much the kind of person a man is, as the kind of situation in which he finds himself that determines how he will act". Instead of examining personalities to explain crimes, he says, we should examine the context, or situation.

Milgram's seminal study was heavily criticized at the time, not least because it painted an unappealing and chilling portrait of human nature. It is easier to believe that there are fundamental differences between the Nazis and the rest of humanity than to accept that in certain situations, many of us are capable of committing extraordinary acts of violence. Milgram held up a light to the dark realities concerning power and the consequences of our tendency to obey authority figures, and in so doing, he simultaneously absolved and made villains of us all. ∎

WHAT HAPPENS WHEN YOU PUT GOOD PEOPLE IN AN EVIL PLACE?
PHILIP ZIMBARDO (1933–)

IN CONTEXT

APPROACH
Conformity

BEFORE
1935 Muzafer Sherif demonstrates how groups quickly come to develop a "social norm" in his autokinetic effect experiments.

1940s Kurt Lewin shows how people's behaviour changes as their situations are altered.

1963 Stanley Milgram conducts his obedience studies, which demonstrate that people will obey authority even if it means committing cruel acts.

AFTER
2002 British psychologists Steven Reicher and Alex Haslam extend Zimbardo's study to explore positive rather than negative group behaviour.

2004 Zimbardo defends a former Abu Ghraib prison guard in court, arguing that the circumstances caused the guard's cruel behaviour.

Stanley Milgram's shocking obedience studies revealed that people will obey authority figures even if this entails acting against their own moral convictions. In the aftermath, Philip Zimbardo set out to discover how people would behave if they were put into a position of authority with unimpeded power. Would they willingly use (or abuse) the power granted to them? In 1971 he carried out the now-famous Stanford Prison experiment, using 24 middle-class American college students who had undergone tests to establish that they were mentally healthy.

On the flip of a coin the students were randomly assigned the role of either "guard" or "prisoner", and one Sunday morning soon afterwards, the prisoners were arrested at their homes, booked at a real police station, then transferred to the basement of the Stanford University psychology department, which had been converted into a mock prison.

The prison environment
In order to make the experience as psychologically real as possible, prisoners were stripped, searched, deloused, and given uniforms and bedding upon their arrival. To heighten their sense of anonymity and dehumanization, they were addressed only by their given numbers, and each had a chain bolted around one ankle to serve as a reminder of their lack of freedom.

The guards wore military-style uniforms and sunglasses (to make eye contact impossible), and carried keys, whistles, handcuffs, and clubs. They were on duty 24 hours a day, and were given complete control over the prisoners, with permission to employ whatever tactics they saw fit in order to maintain order. To the researchers' amazement, the environment quickly

The "prisoners" rebelled against the "guards", but the guards' tactics became more aggressive. They began dividing the prisoners into groups, giving some rewards and others punishments.

became so threatening to participants that the study had to be ended after only six days. Every guard became abusive and authoritarian; prisoners were denied food or bedding, hooded, chained, and made to clean toilet bowls with their hands. As the boredom increased, they used the prisoners as their playthings, making them take part in degrading games. After just 36 hours, one prisoner had to be released because of uncontrolled crying, fits of rage, and severe depression. When other prisoners showed symptoms of acute distress, Zimbardo realized the situation had become dangerous and ended the experiment.

Zimbardo's experiment showed that good people can be induced into behaving in evil ways by immersion in "total situations" that have an apparently legitimizing ideology and approved rules and roles. The implications are vast, as Zimbardo explains: "Any deed that any human being has ever done, however horrible, is possible for any of us to do – under the right or wrong situational pressures". ■

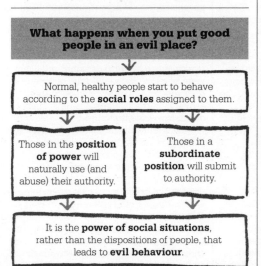

What happens when you put good people in an evil place?

↓

Normal, healthy people start to behave according to the **social roles** assigned to them.

↓ ↓

Those in the **position of power** will naturally use (and abuse) their authority.

Those in a **subordinate position** will submit to authority.

↓

It is the **power of social situations**, rather than the dispositions of people, that leads to **evil behaviour**.

Philip Zimbardo

Philip Zimbardo was born in New York City in 1933 to a Sicilian-American family, and was a classmate of Stanley Milgram at James Monroe High School in the Bronx. He went on to earn his BA degree from Brooklyn College, New York, and a PhD from Yale. He taught at several universities before moving to Stanford in 1968, where he is still a psychology professor.

In 2000, Zimbardo stated that he agreed with George Armitage Miller that it was time to "give psychology away to the public", and his career has reflected this idea. In the 1980s he presented a popular TV series on "discovering psychology". The American Psychological Foundation presented him with an award for Distinguished Lifetime Contributions to General Psychology in 2000, and two years later he was elected president of the American Psychological Association.

Key works

1972 *The Stanford Prison Experiment*
2007 *The Lucifer Effect*
2008 *The Time Paradox*
2010 *Psychology and Life*

DEVELOPM
PSYCHOLO
FROM INFANT TO ADULT

I n the early part of the 20th century, two main approaches in psychology examined the psychological development of humans from childhood to adulthood: the psychoanalytic theory of Freud gave an account of psychosexual development in children, and behaviourism explained the mechanics of the learning process. However, the study of development itself – the psychological, emotional, and perceptual changes that occur during a lifetime – did not evolve until the 1930s, when Jean Piaget overturned conventional thinking with the idea that a child is not just a "miniature adult" gaining knowledge as his or her body matures, but at the same time is also going through radical psychological changes.

Piaget raised some fundamental questions: whether we acquire knowledge gradually or in distinct stages; whether certain abilities are innate or learned; and how the environment affects development. His cognitive development theory suggested that a child's growth into adulthood is divided into several developmental stages, and within each stage the child learns by doing rather than instruction. Piaget's ideas set the stage for the new field of developmental psychology and shaped the curricula of schools up to the present day.

Other developmental theories soon emerged. Although broadly agreeing with Piaget's findings, Lev Vygotsky argued that it was necessary for a child to have adult guidance at various stages in his learning, and also stressed the importance of a child's social and cultural environment. Erik Erikson also built on Piaget's ideas, identifying eight stages of psychosocial development, including the "identity crisis" of adolescence; while Lawrence Kohlberg came up with six stages of moral development in his studies.

With the "cognitive revolution" that followed World War II, psychologists such as Albert Bandura looked at the issue of development again, this time in the light of cognitive models of information processing. Bandura retained elements of both Piaget's stages of development and Vygotsky's social constructivism in his social learning theory. Cognitive psychology also brought new ideas about learning, especially the acquisition of language, and Noam Chomsky's

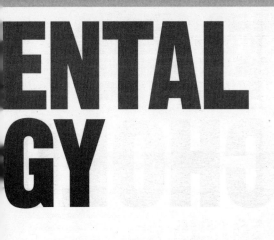

suggestion that this is an innate capability once more opened the nature versus nurture debate.

Attachment theory

While much developmental psychology concerned itself with the process of learning, a growing area of interest arose from the research carried out by the British psychoanalyst and psychiatrist John Bowlby. His study of children who had been separated from their families during World War II led to the formulation of attachment theory, which deals with the way we build and maintain relationships with family and friends, placing a special importance on the attachments made by infants to the people who care for them; Bowlby saw this as a natural impulse for survival. The basic ideas of attachment theory were reinforced by experiments carried out by psychologist Harry Harlow in the US, who showed the effects of isolation and maternal separation on infants. His experiments demonstrated that to build healthy cognitive and social development, infants needed companionship and care. Later research by Mary Ainsworth built on these findings,

adding the concept of a "secure base" from which an infant can explore the world. Bruno Bettelheim developed his own, more controversial, theories of childhood development from the basis of attachment theory, rejecting the importance of the traditional family after his study of children brought up communally in kibbutzim. In the 1960s, social issues such as the civil rights movement and feminism were influencing thought in both social psychology and developmental psychology. How our prejudices are acquired, and at what stage of development, became an area of interest for the African-Americans Kenneth and Mamie Clark, who based their work on studies of child development in Harlem, New York; while Eleanor Maccoby examined the differences in development between the sexes – the first of many similar explorations in the new field of gender studies.

Developmental psychology is currently exploring the causes and treatment of autism and learning difficulties. And, with a growing ageing population, psychology is also looking into issues that confront us as we enter old age. ∎

THE GOAL OF EDUCATION IS TO CREATE MEN AND WOMEN WHO ARE CAPABLE OF DOING NEW THINGS
JEAN PIAGET (1896–1980)

IN CONTEXT

APPROACH
Genetic epistemology

BEFORE
1693 English philosopher John Locke's *Some Thoughts Concerning Education* suggests a child's mind is a tabula rasa, or blank slate.

1780s German philosopher Immanuel Kant introduces the concept of the schema and suggests that morality develops independently of authority figures through interaction with peers.

AFTER
1907 Italian educator Dr Maria Montessori opens the first Montessori school, which encourages independence and respect for natural developmental stages.

1970s–80s Many Western education systems incorporate a more child-centred approach to learning.

Somewhere between his roots as a precocious young biologist and his later fascination with epistemology, Jean Piaget carved out his own niche in a discipline that he called genetic epistemology, the study of how intelligence changes as children grow. Piaget was not interested in comparing levels of intelligence between children of different ages (quantitative cognitive change); his interests lay in the natural development of mental skills over time (qualitative cognitive change). Quantitative studies make possible numerical comparisons, but Piaget wanted to explore differences in the types, experience, and qualities of children's learning, which required "qualitative" research. Breaking away from the prevalent behaviourist model, which had linked child development entirely with environmental factors, Piaget decided to explore the innate, or inborn, capacities that he believed guide children's progression through a series of age-defined developmental stages.

Piaget believed that children are active and autonomous learners, using their senses to interact with the world around them as they move through the developmental stages. He also believed that it is of primary importance to nurture and guide children on this journey, giving them the freedom to experiment and explore on their own, in a very individual, trial-and-error manner. The task of a good teacher is, therefore, simply to support children on their journey through these stages, constantly encouraging their creativity and imagination, because "the goal of education is to create men and women who are capable of doing new things".

Learning is active

One theme that pervades Piaget's theory of intellectual development is the concept of learning as an active personal process. From infancy through childhood, he says, learning arises from a child's natural desire to sense, explore, move, and then master. For this reason Piaget had many misgivings about

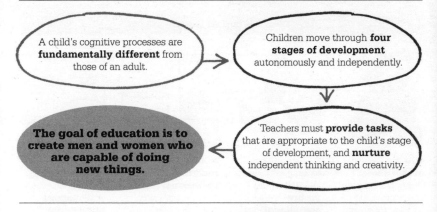

A child's cognitive processes are **fundamentally different** from those of an adult.

Children move through **four stages of development** autonomously and independently.

Teachers must **provide tasks** that are appropriate to the child's stage of development, and **nurture** independent thinking and creativity.

The goal of education is to create men and women who are capable of doing new things.

---

the notion of standardized testing, in which children undergo pre-formatted tests that have "correct" answers to provide quantitative measures of intelligence. While working on standardizing intelligence tests for Alfred Binet in the early 1920s, he became interested less in a child's ability to produce correct answers than in what those answers actually were. Their explanations revealed that children's assumptions about how the world works are very different to those of adults, leading Piaget to believe that children not only think differently to adults, but also that children of different ages have different methods of thinking.

The evolving mind

Since the 17th century, the idea that a child is effectively a miniature adult had held sway. Empiricist philosophers of the time had suggested that a child's brain works exactly like an adult's, but has fewer associations. Another group of thinkers, the psychological nativists, claimed that certain concepts – such as the ideas of time, space, and number – are innate, or "hard-wired" into the brain, so babies are born with an ability to make use of them. Piaget's suggestion that children's mental processes – from infancy to adolescence – are fundamentally different to an adult's was a radical and controversial departure from this view.

Piaget himself claimed that it is vitally important to understand the formation and evolution of intelligence during childhood,

Children are not mini adults who simply do not yet know as much as adults; rather, they see the world differently and interact with it in a wholly distinct way.

because this is the only way we can reach a full understanding of human knowledge. His use of psychotherapeutic interviewing techniques to ask children to explain their answers was inspired, and it became an important tool in all his research. Rather than adhering to a pre-determined and impersonal list of questions, this flexible method allowed the child's answers to determine the subsequent question. By following the child's line of thought, Piaget believed he could better understand the processes underlying it. His rejection of a notion of quantitative or measurable intelligence led to some ground-breaking theories of childhood cognitive development.

Developing the intellect

Piaget initially believed that social factors, such as language and contact with family members and peers, impacted most on »

The Four Stages of Development

1 At the **sensorimotor** stage, babies learn about the world through touch and their other senses.

2 Children begin to arrange objects logically during the **pre-operational** stage.

3 During the **concrete operational** stage, children learn that quantities can take different forms.

4 Verbal reasoning and hypothetical thinking develop in the **formal operational** stage.

children's intellectual development. However, while studying infants, he realized that for them language is less important and their own activity is paramount. In the first few days of life, babies have limited bodily movements – mainly crying and sucking – though they quickly begin to add new actions, such as reaching for a toy. So Piaget concluded that action, rather than social interaction, is the source of thought at this stage.

This discovery formed part of his theory that every child passes through various stages of cognitive development, and that these stages are different in quality and are hierarchical. A child only moves on to the next stage upon genuine completion of the current stage. In studies and observations, Piaget determined that all children pass through the stages in the same sequence, without skipping any or regressing to previous ones. This is not a process that can be rushed, and although children generally tend to go through the same stage at roughly the same age, each individual child has his or her own pace of development.

The four stages defined by Piaget represent levels in the development of intelligence and, as such, they provide a list of the "schemas" that children make use of at that particular moment in their development. A schema is a representation in the mind of a set of ideas, perceptions, and actions that provide a mental structure to help us organize our past experiences, and prepare us for future experiences. During infancy and early childhood, a schema can be as simple as "things I can eat". However, as children grow, their schemas become more complex, offering an understanding of what constitutes "a kitchen", a "best friend", or "democratic government". Intelligent behaviour, according to Piaget, is comprised of a growing collection of schemas.

Four stages of development

Piaget's first stage is called the sensorimotor stage, and this spans the first two years of a child's life. During this period, infants learn about the world primarily through their senses (sensori-) and through physical action or movement (motor). Children at this stage are egocentric, able to see the world only from their own viewpoint. At the beginning of this stage, infants practise reflexes without understanding or intention; later they can extend and coordinate reflexes with objects. Then they begin to coordinate their senses in a way that anticipates events; for example, they can imagine objects that are not present and find hidden ones. They begin to experiment and set goals in their use of objects, and think about a problem before acting. These developments mark the completion of the first stage.

As the child moves towards the development of self-awareness, they now have the tools of representational thought and can begin to develop and use internal images, symbols, and language. This constitutes the second, or pre-operational, stage when a child is primarily interested in how things look or appear. They will demonstrate skills such as arranging objects in a logical order (according to height, for example), or comparing two objects (such as blocks) through shared attributes, focusing on one perceptual quality (such as size or colour) at a time. From years two to four, the child thinks in absolute terms (such as "big" or "biggest"); from four to seven, they begin to use relative terms (such as "bigger" or "heavier"). The ability to think logically is still limited and children remain egocentric, unable to see things from another's perspective.

The third stage is the concrete operational stage, and this is when a child becomes capable of performing logical operations, but only in the presence of actual (concrete) objects. The child now begins to grasp the concept of conservation, understanding that the quantity of an object remains the same despite physical changes in its arrangement. They realize that if you pour liquid from a short, wide glass into a tall, thin one, the amount of liquid remains the same despite the difference in height. Children can also understand that objects can be sorted according to many qualities simultaneously – a marble can be large,

Educators should not insist on a particular way of doing or understanding something, Piaget (pictured left) asserted, but nurture children's natural learning processes.

green, or clear. A little less egocentric now, children begin to incorporate more relativity into their viewpoints.

During the fourth stage – the formal operational stage – children begin to manipulate ideas (rather than simply objects) and are able to reason purely on the basis of verbal statements. They no longer need to refer to concrete objects, and can follow an argument. They start to think hypothetically, and this new capacity for imagination, and their ability to discuss abstract ideas, reveals that they have now become less egocentric.

Reaching equilibrium

In addition to defining the four stages, Piaget identified several fundamental facets of the developmental process that were required through each of the stages; assimilation, accommodation, and equilibrium. Assimilation is the process by which we incorporate new information into existing schemas. Accommodation is required when, in the process of assimilating, we discover that we need to modify existing knowledge or skills. A child who is able to assimilate successfully most or all new experiences is said to be in a state of equilibrium. However, if the existing schemas are inadequate for coping with new situations successfully, then the child is in a state of cognitive disequilibrium, and the schemas need to develop in order to accommodate the necessary information. Essentially, this is the process of adaptation, one of the most basic forms of learning.

Impact on education

Piaget's work inspired the transformation of the education systems of Europe and the US during the 1970s and 80s, bringing about a more child-centred approach to teaching, in theory and in practice. Rather than trying to teach a child to think and behave like an adult, educators were encouraged to view their work as an opportunity to engage children in novel and individual modes of thinking. Piaget believed that education should inspire people to create, invent, and innovate, and actively discourage them from »

Children at this Montessori school bring Piaget's ideas to life. They are encouraged to build their own learning with hands-on activities and plenty of discussion with their peers.

conforming or following established guidelines at the expense of imagination. If the natural process of learning – from infancy onwards – is individual, active, and exploratory, then so too should be a system of education that guides children's formal intellectual development.

Another vitally important aspect of a child-centred education is an awareness of the concept of "readiness", which involves setting limits on learning based on the child's stage of development. One of Piaget's most enduring contributions to the field of education, particularly with regards to mathematics and science, is the acknowledgement that teachers need to be aware of and honour an individual child's capacity to deal with a novel experience or to take on fresh information. The tasks that a teacher sets should reflect, and also be adapted as precisely as possible to, the individual student's cognitive level and capabilities. Piaget believed that children learn from being active rather than from passive observation, and teachers must adapt to this. Interaction between students is of primary significance in the classroom, and having established that one of the best ways to secure knowledge is to teach it to somebody else, it follows that if children are allowed to discuss topics actively among themselves (rather than listening passively to lessons), they are more likely to deepen and consolidate their existing knowledge.

Moral education

As with intellectual development, Piaget believed that children also develop morally in stages and, for the most part, autonomously. Real moral growth is not the product of adult instruction, but is based on a child's own observations of the world. Piaget viewed peer interaction as absolutely crucial for the moral development of children. Peers, not parents or other authority figures, are seen as being vital to moral growth, providing a key source for understanding concepts such as reciprocity, equality, and justice. Consequently, Piaget keenly promoted peer interaction within the classroom as an integral part of the learning experience.

Jean Piaget

Born in Neuchâtel, Switzerland, Jean Piaget grew up with an insatiable interest in the natural world, and at the age of 11 he wrote his first scientific paper. He studied natural sciences and earned a PhD from the University of Neuchâtel at the age of 22. His interest moved to psychoanalysis and he developed his theories of genetic epistemology in France. In 1921, he became the director of the Jean-Jacques Rousseau Institute in Geneva. He married Valentine Châtenay and they had three children, who were the subjects of many of Piaget's observations about cognitive development.

In 1955, he created the International Centre for Genetic Epistemology and was its director until his death in 1980. He was awarded prizes and honorary degrees worldwide.

Key works

1932 *The Moral Judgment of the Child*
1947 *The Psychology of Intelligence*
1952 *The Origins of Intelligence in Children*
1962 *The Psychology of the Child*

The role of the teacher in Piaget's child-centred classroom is, therefore, almost one of a mentor and an enabler rather than that of a standard instructor. Teachers need to assess carefully each student's current level of cognitive development and then set tasks that are intrinsically motivating. Interestingly, teachers must also create cognitive disequilibrium in their students in order to help them advance to the next stage of development, thereby providing genuine learning opportunities. They should focus on the process of learning, rather than on the achievement of end results, by encouraging their students to ask more questions, experiment, and explore, even if that means making some mistakes along the way. Above all, they must engender a collaborative space where students teach and learn from each other.

Criticisms of Piaget's work

Despite his popularity and the broad influence of his work in the fields of developmental psychology, education, morality, evolution, philosophy, and even artificial intelligence, Piaget's ideas were not accepted without scrutiny and criticism. As with all highly influential theories, years of exploration and research have brought to light its problems and weaknesses. Piaget's notion of egocentrism, for instance, has been called into question. Studies by the US psychologist Susan Gelman in 1979 demonstrated that four-

Australian Aboriginal children aged between eight and 14, and living in remote parts of central Australia, were found by Pierre Dasen to progress through the stages identified by Piaget.

year-olds were able to adjust their explanation of something in order to clarify it for a blindfolded person, and would use simpler forms of speech when talking to younger children, which is inconsistent with Piaget's description of an egocentric child who has no awareness of the needs of others.

Piaget's portrayal of children as primarily independent and autonomous in their construction of knowledge and their understanding of the physical world also met with some resistance, as it seemed to ignore the important contribution that other people make to a child's cognitive development. Pioneering psychologist Lev Vygotsky's work focused on proving that knowledge and thought are essentially social in nature, and disproving Piaget's assumption that a child was not really a part of the social whole. His theory suggests human development exists on three levels: the cultural and the interpersonal as well as the individual, and his main concern was with the first two levels. His "zone of proximal development" theory – which states that children require the help of adults or older children to complete some tasks – served as a response to Piaget.

Another area of exploration has been the assumed universality of the developmental stages identified by Piaget. Although he had no compelling evidence to support this assumption at the time, more recent cross-cultural investigations concerning the sensorimotor stage (including one study conducted by Pierre Dasen in 1994) indicated that the sub-stages suggested by Piaget are indeed universal, though environmental and cultural factors seem to affect the rate at which these stages are reached, and how quickly they are then completed.

Piaget's work unquestionably paved the way for many new areas of enquiry into the nature of child development and human cognitive development. He created the context in which a vast body of research took shape in the 20th and 21st centuries, and fundamentally changed the nature of education in the Western world. ■

EARLY EMOTIONAL BONDS ARE AN INTEGRAL PART OF HUMAN NATURE

JOHN BOWLBY (1907–1990)

IN CONTEXT

APPROACH
Attachment theory

BEFORE
1926 Sigmund Freud presents the psychoanalytic theory of "cupboard love", suggesting that infants become attached to caregivers because they fulfil physiological needs.

1935 Konrad Lorenz's research shows that non-humans form strong bonds with the first moving object they encounter.

AFTER
1959 Harry Harlow's work demonstrates that macaque monkeys separated from their mothers in infancy develop social and emotional problems.

1978 Michael Rutter shows that children can become strongly attached to a variety of attachment figures (such as fathers, siblings, peers, and inanimate objects).

I n the 1950s, the prevailing theory on how infants form attachments was based on the psychoanalytical concept of "cupboard love". This suggested that babies form bonds with people who fulfil their physiological needs, such as feeding. At the same time, the animal studies of Konrad Lorenz suggested

---

Infants and mothers are **biologically programmed** to form an attachment with each other…

↓

…within the **critical period** of the child's life (the first 24 months).

↓

If this attachment is broken within the critical period, it will cause **serious and permanent damage** to the child's development.

↓

Attachment behaviour is an integral part of human nature.

---

that animals simply bond with the first moving object they encounter, which is usually the mother.

It was against this background that John Bowlby took a distinctly evolutionary perspective on early attachment. He argued that because newborn infants are completely helpless, they are genetically programmed to form an attachment with their mothers in order to ensure their survival. Mothers, he believed, are also genetically programmed to bond with their babies, feeling the need to keep them in close proximity. Any conditions that threaten to separate mother and child activate instinctive attachment behaviours and feelings of insecurity and fear.

These ideas formed the basis of Bowlby's theory, which developed to explain the lifelong significance of the mother–infant bond, as well as the psychological difficulties that children suffer if this bond is damaged or entirely broken.

Mothers only

One of the most controversial aspects of Bowlby's theory is that infants always attach to a female, never a male. This female figure may not be the natural mother, but she certainly represents a mother-figure. The term he gave for this tendency to attach to a female is "monotropy", and he emphasized that, although an infant may have more than one attachment figure, his attachment to a mother-figure is simply different from and more significant than any other attachment he will form throughout his life. Both the infant and his mother behave in ways that secure this attachment. An infant, for instance, engages in sucking, cuddling, looking, smiling, and crying in order to shape and control his caregiver's behaviour, and a caregiver would be sensitive and responsive to the infant's needs. In this way the two behavioural systems – attachment and caregiving – help to shape one another and create a lifelong bond.

Bowlby believes that this bond is so deeply formative that if it fails to take place, or breaks down within the first few years of life, the child will go on to suffer serious negative consequences in later life. He also argues that there is a critical period during which a mother and infant should develop a secure attachment: it should take place during the first year, or at the very least before the child is two years old. Bowlby thought that any attempts at mothering beyond the age of three would be useless, and the child would be on course to suffer the effects of maternal deprivation.

Maternal deprivation

In 1950, Bowlby was commissioned by the World Health Organization to study children who had suffered maternal deprivation during World War II due to evacuation or being made homeless. He was also asked to investigate the effects of being raised in residential nurseries and other large institutions (such as orphanages). The result of this early work was Bowlby's 1951 report, *Maternal Care and Mental Health*, in which he observed that children deprived of maternal care for prolonged periods of time during early childhood suffered some degree of intellectual, social, or emotional retardation later in life.

Five years later, Bowlby began a second study, this time investigating children who had spent five months to two years in a tuberculosis sanatorium (which offered no substitute mothering) when they had been less than four years old. The children – aged 7 to 13 by the time of the study – were rougher in play, showed less initiative and more over-excitement, and were less competitive than those with a more traditional upbringing.

In extreme cases, Bowlby found that maternal deprivation could even result in "affectionless psychopathy", a clinical condition in which people are unable to care deeply for others and so do not form meaningful interpersonal relationships. Those who suffer from it display a higher incidence of juvenile delinquency and antisocial behaviour without any sign of remorse, as they are unable to experience feelings of guilt. In Bowlby's 1944 study of juvenile thieves, he found that many of the young criminals had been separated from their mothers for a period of more than six months before they were five years old, and of these, 14 had developed the condition of affectionless psychopathy. »

> ❝ Mother love in infancy is as important for mental health as are vitamins and proteins for physical health.
> **John Bowlby** ❞

> 66 Attachment behaviour is held to characterize human beings from the cradle to the grave.
> **John Bowlby** 99

The reason why this primary, secure attachment is so important, Bowlby says, is that it is essential for the development of an inner working model, or framework, that the child uses to understand himself, others, and the world. This inner working model guides a person's thoughts, feelings, and expectations in all of his personal relationships, even into adulthood. Because the primary attachment serves as a prototype for all future relationships, the quality of the attachment will determine whether or not a child grows to trust others, view himself as valuable, and feel confident in society. These working models are resistant to change; once formed, they determine how people behave and the kind of bond they will form with their own children.

The father's role

Bowlby's attachment theory has been criticized for exaggerating the importance of the mother–child

Bowlby predicted that child evacuees would suffer long-term attachment problems as a result of enforced separation from their mothers; later studies found this to be the case.

relationship and undervaluing the father's contribution. Bowlby sees the father as having no direct emotional significance for the infant, contributing only indirectly by supporting the mother financially and emotionally. The evolutionary basis of Bowlby's theory suggests that women are naturally inclined to be parents, with inborn maternal instincts that guide them through the process of child-rearing, whereas men are more naturally suited for being providers.

However, British psychologist Rudolph Schaffer – who worked under Bowlby at the Tavistock Clinic in London – found that there is considerable cultural variation in the extent to which fathers are involved in childcare. Increasing numbers of fathers are taking on the role of principal parent, which suggests that parenting roles are a consequence of social convention rather than biology.

Bowlby's view implies that men will inevitably be inferior parents, but research by Schaffer and the American psychologist Ross Parke suggests that men are equally capable of providing warmth and sensitivity to their infants. They also found that a child's developmental outcome is not determined by the parent's gender, but rather by the strength and quality of the bond that is forged. In a further study, Schaffer and psychologist Peggy Emerson found that infants and young children display a wide range of attachment behaviours towards many people besides their mothers, and that multiple attachments may actually be the rule rather than the exception.

These later findings were especially important for working women, because the implication of Bowlby's theories was that women should not work once they become mothers; they should stay with the child, fulfilling the role of essential primary caregiver. For decades after Bowlby's theory was posited, generations of working women were saddled with guilt, but many studies since then have questioned this aspect of Bowlby's theory. For instance, in the 1970s, psychologists Thomas Weisner and Ronald Gallimore showed that mothers are the exclusive

> Direct observations of men in their fathering role has shown them to be as capable of as much warmth and sensitivity as women.
> **H. Rudolph Schaffer**

caregivers in only a very small percentage of human societies, and it is not uncommon for groups of people (including relatives and friends) to share responsibility for raising children. Schaffer also points to evidence suggesting that children of mothers who are happy in their work develop more successfully than children whose mothers are frustrated from staying at home.

Ground-breaking work

Despite the many criticisms and revisions that it has provoked, Bowlby's work remains the most comprehensive and influential account of human attachment to date, leading to the ground-breaking experiments of Harry Harlow and Mary Ainsworth. Psychologists have used Bowlby's basic premise to delve more

Bowlby claimed that crèches are not suitable for the care of infants, because maternal deprivation leads to juvenile delinquency; this created a real dilemma for working mothers.

deeply into childhood attachment patterns, and to develop theories of adult attachment by exploring how the bond between parent and child can influence the future bond between spouses and romantic partners. Bowlby's theories have also had many beneficial effects on various aspects of child-rearing, such as the improvement of institutional care and the growing preference for fostering as an alternative. ■

John Bowlby

John Bowlby was the fourth of six children born to a London-based, upper-middle-class family. He was raised primarily by nannies and sent to boarding school at the age of seven. These experiences made him particularly sympathetic to the attachment difficulties faced by young children. He studied psychology at Trinity College, Cambridge, then spent some time teaching delinquent children. He later earned a medical degree and qualified as a psychoanalyst.

During World War II, Bowlby served in the Royal Army Medical Corps, and in 1938 married Ursula Longstaff, with whom he had four children. After the war, he became director of the Tavistock Clinic, where he remained until retirement. In 1950, he carried out a major study for the World Health Organization. He died at his summer home on the island of Skye in Scotland, aged 83.

Key works

1951 *Maternal Care and Mental Health (WHO Report)*
1959 *Separation Anxiety*
1969, 1973, 1980 *Attachment and Loss (three volumes)*

GIRLS GET BETTER GRADES THAN BOYS

ELEANOR E. MACCOBY (1917–)

IN CONTEXT

APPROACH
Feminist psychology

BEFORE
Early 20th century First research into sex differences by female psychologists.

1970s Studies of the sexes tend to emphasize differences between men and women.

AFTER
1980s Studies suggest structural differences between the male and female brain.

1993 Anne Fausto-Sterling claims biological graduations exist between "male" and "female" such that we could identify five different sexes along the spectrum.

2003 Simon Baron-Cohen argues that the female brain is predominantly hard-wired for empathy, and the male brain for understanding systems.

There is no significant difference in the overall **intellectual aptitude** of boys and girls.

↓

But because girls tend to put in a greater effort at school, and have greater interest and better work habits…

↓

…girls get better grades than boys.

The emergence of feminist psychologists during the 1970s revived an interest in the study of sex differences, which had waned during the rise of behaviourism. Feminist concerns became increasingly important to US psychologist Eleanor Maccoby. Frustrated by the tendency of psychological literature to report on research findings that emphasized the differences between men and women rather than the similarities, Maccoby, with student Carol Jacklin, reviewed more than 1,600 studies of gender differences. They published their findings in *The Psychology of Sex Differences* (1974) with the aim of showing that what most consider essential differences between the sexes are in fact myths, and that many gender stereotypes are untrue. Although some findings had shown boys to be more aggressive and more adept at mathematics and spatial reasoning than girls, and girls to have superior verbal abilities, subsequent studies revealed that these differences are either negligible or are more complex than they initially appear.

One difference that was consistent and undeniable was that "girls get better grades than boys" in school. Maccoby found this particularly interesting, especially considering that girls did not obtain higher aptitude test scores when all of the subject matter areas were reviewed. Furthermore, previous research into achievement motivation seemed to suggest that boys should outperform their female peers. Males were arguably more oriented towards achievement for its own sake than girls, showing greater task involvement, and more exploratory behaviour; females were primarily interested in achievement relating to interpersonal relationships – exerting effort to please others, and demonstrating low self-confidence with respect to many tasks.

Challenging stereotypes

Maccoby systemically argued against these assumptions, pointing to the fact that girls are higher academic achievers than boys, show greater interest in school-related skills from an early age, and are less likely to drop out before completing high school. Maccoby concluded that their better grades clearly reflect some combination of greater effort, greater interest, and better work habits than their male peers. Whatever discrepancy exists between boys and girls in terms of achievement motivation does not reflect school-related motivation. This motivation could prove significant throughout girls' lives, as performance at school is also relevant to job performance.

Girls show greater responsiveness to teacher's expectations and are more willing to work, according to Maccoby's research, which makes them more likely to do better at school than boys.

The ongoing debate over inherent sex differences is tied up with general political questions about how society should be organized, and the roles that men and women are "naturally" equipped to fill. By pointing out that psychological literature tends to publish results indicating sex differences, while ignoring those indicating equality, Maccoby has fought against the assignment of men and women to stereotypical professions. ∎

Eleanor E. Maccoby

Born in Tacoma, Washington, Eleanor Maccoby (née Emmons) earned a bachelor's degree from the University of Washington and a master's and PhD in experimental psychology from the University of Michigan. In the 1940s, she worked for the Department of Agriculture, and then at Harvard University, supervising research on child-rearing practices. Perceiving that gender bias was holding her back, she moved to Stanford University, where she became the first woman to serve as Chair of the Psychology Department. Maccoby went on to receive a Lifetime Achievement Award from the American Psychology Foundation, and The American Psychological Association introduced an award in her name. Maccoby's work to debunk stereotypes is considered fundamental to understanding children's socialization and gender differences.

Key works

1966 *The Development of Sex Differences*
1974 *The Psychology of Sex Differences*
1996 *Adolescents after Divorce*

MOST HUMAN BEHAVIOUR IS LEARNED THROUGH MODELLING
ALBERT BANDURA (1925–)

IN CONTEXT

APPROACH
Social learning theory

BEFORE
1938 B.F. Skinner proposes the behaviourist notion of operant conditioning, which explores positive and negative reinforcements in learning.

1939 US psychologist John Dollard argues that aggression is always a consequence of frustration, and that frustration always leads to aggression.

AFTER
1966 American pychologist Leonard Berkowitz claims environmental cues, such as those associated with aggressive behaviour, must be present for aggression to follow anger.

1977 US psychologist Robert A. Baron suggests that Bandura's experiment implies that violence in the media contributes to violence in society.

We are surrounded by people talking and acting in different ways.

↓

We notice and remember these **observed actions**...

↓

...which we then **mentally rehearse**...

↓

...and, if motivated, **physically reproduce** ourselves.

↓

Most human behaviour is learned through modelling.

I n the 1940s and 1950s, learning was understood primarily in behaviourist terms, with B.F. Skinner's theory of operant conditioning – in which learning is wholly determined by rewards and punishments – dominating the field. From this context emerged Albert Bandura's interest in studying childhood aggression – an area he felt was too complex to explain in terms of operant conditioning – as a learned behaviour.

Bandura's hypothesis was that children learn aggression through observing and imitating the violent acts of adults – particularly family members. He believed that the key to the problem lies at the intersection of Skinner's operant conditioning and Freud's psychoanalytic theory of identification, which explores how people assimilate the characteristics of others into their own personalities. Bandura's work culminated in his famous Bobo doll experiment, and his hugely influential 1977 treatise *Social Learning Theory*.

Social learning theory

Bandura's belief that people learn not through reinforcement (rewards and punishments), but through observing others, is at the heart of social learning theory. This theory suggests that learning is achieved by mentally rehearsing and then imitating the observed actions of other people, who serve as models of appropriate or acceptable behaviour. Bandura argued that "most human behaviour is learned through modelling".

Bandura noted four conditions that are necessary for a person to successfully model the behaviour of another: attention, retention, reproduction, and motivation. Learning requires that the learner is paying attention to the behaviour in the first place, that he remembers what he saw or heard, that he is actually able to physically reproduce the behaviour, and that he has a good motive or reason to reproduce it, such as the expectation of reward.

Although the concept of reward is part of his social learning theory, Bandura's move away from behaviourism is evident in his radical, anti-behaviourist ideas about the relationship between a person's environment and his or her behaviour. According to behaviourism, environmental circumstances entirely determine behaviour, but Bandura believes in "reciprocal determinism" – the idea that a person influences the environment just as the environment influences him. Bandura conceived of personality as an interaction between three different components: the environment, behaviour, and psychological processes (the ability to use language and entertain images in the mind). All of these components are relevant to the study of childhood aggression, which, Bandura argued, was learned by watching and modelling adults.

Bobo doll experiment

Bandura's social learning point of view was the basis for his 1961 Bobo doll experiment on childhood aggression, which sought to explain how aggressive behaviour develops, what provokes people to carry out aggressive acts, and what determines whether they will continue to

Children attack the Bobo doll in Bandura's 1961 experiment on aggressive behaviour. In some cases, subjects devised new ways to attack the doll by using other toys in the room.

behave aggressively. By proving that a child will imitate the behaviour of an adult role model, the experiment showed the power of examples of aggression in society.

For the experiment, 36 boys and 36 girls, all between the ages of three and six, were recruited from a local nursery school. They were divided up into three groups of 24, each comprising 12 boys and 12 girls. The first group was the control group (which did not see any adult role model); the second group was exposed to an adult modelling aggressive behaviour towards an inflatable Bobo doll; the third group was exposed to a passive adult model. All of the children in the experiment were tested individually to ensure that they would not be influenced by their peers.

In the experiments on the second group, each child watched an adult performing physically and verbally aggressive acts towards the doll. The adult pummelled the large Bobo toy with a mallet, flung it in the air, kicked it, threw it down on the floor, and beat it. When each child was later left alone in a room of toys that included a Bobo doll, he or she imitated a good deal of the aggressive acts performed by the adult models, even creating novel acts of violence against the doll. Children in this group were also generally less inhibited than those in the other groups, showing an increased attraction to guns despite the fact that playing with guns was not modelled. »

By contrast, children who were either in the control group or who were exposed to a passive adult model only rarely demonstrated any kind of physical or verbal aggression. Although Bandura did consider the possibility that observing aggressive acts merely weakened any inhibitions that the children may have already had about behaving violently, the fact that they often imitated the exact behaviour they had just seen suggests that observational learning was taking place.

Violence in the media

Bandura's research has raised many important questions surrounding the prevalence of violence in the media. If a stranger performing aggressive acts can be a model of aggression for children, you might argue that television programmes could also be considered a source of behaviour modelling. Modern films and television shows include graphic violence, which is often expressed as an acceptable (or at least expected) form of behaviour, which children who are regularly exposed to the media may feel inclined to imitate. This idea has been hotly debated. Many studies indicate that violent films and television shows do not increase a child's tendencies towards violence. Some studies even indicate that exposure to violence can actually decrease the amount of aggression in children. This theory – known as the Catharsis effect – suggests that an individual may be able to relate to a violent on-screen character and release negative feelings, thereby becoming less aggressive personally than prior to the viewing.

Other psychologists regard television as a form of education, and believe that, as characters often serve as role models for children, they should be positive models in order to help decrease the general level of violence prevalent in society.

> 66 Exposure to aggressive modelling is hardly cathartic.
> **Albert Bandura** 99

Violence in computer games, and in the media generally, has been cited as a potential source of behaviour modelling, although this view has not been strongly supported by studies.

Although Bandura himself does not believe in the Catharsis effect of viewing aggressive behaviour, he was careful to note that there was a distinction between learning and performance. Children, he thought, could certainly learn aggressive behaviour from viewing it, but knowledge of violent acts would not necessarily result in committing these acts themselves. He warned against assuming a more direct and causal relationship between violence in the media and real-world aggression.

Social learning theorists accept that cognition has a part to play in modelling, and that cognitive factors mediate the process between viewing violence and actually imitating it. For instance, the perception and interpretation of TV violence, and how realistic the programme is, are both important intervening variables. Bandura also considers that environmental experiences are another influence in the social learning of aggression in children. Unsurprisingly, people living in neighbourhoods with high crime rates are more likely to commit acts of violence than those living in low-crime areas.

Gender development

The social learning theory underlying Bandura's research on childhood aggression has important implications for our understanding of the development of gender identity. According to the gender development theory, one reason why boys and girls tend to exhibit differences in their behaviour is that they are treated differently by their parents (as well as other significant adults and peers). It has been shown that people unwittingly tailor their behaviour towards children from birth to match their own gender-role expectations; this encourages children to behave according to what are considered gender norms.

According to Bandura's findings, children also learn how to behave through reinforcement and observation learning. By imitating the behaviour of others, children are highly likely to receive positive reinforcement for the type of behaviour that is considered most appropriate to their sex. They will also be either directly or subtly discouraged from behaving in ways that are not sex-appropriate.

Although there has been some criticism of Bandura's work (often centred on whether his idea is truly a theory of cognitive development), his findings and theories are still cited and debated half a century later, reflecting the breadth and scope of his influence. His ground-breaking contributions span many of the fields of psychology, including social cognitive theory, personality theory, and even therapeutic practices. His ideas also serve as a bridge between preceding behaviourist learning theories and subsequent cognitive learning theories.

Bandura's focus on processes such as attention, memory, and motivation marked a departure from studying only observable and measurable variables (the sole concern of behaviourists) and looked instead to the mental realm – the mind – for information about how people learn. For these reasons, Bandura is considered by many of his peers to be one of the most distinguised and influential psychologists of all time. ∎

Behaviour seen as sex-appropriate in children, such as independence (in boys) or empathy (in girls), is often positively reinforced by adults' expectations, as well as by children's imitation of adults and peers.

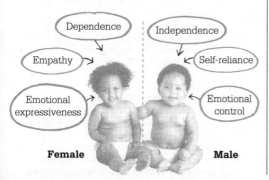

Dependence — Independence
Empathy — Self-reliance
Emotional expressiveness — Emotional control

Female — **Male**

Albert Bandura

Albert Bandura was born to Polish parents in the small town of Mundare in Alberta, Canada. He graduated from the University of British Columbia, moving on to take his master's degree and doctorate at the University of Iowa, where his interest in learning theory developed. In 1953, he took up a teaching post at Stanford University, California, where he is a professor emeritus.

One of the world's most eminent and influencial psychologists, Bandura has received numerous awards, including the Thorndike Award for Distinguished Contributions of Psychology to Education (1999), and a Lifetime Achievement Award from the Association for the Advancement of Behavior Therapy (2001). He also has more than 16 honorary degrees, and in 1974 was elected president of the American Psychological Association.

Key works

1973 *Aggression: A Social Learning Analysis*
1977 *Social Learning Theory*
1986 *Social Foundations of Thought and Action: A Social Cognitive Theory*

THE LANGUAGE ORGAN GROWS LIKE ANY OTHER BODY ORGAN
NOAM CHOMSKY (1928–)

IN CONTEXT

APPROACH
Nativism

BEFORE
1958 B.F. Skinner uses operant conditioning to explain language development, arguing that children learn words and phrases through reinforcement.

1977 Albert Bandura argues that children may imitate the general form of sentences, and fill in these with specific words.

AFTER
1994 Steven Pinker argues that language is an instinct from an innate programme hard-wired in the brain, which arose because it was adaptive for human survival.

2003 Psychologists Stan Kuczaj and Heather Hill claim parents offer children better examples of grammatical sentences than Chomsky suggests.

In the middle of the 20th century, learning theory as explained by B.F. Skinner and Albert Bandura dominated psychologists' conception of language development. These behaviourists believed that language – like all other human faculties – was a direct result of environmental input and learning, developed through the reinforcement and reward techniques at the heart of operant conditioning. Skinner noted that when children imitate verbal sounds, and form correct words, they receive immediate reinforcement and approval from their parents, which motivates them to continue learning new words and phrases. Bandura broadened the concept of imitation, noting that children imitated not only specific words and sounds, but also the general form and structure of sentences, as though filling in templates with specific words.

Linguist Noam Chomsky, however, did not believe that operant conditioning adequately explained the productivity, creativity, and innovation of language. It also seemed insufficient to explain children's spontaneous use of grammatical rules that they have neither heard nor learned, as well as their ability to understand the meaning of an entire sentence without necessarily understanding the meaning of each word. For Chomsky, this ability is innate in humans – he claimed that "the language organ grows like any other body organ", likening it to other features acquired through heredity.

Nativism
Chomsky maintained that, although a child's environment supplies the content of language, grammar itself is an in-built and biologically determined human capacity. To illustrate his point, he refers to other aspects of human development that we accept as being an inevitable outcome of

Young children **spontaneously use grammatical rules** that they have never been taught.

Young children can **understand the meaning** of an entire sentence without understanding all the words.

Verbal imitation combined with approval and praise does not explain the **productivity and creativity** of language.

The human capacity to understand grammar is **innate and biological**.

The language organ grows like any other body organ.

heredity. The onset of puberty, for instance, is an aspect of human growth that is like the "growth" of the language organ. We assume unquestioningly that it is a genetically determined milestone, and though the specific details of its onset depend on several variable environmental influences, the fundamental process is the same across the human species. We take for granted that this is a result of basic biological programming. Language growth, Chomsky emphasizes, is another genetically programmed inevitability of human development, on a par with the processes that determine that we have arms instead of wings, or that build the structure of our visual or circulatory systems. The concept that language is a part of our growth process is important because it highlights Chomsky's belief that it is not a consequence of learning. He

adopts a nativist perspective, focusing on the inherited contributions to behaviour and minimizing the importance of environmental input. However, he believes that the environment plays a role in determining the specific direction of language growth, insofar as an individual's language organ develops according to early experiences. For instance, because Chomsky grew up in Philadelphia, Pennsylvania, USA, he absorbed knowledge of that particular English dialect and his language organ's structure was tailored accordingly. The same process occurs for everyone, whether they have grown up in Paris, Tokyo, or London.

Universal grammar

But where is the proof that language acquisition is inborn rather than learned? According to Chomsky, the most convincing evidence for this claim is that there are aspects of grammar that are so intuitive and self-evident that they need never be discussed or learned in order to be understood, (they are therefore part of our biological inheritance). For instance, there are certain constructions in the English language that permit the dropping of pronouns, and others that do not. The difference between the two is subtle, yet even by the age of six, native English-speaking children will use the constructions flawlessly. This implies that certain aspects of grammar are understood without requiring any instruction, and that the knowledge is therefore innate. This is the only way to explain how people have such a rich grammatical understanding and how children can use language so creatively by the age of six.

Chomsky claims that "universal grammar" is found worldwide, with modifications according to people's native languages. It is a predefined mechanism **»**

Language is a process of free creation.
Noam Chomsky

that acts as the basis for the acquisition of any language. He argues that this is demonstrated by the way that all children are equally able to learn any language to which they are exposed. He says that a common set of linguistic features is built into the language organ through heredity, and it includes elements of grammar, meaning, and speech. It is what makes it possible for us to speak and learn human languages, and may make it impossible for us to learn any language that violates these principles.

Language device

Chomsky proposes a name for our innate language organ: the Language Acquisition Device (LAD). He bases his claim for its existence on three things: the fact that children are born with the capacity to formulate and understand all kinds of sentences despite never having heard or learned them; that every human language appears to have certain universal elements; and that some grammatical principles are acquired by individuals regardless of their culture or intelligence. There is other supporting evidence as well, including the fact that the human vocal organs, breathing apparatus, auditory system, and brain are all specialized for spoken communication. Chomsky argues that, in light of the frequency with which

Deaf children communicate using a "gestural language", which has the same characteristics as spoken language, suggesting that knowledge of grammar and syntax is innate.

children are exposed to the ungrammatical and incomplete speech uttered by their parents and other adults, only some kind of LAD can explain the fact that children seem to possess knowledge of grammatical rules. Finally, studies of deaf children provide further evidence for an LAD, revealing the untutored emergence of a "gestural language" that shares the basic principles of spoken language.

Evaluation

Cognitive scientist Steven Pinker agrees that language is an instinct stemming from an innate programme that is hard-wired in the human brain, but says that it arose

Noam Chomsky

Linguist, philosopher, cognitive scientist, and social activist Noam Chomsky was born in Pennsylvania, USA, to Jewish parents. He studied philosophy and linguistics at the University of Pennsylvania, where he earned his bachelor's, master's, and doctoral degrees. Chomsky joined the Massachusetts Institute of Technology in 1955, becoming an Institute Professor in 1976.

Chomsky is widely known as one of the fathers of modern linguistics, but he is also a political dissident and anarchist. His criticisms of US foreign policy have made him a highly controversial figure. He has won several honorary degrees as well as being a recipient of the Distinguished Scientific Contribution Award, the Dorothy Eldridge Peacemaker Award, and the Orwell Award. He was married to linguist Carol Schatz for 59 years until her death in 2008.

Key works

1957 *Syntactic Structures*
1965 *Cartesian Linguistics*
1968 *Language and Mind*

through evolution and was therefore adaptive, helping our ancestors to survive. Chomsky disagrees with Pinker about how language evolved, arguing that language represents a distinct mental module that is unique to human beings and completely independent of general cognitive ability.

Linguist Jean Aitchison is also in agreement with Chomsky's claim that children are hard-wired with knowledge of linguistic rules, but her view is that children have built-in problem-solving abilities that enable them to process linguistic data (and other forms of data). Chomsky maintains, however, that human beings' innate language ability exists independently of other abilities, and because the mind is constructed of mental organs similar to those of the body, language can easily be isolated from other mental faculties.

Criticism also comes from Robin Chapman, an expert in communicative disorders, who argues that the study of language development should also be understood within the context of children's social interactions. She notes that language structure is acquired piecemeal over several years, and that there are wide variations in how rapidly children acquire it, suggesting that social environment could also be a factor. There is also some degree of doubt surrounding Chomsky's

> ❝ We are designed to learn languages based upon a common set of principles, which we may call universal grammar.
> **Noam Chomsky** ❞

assumption that language is unique to human beings. Data from studies with chimpanzees and gorillas has suggested that the difference between ape and human language is quantitative rather than qualitative, which raises questions about how species-specific language really is.

Chomsky's work has been highly influential across linguistics, psychology, philosophy, and even mathematics. Although the idea that children are predisposed to learn language is widely accepted, his claim that children have an innate knowledge of language that is not deeply influenced by their parents is highly controversial. He has been widely considered the most extreme nativist in the history of psychology, and although a biological source for language development is widely thought to be nearer the truth than one involving operant conditioning, it is still unlikely to offer the complete picture. Chomsky's work has led to the emergence of more integrated views, which will no doubt lead to new research and understanding. ■

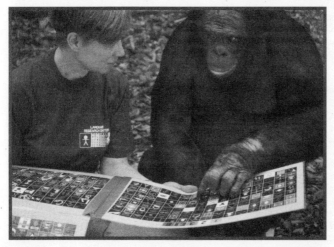

Studies of how chimpanzees communicate with each other shows that their language is complex, although it appears to have less content and variation than human language.

PSYCHOLO OF DIFFER

PERSONALITY AND INTELLIGENCE

T heoretical psychology has largely been concerned with identifying and examining aspects of the mind and behaviour that are common to us all, yet philosophers, and later scientists, have always recognized that there are differences in our psychological make-up that render us individuals. Some of the early philosophers explained differences in personality using the idea of the four humours or temperaments, but it was not until the 20th century that there was any truly scientific study of personality.

Behaviourists, as one would expect, saw personality as a product of conditioning, and psychoanalytical theory described personality as the effect of past experience on the unconscious – but these explanations resulted from research into more general theories rather than a study of personality itself. The first psychologist to systematically approach the subject was Gordon Allport, who felt that existing ideas of personality were inadequate. As one of the pioneers of what is now called "trait theory", he identified a number of different personality traits, which he suggested showed themselves in three different levels in a combination unique to each

person. The idea of traits became central to personality psychology and, following Allport's work, it became a major new area of study.

Personality traits

New ways of analysing traits, such as Raymond Cattell's factor analytical method, which identified 16 personality factors, led to refinement of Allport's theories: reducing the number of traits that combined to form an individual personality. The prominent traits of introversion and extraversion were common to most of these models, and the distinction between them was felt to be a major factor in determining personality. They were incorporated into Hans Eysenck's three-factor model, with its basic traits of extraversion–introversion, neuroticism, and psychoticism.

One assumption that was questioned was whether personality traits would result in consistent behaviour. Research conducted by Walter Mischel showed that different situations produced different behaviour, and suggested that personality traits should be considered in the context of an individual's perception of and reaction to various circumstances. Not only was personality found to be less consistent than had been assumed, but in some cases there was the possibility of an individual having more than one distinct personality. In a case made famous by a book and film, *The Three Faces of Eve*, psychiatrists Corbett H. Thigpen and Hervey M. Cleckley described multiple personality disorder, now called dissociative identity disorder.

The intelligence factor

Another factor that distinguishes us as individuals is intelligence. This had been studied from the earliest days of psychology, but had proved difficult to define or measure. Studies are also frequently controversial; since the time of Darwin and Galton, intelligence was assumed to be an inherited characteristic (and carried with it connotations of racial stereotypes and eugenics) rather than one influenced by environment. The issue of nature versus nurture in determining intelligence became key, with psychologists including Raymond Cattell and Hans Eysenck defending a hereditary viewpoint, and others arguing that not only is intelligence affected by environment, but the way it is tested is culturally biased, giving distorted results.

In the early 20th century, British psychologist Charles Spearman had laid the foundations for a more objective, scientific study of intelligence by using statistical techniques to test and measure intelligence. He identified a single factor, the "g factor", that correlated to all the mental abilities that make up general intelligence. This notion of a single measure of intelligence was challenged by J.P. Guilford, who believed that intelligence consists of a number of different abilities, an idea that led to Raymond Cattell's theory of fluid and crystallized intelligence – two levels of reasoning and critical thinking.

Research into other areas of psychological difference has included emotions and facial expressions, pioneered by Paul Ekman and Nico Frijda, and psychological disorders, though David Rosenhan's experiment showed that it is not easy to distinguish the "normal" from the "abnormal". Individual differences appear to be points on a spectrum, rather than easily labelled divisions – highlighting the complexity and diversity of human psychology. ∎

NAME AS MANY USES AS YOU CAN THINK OF FOR A TOOTHPICK

J.P. GUILFORD (1897–1987)

IN CONTEXT

APPROACH
Intelligence psychometrics

BEFORE
19th century Wilhelm Wundt, Gustav Fechner, and Francis Galton claim that individual differences in people's cognitive abilities can be empirically measured.

1904 British psychologist Charles Spearman claims intelligence can be summed up in a single number.

1938 British psychologist L.L. Thurstone identifies seven independent factors that make up a person's "primary abilities" or intelligence.

AFTER
1969 Philip E. Vernon estimates that intelligence is 60 per cent inborn.

1974 US psychologist Ellis Paul Torrance produces his own tests of creativity, which are most widely used today.

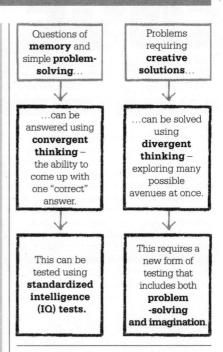

Questions of **memory** and simple **problem-solving**...

...can be answered using **convergent thinking** – the ability to come up with one "correct" answer.

This can be tested using **standardized intelligence (IQ) tests.**

Problems requiring **creative solutions**...

...can be solved using **divergent thinking** – exploring many possible avenues at once.

This requires a new form of testing that includes both **problem-solving and imagination**.

A lthough intelligence, and what makes up intelligence, had been discussed since the time of ancient Greece, the first systematic method of measuring intelligence was not developed until 1905, when the French psychologist Alfred Binet was asked to identify children who might benefit from educational assistance. Together with researcher Theodore Simon, he created the "Binet–Simon Scale", which used memory, attention, and problem-solving tasks to measure and produce a number, or "quotient", that summarizes intellectual ability. The average intelligence quotient (IQ) was set for convenience at 100, allowing psychologists to categorize people in relation to this score. In practice, around 95 per cent of the general population score

Creative minds see even toothpicks as potentially having hundreds of uses. Guilford's "Alternative Uses Test" scores people on their ability to think of many original and widely assorted alternatives.

between 70 and 130, and the top 0.5 per cent score over 145, the "genius" level.

Although the scale is still used for most IQ tests today, US psychologist J.P. Guilford believes it has fundamental flaws. Standard intelligence tests, he says, ignore creativity and assume that there is a "general intelligence" that can be represented by an IQ score.

Measuring creativity

By definition, creativity means there is more than one answer to any problem. It requires a different kind of thinking, which Guilford calls "divergent", since it goes in different directions and produces multiple solutions to a problem. In contrast, traditional IQ tests require thinking that ends up with a single answer: "convergent" thinking.

Guilford thought that creativity was measurable – it is indicated by the number of directions in which a person's thoughts travel. He devised a number of tests to quantify divergent thinking, including his 1967 "Alternative Uses Test", which asks participants to write as many uses as they can think of for: (a) a toothpick, (b) a brick, and (c) a paper clip. In his "Consequences Test", subjects were asked to imagine all the things that might possibly happen if all national and local laws were suddenly abolished. Guilford scored the answers on levels of four key components: originality, fluency, flexibility, and elaboration.

Guilford claims that intelligence is not made up of just one "general factor", but of three different groups of activities. "Operations" are the intellectual processes we use; there are six types of these, including memory, cognition, and evaluation. "Content" is the type of information or data involved – there are five of these, including visual and auditory content. "Products" are the results of applying operations to content, such as classes or relations, and there are six of these. The many ways in which we combine and use these different types means there may be anything up to 180 (6 × 5 × 6) types of intelligence – more than 100 of these have already been verified.

The complexity of Guilford's theory and problems with testing mean that his tests are used less frequently than standard IQ tests, but his work has influenced research into intelligence and creativity. ∎

J.P. Guilford

Joy Paul Guilford was born on a farm in Nebraska, USA. Always markedly intelligent, he was the valedictorian of his high school class. His bachelor's degree in psychology was interrupted by a spell in the army as a private, but he went on to earn a PhD from Cornell University.

In 1928, he returned to Nebraska as an associate professor, then took up a position at the University of Southern California (USC) in 1940, remaining there – apart from a short secondment during World War II – until his retirement in 1967. Described as a devoted family man of enormous integrity and generosity, his shyness earned him the

nickname the "grey ghost" during his time in the army. An influential and prolific researcher, Guilford produced more than 25 books, 30 tests, and 300 articles.

Key works

1936 *Psychometric Methods*
1967 *The Nature of Human Intelligence*

DID ROBINSON CRUSOE LACK PERSONALITY TRAITS BEFORE THE ADVENT OF FRIDAY?

GORDON ALLPORT (1897–1967)

IN CONTEXT

APPROACH
Trait theory

BEFORE
2nd century BCE Galen classifies human temperament according to the four humours.

1890 In *Principles of Psychology*, William James makes an early attempt to define the self as having both an "I" (the knowing self) and a "me" (the experiencing self).

AFTER
1946 Raymond Cattell develops his 16PF (Personality Factors) questionnaire, based on Allport and Odbert's lexical hypothesis.

1970s Hans J. Eysenck creates the PEN (Psychoticism, Extraversion, Neurotisicm) personality questionnaire.

1993 American psychologist Dan P. McAdam demonstrates the idiographic method in his book *The Stories We Live By.*

ordon Allport is sometimes referred to as one of the founding fathers of personality psychology, as he was the first psychologist of modern times to embark on a dedicated study of personality. Since the early work on the four temperaments by Hippocrates (c.400 BCE) and Galen (c.150 CE), there seems to have been no attempt to classify personality in any detail. In the 19th century, personality was barely mentioned in psychology, though there was much discussion of the self, or "ego".

In the early 20th century, the two predominant schools of psychology – psychoanalysis and behaviourism – were polar opposites in approach. Both were highly developed and influential schools that remain powerful (as well as enduringly controversial) to this day. Behaviourism, being interested only in how we acquire (or learn) our behaviour, had nothing to say about personality; while psychoanalysis offered an in-depth approach, arguing for the existence of an unknowable unconscious that controls personality but reveals itself only fractionally and accidentally by slips of the tongue and in dream symbols.

The American psychologist Gordon Allport had fundamental problems with both of these approaches. He thought that behaviourism was wrong to discount the "person" doing the learning, because each person is unique and their perception is part of the process. He also considered psychoanalysis to be inadequate for explaining personality and behaviour because it placed too much importance on a person's past, ignoring their current context and motivations. His view was affirmed when, as a young college graduate, he paid a visit to Sigmund Freud in Vienna. On first meeting, to make small talk, Allport told Freud of a small boy he had met on the train on the way, who was afraid of getting dirty and refused to sit near anyone dirty, despite his mother's encouragement. Perhaps, Allport suggested, the child had learned this dirt phobia from his mother, a neat and rather domineering woman. Freud then asked, "And was that little boy you?" Freud's reduction of this small observation of Allport's to some unconscious episode from his own childhood seemed, to Allport, dismissive of all his current motivations and intentions. Throughout his work, Allport emphasizes the present over the past, though later in his life he paid more attention to psychoanalysis as a supplement to other methods. Allport argued for an approach to the study of human learning and personality that was reasoned, eclectic, and conceptually open-minded. He took some of what he believed from prevailing approaches, but his central belief is that the uniqueness of each individual and his or her personality is largely – but not exclusively – forged in human relationships.

Theory of personality

Allport's idea of personality is a complex amalgam of traits, human relationships, current context, and motivation. He identified two distinctly different approaches to the study of personality – the nomothetic and idiographic methods – both of which had been devised by the German philosophers Wilhelm Windelband and Wilhelm Dilthey, but had first been put into practice by Allport's university tutor, William Stern.

The first method, the nomothetic, aims to be as objective and scientific as possible, and it is exemplified in the study of human intelligence. This involves obtaining test results from large populations of people, on personality traits such as extraversion and introversion. Results can be submitted to a sophisticated analysis, resulting in a number of general conclusions, such as the percentages of people who are extravert or introvert, or variations linked to age, gender, or geography. However, this method does not aim to comment in any way on traits at the individual level; it focuses on comparative comments and conclusions about a certain trait, rather than any particular person. This was the method that the behaviourist B.F. Skinner used for his observations of rat behaviour.

The second method, the idiographic, stands in direct opposition to the nomothetic method; it studies one individual in breadth and depth, taking into account their biography, their personality traits, and their relationships, as well as how they are seen and experienced by others. This method is much closer to the psychoanalytic method with its focus on one person, one life.

Allport said that while the nomothetic method was a way of describing traits, it had little explanatory power; whereas the idiographic method, though unable to draw any general conclusions, could explain one person in illuminating detail. He was to use both methods, though his work in general is not known for its focus on empirical research; he was more of a theorist, almost a philosopher. Yet his very first paper, »

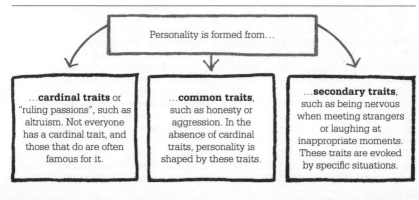

Personality is formed from…

…**cardinal traits** or "ruling passions", such as altruism. Not everyone has a cardinal trait, and those that do are often famous for it.

…**common traits**, such as honesty or aggression. In the absence of cardinal traits, personality is shaped by these traits.

…**secondary traits**, such as being nervous when meeting strangers or laughing at inappropriate moments. These traits are evoked by specific situations.

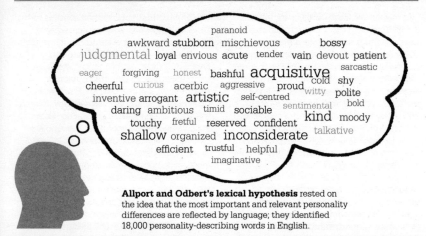

Allport and Odbert's lexical hypothesis rested on the idea that the most important and relevant personality differences are reflected by language; they identified 18,000 personality-describing words in English.

Personality Traits: Their Classification and Measurement, co-written with his brother Floyd, was an excellent example of the nomothetic method. One of his last major pieces of work, the analysis of Jenny Masterson, was an extraordinarily detailed example of the idiographic method.

The lexical hypothesis

In his first study, Allport and his brother reported their research on personality traits. They asked the participants to complete a personality questionnaire, and to ask three people who knew them well to complete it too; this reflected the Allport brothers' view that personality is forged in relationship to others. They concluded from their results that there is a case for identifying traits, and for attempting to measure them. They also believed they had proven the possibility of developing a complete and sensitive instrument for the measurement of personality. In 1936, Allport and his colleague H.S. Odbert proposed that individual differences that are most salient and socially relevant in people's lives eventually become expressed through language; and the more important the difference, the more likely it is to be expressed as a single word. This idea is known as the lexical hypothesis. The two researchers went on to study the most comprehensive dictionaries of the English language available at the time, to find 18,000 words that described personality. They narrowed this down to 4,500 adjectives that they considered to be observable and stable personality traits.

Cardinal traits

Based on a further analysis of his lexical study, Allport defined three distinct categories of traits: cardinal, common, and secondary. Cardinal traits are those that are fundamental to a person, governing their entire approach to life. Not everyone has a cardinal trait, according to Allport, but when they do, they may even be famous for them; in fact some people are so famous for them that their name becomes a byword for that trait, giving us terms such as Byronic, Calvinistic, and Machiavellian. On a less iconic scale, a person's cardinal trait might be something like "a fear of communism", where this is so central and important to someone that it guides and unifies their life in both conscious and unconscious ways; virtually every act is traceable to its influence.

In his later years, Allport considered a person's cardinal traits as contributing to the *proprium*: the essential drives, core needs, and desires of a person. This concept goes beyond the idea of temperament, and is more akin to a guiding purpose that will always press for expression. As an example of the *proprium*, Allport gave the Norwegian polar explorer Roald Amundsen, who had one dominant passion from the age of 15: he wanted to be a polar explorer. The obstacles to his ambition seemed insurmountable, and the temptation to relinquish his dreams was great, but the "propriate" striving persisted, and though he welcomed each success, it simply raised his level of aspiration. Having sailed the Northwest Passage, Amundsen embarked upon the project that led to his success in reaching the South Pole. Then, after years of planning and discouragement, he flew over the North Pole. His commitment never wavered, and he eventually died attempting to save the life of a less experienced explorer.

Less fundamental traits

In contrast to cardinal traits, common traits are general characteristics, such as honesty, that are found in most people. These are the building blocks that shape our behaviour, but they are less fundamental than cardinal traits. Common traits, Allport said, develop largely in response to parental influences, and are a result of nurture. They are shared among many people within a culture but in varying degrees; aggressiveness, for instance, is a common trait that varies by degrees. According to Allport, most of us have personalities made up of five to ten of these traits at a level whereby they have become our "outstanding characteristics".

Over time, common traits may achieve "functional autonomy", by which Allport means that although we start doing something for one reason, we may carry on doing it for quite another. This is because our motives today are not continuously dependent on the past. We may start learning to draw, for instance, to compete in popularity with another child in class, but ultimately become more interested in perfecting the craft for its own sake. This means that how we think and act today is only indirectly affected by our past. Functional autonomy is also thought to explain obsessive and compulsive acts and thoughts: they may be manifestations of functionally autonomous traits, where someone has no idea why he is doing something, but can't stop himself from doing it.

Allport's third category of traits, known as secondary traits, exert much less influence on us than cardinal or common traits. They are only seen in certain circumstances, because they are determined by context or situation. For instance, we might say of someone "he gets very cross when tickled" or "she gets nervous on flights". These traits express preferences or attitudes that are open to change. In the absence of another person, secondary traits might be present but quite invisible. Added to the common and »

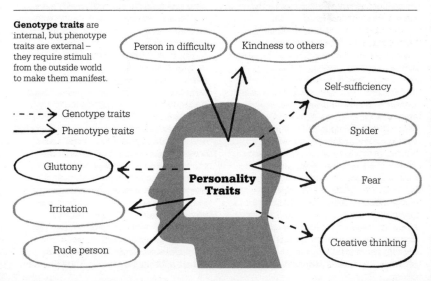

Genotype traits are internal, but phenotype traits are external – they require stimuli from the outside world to make them manifest.

· – – ➤ Genotype traits
——➤ Phenotype traits

Person in difficulty — Kindness to others — Self-sufficiency — Spider — Gluttony — Fear — Irritation — **Personality Traits** — Rude person — Creative thinking

Robinson Crusoe, Allport concluded, must always have had many distinctive personality traits, but some were only uncovered by new circumstances after he was shipwrecked and met Friday.

cardinal traits, they provide a complete picture of human complexity.

Traits and behaviour

Allport was interested in how traits are forged in a person, and their connection with behaviour. He suggested that a combination of internal and external forces influence how we behave. Certain internal forces, which he called "genotypes", govern how we retain information and use it to interact with the external world. At the same time, external forces, which he named "phenotypes", determine the way individuals accept their surroundings and how they allow others to influence their behaviour. These two forces, he said, provide the groundwork for the creation of individual traits.

Applying these ideas to the story of Robinson Crusoe, Allport saw that, prior to his meeting with Friday, Crusoe's genotypes, or inner resources, along with some phenotype aspects, helped him to survive alone on a desert island. He had the resilience to overcome his initial despair, and fetched arms, tools, and other supplies from the ship before it sank. He built a fenced-in compound around a cave, and kept a calendar. He hunted, grew corn and rice, and learned to make pottery and raise goats, and he also adopted a parrot. He read the Bible and became religious. These activities demonstrated the expression of Crusoe's genotypical traits and resulting behaviours. However, it was only with the arrival of Friday that other aspects of his phenotypic behaviours could find expression: he helped Friday to escape from his captors;

he named him; he had the patience and persistence to teach him to speak English, and the capability to convert him to Christianity. While Crusoe always had these personality traits, they remained unexpressed on the island until he formed a relationship with Friday. The idea is similar to a well-known philosophical puzzle: if a tree falls down in a forest, and there is nobody there, does it make a noise? For Allport, traits make behaviour consistent; they are always there, even if no one is around to evoke them or witness them in action.

An idiographic study

After the publication of *Personality: A Psychological Interpretation* in 1937, Allport turned his attention to the topics of religion, prejudice, and ethics. But in 1965 he returned to the subject of personality by undertaking an idiographic study of the personality traits of Jenny Masterson, who lived from 1868 to 1937. During the last 11 years of her life, Jenny wrote 300 personal letters to a married couple with whom she was friendly. Allport used these letters for his analysis, asking 36 people to characterize Jenny's personality traits from her letters. Eight trait "clusters" encompassing 198 individual traits were relatively easy to identify, with broad agreement from all the people rating the documents. These traits were: quarrelsome–suspicious; self-centered; independent–autonomous; dramatic–intense; aesthetic–artistic; aggressive; cynical–morbid; and sentimental.

However, Allport concluded that this trait analysis of Jenny was somewhat inconclusive, and so he went on to use a number of other frameworks, including Freudian and Adlerian analysis. Assisted by his students Jeffrey Paige and Alfred Baldwin, he also applied "content analysis" to the material. This was a new form of computerized analysis, where the computer was programmed to count the number of times words or phrases occur that are related to a given topic or emotion. Allport was particularly impressed by this new method because of its potential to analyse idiographic data, confirming his belief that the idiographic approach can identify subtleties of an individual character that trait questionnaires alone cannot reveal. In 1966, Allport published a paper entitled *Traits*

Revisited suggesting that the aim of personality study should not be the microanalysis of individual traits, but the study of the psychic organization of the whole person. He stated that his early writings about traits were written in an age of psychological innocence, although he maintained his belief that traits are a reasonable starting point for the description of personality.

Allport's influence

Allport's work forms the basis of many contemporary schools of thought, though he is rarely credited directly. Much of modern personality testing derives from the work of Raymond Cattell and Hans Eysenck, and both of these psychologists drew upon Allport's lexical study. Cattell's "16 Personality Factor Questionnaire", which is still used by psychologists today, uses 16 traits identified by Cattell through computer analysis of Allport and Odbert's original 4,500 adjectives.

Humanistic psychology, which forms the basis of most counselling and therapeutic practices, also relies heavily upon Allport's ideas, particularly his idiographic method and insistence upon the uniqueness of each and every person. Increased focus on the practitioner–client relationship as a vehicle for the expression and development of personality has its roots in Allport's assertion that personality is largely a function of relationships.

Allport was also one of the first to point out that even those psychological theories that attempt to explore positive human experience are based "largely upon the behaviour of sick and anxious people or upon the antics of captive and desperate rats". He wondered why there were no theories based on the study of healthy human beings, and those who strive to make life worth living. He pointed out that most studies are of criminals, not of law abiders; of fear, not courage; and focus on the blindness of humans, rather than their vision. The burgeoning school of positive psychology, led by Martin Seligman, has taken up this idea and aims to develop a scientific psychology of positive experience.

By 1955, when Allport wrote *Becoming*, his thinking had developed further; he now saw human striving towards a higher level of consciousness and realization as the true motive of personality. The idea that "becoming" is the ultimate goal of human beings was also developed by the psychologists Carl Rogers and then Abraham Maslow, who renamed it "self-actualization". Although Allport's work is cited less often than other well-known figures, he had a profound and lasting influence on the field of psychology. ∎

Gordon Allport

Gordon Willard Allport was born in Montezuma, Indiana, USA in 1897. The youngest of four sons, Allport was shy and studious as a child, but as a teenager he became editor of his school newspaper and ran his own printing business.

During World War I, Allport performed military duties, before winning a scholarship to Harvard University to study philosophy and economics. After graduating in 1919, he taught for a year in Turkey, then went back to Harvard, where he gained his doctorate in psychology in 1922. He also studied with the Gestalt School in Germany, and at Cambridge University in the UK.

In 1924, Allport again returned to Harvard to teach the first course in personality studies in the USA. Apart from four years at Darmouth College, New Hampshire, he remained at Harvard until his death from lung cancer, aged 70, in 1967.

Key works

1937 *Personality: A Psychological Interpretation*
1954 *The Nature of Prejudice*
1955 *Becoming*
1961 *Pattern and Growth in Personality*

THERE IS AN ASSOCIATION BETWEEN INSANITY AND GENIUS
HANS J. EYSENCK (1916–1997)

IN CONTEXT

APPROACH
Personality

BEFORE
1926 American psychologist
Catharine Cox tests the intelligence
and personalities of 300 geniuses and
finds the average IQ to be 165+; key
characteristics are tremendous
persistence and motivation.

1956 J.P. Guilford develops the
concept of divergent thinking
to discuss creativity.

AFTER
2009 In *Genius 101: Creators,
Leaders, and Prodigies,* American
psychologist Dean Keith Simonton
argues that geniuses are the result of
good genes and good surroundings.

2009 Swedish psychologist
Anders Ericsson attributes
expert performance to 10,000
hours of practice.

A capacity for **over-inclusive thinking** can lead to original and creative ideas…

…and combined with an **IQ of 165** or above…

…but combined with **psychotic symptoms**…

…this can lead to genius.

…this can lead to insanity.

Discussion about genius has been
dominated for most of its history
by the nature-versus-nurture
debate: is a genius born or made? Prior to
the early 1900s, ideas about genius were
based largely on stories of people who were
perceived as geniuses, such as Leonardo
da Vinci and Beethoven. As early as
Aristotle, creative genius and madness
were seen as linked, and both assumed to
be largely genetic in nature. In 1904, British
psychologist Havelock Ellis's *A Study of
British Genius,* reported controlled studies
of both psychotic patients and creative
people to establish a link between the
two. Seventy years later the German
psychologist Hans Eysenck reviewed the
early evidence and concluded that it is not
psychosis (full blown insanity) that is
related to genius, but psychoticism, which
he defined as an underlying disposition to
develop psychotic symptoms.

Temperament and biology
Many psychologists have defined and
measured personality traits, but Eysenck's
interests focused on human temperament
rather than the detailed characteristics that
make up a whole person. He was a biologist,

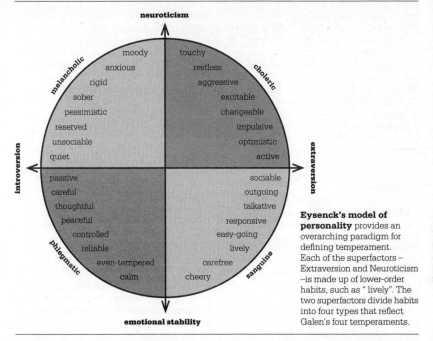

Eysenck's model of personality provides an overarching paradigm for defining temperament. Each of the superfactors – Extraversion and Neuroticism – is made up of lower-order habits, such as "lively". The two superfactors divide habits into four types that reflect Galen's four temperaments.

and like others before him, notably the ancient Greek physicians Hippocrates and Galen, he believed that physiological factors account for temperament. Hippocrates had suggested that personality type arises from an excess or deficit of a particular type of bodily fluids, known as humors. Galen expanded upon this idea to suggest there are four types of temperament: sanguine, choleric, phlegmatic, and melancholic. He claimed that sanguine people have an excess of blood, and are cheerful and optimistic. Those with a choleric temperament, stemming from an abundance of bile, are quick and hot-tempered. Phlegmatic individuals, with too much phlegm, are slow, lazy, and dull. Melancholics, who suffer from black bile, are sad, pessimistic, and depressed. Galen's biological approach appealed to Eysenck, who considered temperament to be physiological and genetically determined. He proposed a measure of two dimensions, or overarching "superfactors" of personality, that encompass all the detailed traits: Neuroticism and Extraversion–Introversion,

which he then mapped against Galen's four temperaments.

Eysenck's scales

"Neuroticism" was Eysenck's name for a personality dimension that ranges from emotionally calm and stable at one extreme, to nervous and easily upset at the other. He claimed that neurotics (at the less stable end of the spectrum) have a low activation threshold in terms of triggering the sympathetic nervous system, which is the part of the brain that activates the "fight or flight" response. People with this more responsive system are hyperactive in this regard, so they respond to even minor threats as though they are seriously dangerous, experiencing an increase in blood pressure and heart rate, sweating, and so on. They are also more likely to suffer from the various neurotic disorders. However, Eysenck was not suggesting that people who scored at the nervous end of this dimension are necessarily neurotic in practice, merely that they would be more likely to develop a variety of nervous disorders. Eysenck's second dimension of » temperament was "Extraversion–Introversion". He used these terms very much as we use them to describe people around us: extraverts are outgoing and talkative, while introverts are shy and quiet. Eysenck claimed that variations in brain activity explain the difference: introverts are chronically over-aroused and jittery, while extraverts are chronically under-aroused and bored; so the brain must either wake itself up through seeking further excitement with other people (extraverts) or calm itself down through seeking peace and solitude (introverts).

Psychoticism

Eysenck tested his ideas on large groups of people, but realized there were some sections of society that he was missing; so he took his studies into mental institutions. Through this work, he identified a third dimension of temperament, which he labelled "psychoticism", a term that has largely replaced the word "insanity" in general use. In personality theory, this was quite a departure: most personality theorists were attempting to define and measure the normal (sane) personality. However, Eysenck said that, as with the neuroticism dimension, psychoticism ranges along a scale; his tests looked for the occurrence of personality traits commonly found among psychotics.

Eysenck found that a number of personality traits relate to each other to produce psychoticism; those who score highly on this scale are usually aggressive, egocentric, impersonal, impulsive, antisocial, unempathic, creative, and tough-minded. A high score on the scale does not mean a person is psychotic, and it is not inevitable that they will become so; they simply share characteristics with psychotic patients. In controlled studies, such as those by Norwegian psychologist Dan Olweus and his colleagues in 1980, the aggressive element of psychoticism has been related biologically to increased testosterone levels.

Studying genius

A clear psychological definition of creativity has proved slippery, but there is broad agreement that it involves originality and novelty, and is based on aspects of both intellectual ability and personality. In his paper, *Creativity and Personality: Suggestions for a Theory*, Eysenck aimed to throw some light on the nature of creativity and its relationship to intelligence, personality, and genius.

Genius is held to be the highest form of creativity, and it rests upon very high intelligence: an IQ score of at least 165 is considered to be a prerequisite. However, a high IQ is not enough on its own. Another relevant component of intelligence is the mental search process which we use to find solutions, by bringing together different ideas from memory to form new answers to problems. This mental scanning is guided by ideas of relevance: what past ideas and experiences do I have that are relevant to this problem? Each of us performs this differently, and it is an ability that is independent of our IQ. The ability runs along a scale, ranging from an expansive, over-inclusive idea of what is relevant (seeing too many things as potential possibilities), to an overly narrow one (seeing few possibilities); at the centre sits a more conventional sense of what might apply to any problem at hand. Over-inclusive thinking can be measured by word-association tests, which analyse two features: the number of responses to any given word, and the

Professor Frankenstein creates a monster in Mary Shelley's novel, and exhibits classic psychotic symptoms: recklessness, disregard for conventions, and tough-mindedness.

Creative geniuses, such as the artist Vincent van Gogh, exhibit traits from Eysenck's psychoticism dimension, particularly over-inclusive thinking, independence, and non-conformity.

originality of responses. For example, when presented with the word "foot", those with a narrow range of responses are most likely to respond with the word "shoe"; a slightly wider range of inclusive thinking might contain the words "hand" or "toe", while an over-inclusive person might generate words such as "soldier" or "sore". This kind of test makes it possible to measure people's creativity.

It is the element of over-inclusive thinking that Eysenck demonstrated to be a common feature of both psychoticism and creativity. When over-inclusive thinking and high IQ are present together, creative genius will result, because the combination generates creative and original ideas. This is the cognitive characteristic that lies at the base of creativity. When over-inclusive thinking and psychotic symptoms are present together, psychosis, in varying degrees, may result.

Creativity and personality

Eysenck believed that creativity is a personality trait that provides the potential for creative achievement, but the realization of that potential lies in the character trait of psychoticism (in the absence of psychosis). The drive to translate the trait of creativity into achievement, for example by creating works of art, comes from aspects of the psychotic temperament, in particular the over-inclusive thinking style. Eysenck was not suggesting a causal link between genius and insanity; while the two things have something in common – over-inclusive thinking – this combines with other features of genius or insanity to lead to very different results.

Research into creativity faces a number of difficult challenges: with some researchers claiming that creativity can only be judged on what it produces. Eysenck felt unable to propose a fully developed theory of creativity, only a suggestion for one. As he said, "I am linking several fuzzy theories". His work ranged over many areas, though he is best known for his exploration into personality and intelligence. His PEN (Psychoticism, Extraversion, Neuroticism) model was hugely influential, and acted as the basis for much of the later research into personality traits. ∎

Hans J. Eysenck

Hans Jurgen Eysenck was born in Berlin, Germany, to artistic parents; his mother was a well-known film actress, and his Catholic father, Eduard, was a stage performer. His parents separated soon after his birth, and he was raised by his maternal grandmother. In 1934 he discovered that he could only study at Berlin University if he joined the Nazi party, so he travelled to England to study psychology at University College London.

He married in 1938 and after narrowly escaping internment as a German citizen during World War II, he completed a PhD, and took up work as a psychologist at an emergency hospital. He later founded and then headed the Institute of Psychiatry at the University of London. Eysenck married again in 1950, and became a British citizen in 1955. He was diagnosed with a brain tumour in 1996 and died in a London hospice in 1997.

Key works

1967 *The Biological Basis of Personality*
1976 *Psychoticism as a Dimension of Personality*
1983 *The Roots of Creativity*

EMOTION IS AN ESSENTIALLY UNCONSCIOUS PROCESS
NICO FRIJDA (1927–2015)

IN CONTEXT

APPROACH
Psychology of emotion

BEFORE
1872 Biologist Charles Darwin publishes the first scientific study of human emotions in *The Expression of the Emotions in Man and Animals*.

Late 1800s William James and Danish physiologist Carl Lange propose the James–Lange theory of emotion: that emotions are the result of bodily changes, and not the cause of them.

1929 Physiologists Walter Cannon and Philip Bard say we experience physiological arousal and emotion at the same time, in the Bard–Cannon theory.

AFTER
1991 In *Emotion and Adaptation*, psychologist Richard Lazarus says a thought must precede any emotion or physiological arousal.

Emotion is an essentially unconscious process.

Emotions are motivating forces, preparing us for action.	**Feelings** are how we interpret the emotions we experience.
They are **spontaneous biological processes** that are out of our control.	We are **consciously aware** of our feelings and can make **decisions** based on them.
They can be **understood by others** through spontaneous physical expression, such as laughter.	As we have control of our feelings, **others cannot guess** at our feelings through our behaviour.

O ur emotions and feelings are idiosyncratic; they seem to be purely subjective, and the mysticism surrounding them may explain why the psychology of emotion has advanced so slowly. But during the last 30 years, this situation has changed, as scientific findings regarding the "site" of emotions have led to renewed interest. Evolutionary psychologists have also posed questions. What is the purpose of emotions? How have they helped us survive and thrive?

Nico Frijda's ground-breaking book, *The Laws of Emotion*, explores the substance and rules of emotions. He sees them as lying at the crossroads of biological and cognitive processes: some, such as fear, are biologically inherent or innate, and these basic emotions are the ones we share with other animals. Others arise in us in response to thoughts, so are clearly cognition-based. They may even – as in the case of indignation or humiliation – be shaped by culture.

Frijda makes clear distinctions between emotions and feelings. Emotions are beyond our control; they spontaneously arise and alert us to their presence by physical sensations, such as a tightening in the gut when we feel fear. For this reason he says that "emotion is an essentially unconscious process". Feelings, on the other hand, are our interpretations of whatever emotions we are experiencing, and have a more conscious element to them. When we feel something, we are able to have thoughts and make decisions about it. We are not suddenly hijacked by our feelings as we are by our emotions.

Action and thought

Frijda points out that emotions and feelings are also displayed differently. Emotions prepare us for action; in situations that induce fear, they are motivating forces that prepare the body to flee or stand and fight. Other people are able to understand, or at least guess at, our emotions from our behaviour. Feelings, however, may or may not be consistent with behaviour, because we can choose to behave in a way that hides them.

Frijda sees the basic emotions as an opportunity for greater self-awareness.

Emotions, such as fear, Frijda says, are always "about something". They are spontaneous responses to changing circumstances, and reveal much about our relationship with our environment.

They accompany a biological arousal that makes us notice them and become more aware of our feelings. This allows us to factor them into choices we make, and with honest reflection, to deepen self-awareness. But Frijda confines basic emotions to anger, joy, shame, sadness, and fear. Others, such as jealousy and guilt, do not have the same biological imperative.

In defining and describing a very specific set of laws by which emotions operate, Frijda shows that they emerge, wax, and wane in a predictable way. Reason interprets them like a barometer, to ensure our mental wellbeing. "Our emotional selves and reasonable selves are not compartmentalized," Frijda says, "on the contrary, they are connected much more than they seem". ∎

Nico Frijda

Nico Henri Frijda was born in Amsterdam to an academic Jewish family, and lived in hiding as a child to avoid the persecution of the Jews during World War II. He studied psychology at Gemeente Universiteit, Amsterdam, where he was awarded a PhD in 1956 for his thesis *Understanding Facial Expressions*. He attributes his initial interest in emotions to being in love, as a student, with "a very expressive girl".

From 1952 to 1955, Frijda worked as a clinical psychologist at the Dutch Army Neurosis Centre, before returning to research and teaching. For the next 10 years he was assistant professor at the University of Amsterdam, then professor in experimental and theoretical psychology.

Frijda held visiting posts in universities across Europe, including Paris, Italy, Germany, and Spain. He died on 11 April 2015, at the age of 87.

Key works

1986 *The Emotions*
2006 *The Laws of Emotion*
2011 *Emotion Regulation and Free Will*

BEHAVIOUR WITHOUT ENVIRONMENTAL CUES WOULD BE ABSURDLY CHAOTIC
WALTER MISCHEL (1930–)

IN CONTEXT

APPROACH
Personality theory

BEFORE
c.400 BCE Ancient Greek physician Hippocrates suggests personality depends on the levels of the four humours in the body.

1946 Raymond Cattell begins developing his 16-factor model of personality.

1961 American psychologists Ernest Tupes and Raymond Christal propose the first "Big Five" personality-factor model.

AFTER
1975 Hans J. Eysenck's Personality Questionnaire identifies two biologically based, independent dimensions of personality.

1980 US psychologists Robert Hogan, Joyce Hogan, and Rodney Warrenfeltz develop comprehensive personality tests based on the "Big Five" model of personality.

U ntil the late 1960s, personality was most often described as a series of individual behavioural traits that were genetically inherited. Psychologists worked to define and measure these traits, because this was thought to be essential to understanding and reliably predicting a person's behaviour. Raymond Cattell identified 16 different personality traits; Hans J. Eysenck suggested there were only three or four. In 1961, Ernest Tupes and Raymond Christal proposed that there are five major personality traits (the "Big Five"): openness, conscientiousness, extraversion, agreeableness, and neuroticism or emotional stability. Then, in 1968, Walter Mischel shocked the world of personality theory when he proclaimed in *Personality and Assessment* that the classic personality test was almost worthless. He had reviewed a number of studies that tried to predict behaviour from personality test scores, and found them to be accurate only 9 per cent of the time.

External factors

Mischel drew attention to the part played by external factors, such as context, in determining behaviour, believing that it

Resisting temptation, rather than succumbing to short-term gratification, often indicates a capacity for greater achievement in life, as Mischel's studies of behaviour in young children revealed.

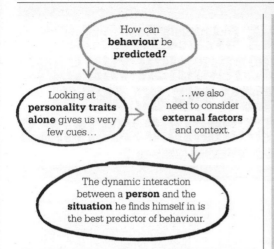

How can **behaviour** be **predicted?**

Looking at **personality traits alone** gives us very few cues…

…we also need to consider **external factors** and context.

The dynamic interaction between a **person** and the **situation** he finds himself in is the best predictor of behaviour.

Walter Mischel

Walter Mischel was born in Austria, but emigrated with his family to the USA in 1938. He grew up in Brooklyn, New York, receiving his PhD in clinical psychology from Ohio State University in 1956. He then went on to teach at the Universities of Colorado, Harvard, and Stanford, moving in 1983 to Columbia University in New York City, where he is the Robert Johnston Niven Professor of Humane Letters.

Numerous honours have been heaped on Mischel. These include the Distinguished Scientific Contribution Award as well as the Distinguished Scientist Award of the American Psychological Association, and the prestigious Grawemeyer Award in psychology in 2011. Mischel is also a prolific and talented artist.

Key works

1968 *Personality and Assessment*
1973 *Is Information About Individuals More Important Than Information About Situations?*
2003 *Introduction to Personality*

was necessary to look at the dynamic interaction of people and the situation they find themselves in. Imagine how absurd it would be if people's behaviour appeared to be independent of external factors. He proposed that an analysis of a person's behaviour, in different situations, observed on numerous occasions, would provide clues to behaviour patterns that would reveal a distinctive signature of personality, as opposed to a list of traits. Individual interpretation of a situation was also considered.

Later, Mischel explored habits of thinking, which might endure over time and across different situations. In his famous marshmallow experiments, aimed at testing willpower, four-year-old children were presented with a single marshmallow and told they could either eat it immediately, or wait 20 minutes and then have two. Some children were able to wait, others were not. Mischel monitored each child's progress into adolescence, and reported that those who had resisted temptation were better adjusted psychologically and more dependable; they did better at school, were more socially competent, and had greater self-esteem. Ability to delay gratification seemed to be a better predictor of future success than any previously measured trait.

Mischel's work led to a shift in the study of personality – from how personality predicts behaviour to how behaviour reveals personality. It also changed the way personality profiling is used in assessing job candidates. Tests that were once considered an accurate basis for staff recruitment are now seen as a guide, to be interpreted in the context of the situations that are likely to arise in doing a job. ■

WE CANNOT DISTINGUISH THE SANE FROM THE INSANE IN PSYCHIATRIC HOSPITALS
DAVID ROSENHAN (1932–2012)

IN CONTEXT

APPROACH
Anti-psychiatry

BEFORE
1960 In *The Divided Self: An Existential Study in Sanity and Madness*, R.D. Laing emphasizes the family as a source of mental illness.

1961 Psychologists E. Zigler and L. Phillips demonstrate huge overlaps in the symptoms of different categories of psychiatric disorder.

1961 Hungarian-American psychiatrist Thomas Szasz publishes the controversial *The Myth of Mental Illness*.

1967 British psychiatrist David Cooper defines the anti-psychiatry movement in *Psychiatry and Anti-Psychiatry*.

AFTER
2008 Thomas Szasz publishes *Psychiatry: The Science of Lies*.

Psychiatrists say that mental disorders **can be accurately diagnosed through symptoms** that can be categorized into diseases.

↓

So they should be able to **tell the difference** between the sane and the insane.

↓

A first experiment showed that sane people can be judged insane.

A second experiment showed that people with genuine mental health disorders can be judged to be faking them.

↓

We cannot distinguish the sane from the insane in psychiatric hospitals.

↓

Psychiatric diagnoses are not objective, but exist only in the minds of the observers.

During the 1960s, psychiatry faced a vocal challenge to its fundamental beliefs by a number of experts known as the "anti-psychiatrists". This informal group of psychiatrists, psychologists, and welfare workers claimed that psychiatry is a medical model of mental health, yet there are no physical symptoms, and its treatment regimes largely ignore the patient's needs and behaviours.

In 1973, David Rosenhan carried out a field study in the USA that explored the validity of psychiatric diagnosis and resulted in the dramatic conclusion that we cannot distinguish the sane from the insane in psychiatric hospitals.

In the first part of the study, Rosenhan assembled a group of eight sane people (including himself), made up of women and men of different occupations and ages, and designated them as pseudo-patients. They were briefed to make an attempt to be admitted as patients to different mental hospitals in five US states, first by telephoning the hospital to ask for an appointment. Later, at the admissions office, they were to complain of hearing an unfamiliar voice in their heads, which was unclear but used words such as "empty" and "thud". This suggested existential feelings of pointlessness. They were instructed to give false names and occupations, but otherwise true personal histories. As a result, all the pseudo-patients were admitted to hospital with a diagnosis of schizophrenia, despite showing no symptoms of the disorder. Their hospital stays lasted an average of 19 days, during which time letely normally. They maintained journals of their experiences, surreptitiously at first but then openly, as it was never questioned. Demonstrating how even normal behaviour might be interpreted as evidence of a psychiatric condition, Rosenhan found that a common comment in their medical notes was "patient engages in writing behaviour". The "patients" themselves described their experience in hospital as one of depersonalization and powerlessness. Their records showed that the average daily time they spent with medical staff was less than seven minutes. Although they were undetected by the hospital staff, other patients challenged their sanity, sometimes quite vigorously: "You're not crazy. You're a journalist checking up on the hospital."

Judging the insane sane

In the second part of Rosenhan's study, he falsely informed the staff at a teaching and research hospital (who were aware of the first study) that during the next three months, one or more pseudo-patients would try to be admitted to the hospital, and they were asked to rate each new patient on the likelihood of them being a pseudo-patient. Of 193 genuine new admissions, 41 were judged suspect by at least one member of staff, and 23 were flagged as possible pseudo-patients by at least one psychiatrist.

Rosenhan's work generated an explosion of controversy, and led many institutions to take steps to improve their care of patients. ∎

David Rosenhan

David Rosenhan was born in the USA in 1 932. After gaining a BA in psychology from Yeshiva College, New York City, he moved to the city's Columbia University to study for his MA and PhD. He specialized in clinical and social psychology, and became an expert in legal trial tactics and decision-making. From 1957 to 1970, he taught at Swarthmore College, Princeton University, and Haverford College, then moved to Stanford, where he taught for nearly 30 years. He later became the university's professor emeritus of psychology and law. He was a fellow of the American Association for the Advancement of Science and was a visiting fellow at Oxford University. He founded the Trial Analysis Group and was a major advocate for the legal rights of mental health patients.

Key works

1968 *Foundations of Abnormal Psychology* (with Perry London)
1973 *On Being Sane in Insane Places*
1997 *Abnormality* (with Martin Seligman and Lisa Butler)

INDEX

ACKNOWLEDGMENTS

Dorling Kindersley would like to thank Shriya Parameswaran, Neha Sharma, Payal Rosalind Malik, Gadi Farfour, Helen Spencer, Steve Woosnam-Savage, and Paul Drislane for design assistance; Steve Setford for editorial assistance; and Stephanie Chilman for composing the Directory.

PICTURE CREDITS

The publisher would like to thank the following for their kind permission to reproduce their photographs:

(Key: a-above; b-below/bottom; c-centre; f-far; l-left; r-right; t-top)

13 Corbis: Bettmann (tr). **Getty Images:** Hulton Archive (tl). **15 The Bridgeman Art Library:** Birmingham Museums and Art Gallery (bl). **Getty Images:** Hulton Archive (tr). **17 Alamy Images:** Interfoto (bc). **18 Corbis:** Bettmann (tr, tl). **21 Corbis:** (tr). **23 Corbis:** The Gallery Collection (tl). **24 Corbis:** Underwood & Underwood (br). **25 Science Photo Library:** Chris Gallagher (tr). **27 Corbis:** Bettmann (bl); Bill Varie (tr). **29 Science Photo Library:** US National Library of Medicine (tr). **30 Corbis:** Bettmann (tl). **33 Alamy Images:** Eddie Gerald (cr). **Lebrecht Music and Arts:** Rue des Archives / Varma (bl). **37 Corbis:** Bettmann (bl). **LawtonPhotos.com :** (tl). **41 Corbis:** Jose Luis Pelaez, Inc. (bl). **Science Photo Library:** Humanities and Social Sciences Library / New York Public Library (tr). **43 Corbis:** Underwood & Underwood (bl). **45 The Advertising Archives:** (br). **47 Corbis:** Sandy Stockwell / Skyscan (cr). **Magnum Photos:** Wayne Miller (bl). **49 Science Photo Library:** OMIKRON (bl). **50 Getty Images:** Nina Leen / Time & Life Pictures (tr). **51 Getty Images:** Joe Raedle (tl). **Corbis:** Bettmann (br). **52 Alamy Images:** Monashee Frantz (tl). **57 Getty Images:** Imagno / Hulton Archive / Sigmund Freud Privatstiftung (tl). **59 Alamy Images:** Bjanka Kadic (bl). **60 The Bridgeman Art Library:** Museum of Modern Art, New York / © Salvador Dali, Fundació Gala-Salvador Dali, DACS, 2011 (b). **61 Corbis:** Hulton-Deutsch Collection (tr). **63 Corbis:** Guo Dayue / Xinhua Press (tl). **Getty Images:** Imagno / Hulton Archive (tr). **65 Getty Images:** Imagno / Hulton Archive (bc). **66 Getty Images:** Apic / Hulton Archive (bl). **67 akg-images:** Walt Disney Productions (tl). **Getty Images:** Imagno / Hulton Archive (tr). **68 Corbis:** Robbie Jack (cra). **69 Wellcome Images:** (tr). **72 Corbis:** Robert Wallis (bl). **73 Alamy Images:** Harvey Lloyd / Peter Arnold, Inc. (bl). **Science Photo Library:** National Library of Medicine (tr). **75 Getty Images:** Hulton Archive (bl). **76 Corbis:** Nancy Honey (br). **79 Getty Images:** Ryan McVay (tl). **Lebrecht Music and Arts:** Rue des Archives / Collection Bourgeron (bl). **81 Corbis:** Michael Reynolds / EPA (tr). **82** Getty Images Roger-Viollet (bc). **83 Getty Images:** Leonard Mccombe / Time & Life Pictures (bc). **86 Corbis:** Pascal Deloche / Godong (tl). **87 Getty Images:** David Malan / Photographer's Choice (tr). **88 Corbis:** Roger Ressmeyer (bl). **89 Getty Images:** Peter Cade / Iconica (tr). **94 Corbis:** Bettmann (bl). **Getty Images:** Mark Douet (tr).

97 Corbis: Jutta Klee (tl/computer); Roy Morsch (tc/blamer); Larry Williams (tr/placator). **Getty Images:** Nathan Blaney / Photodisc (tc/leveller). **99 Corbis:** Allen Ginsberg (tr); Robbie Jack (bl). **103 TopFoto.co.uk:** Topham Picturepoint (tl, tr). **105 Press Association Images:** (tr). **107 Science Photo Library:** Estate of Francis Bello (bl). **111 Corbis:** William Whitehurst (tl). **Jon Roemer:** (tr). **113 Beck Institute for Cognitive Behavior Therapy:** (tr). **114 Corbis:** Bettmann (br). **117 Alamy Images:** David O. Bailey (bl). **Science Photo Library:** Corbin O'Grady Studio (tr). **118 Corbis:** Carol Kohen (bl). **120 Corbis:** H. Armstrong Roberts / ClassicStock (bc, br). **Getty Images:** George Marks / Retrofile / Hulton Archive (bl). **121 Corbis:** Monty Rakusen (tr). **124 Courtesy of Baycrest:** (bl). **127 Corbis:** Ocean (cr). **129 Getty Images:** Purestock (bl). **Positive Psychology Center, University of Pennsylvania. :** (tr). **133 Courtesy of UC Irvine:** (bl). **Corbis:** Guy Cali (cr). **134 Lebrecht Music and Arts:** Matti Kolho (bc). **135 University of Bath:** (tr). **139 Getty Images:** Chris Ryan / OJO Images (tl). **140 Corbis:** Moment / Cultura (tl). **141 Alamy Images:** Interfoto (bl). **Corbis:** K.J. Historical (tr). **143 Solomon Asch Center for Study of Ethnopolitical Conflict:** (tr). **145 Corbis:** Bettmann (bl). **148 Corbis:** Claro Cortes / Hanoi, Vietnam (tl). **149 Corbis:** Hannes Hepp (bl). **Stanford News Service. :** Linda A. Cicero (tr). **151 Manuscripts and Archives, Yale University Library:** Courtesy of Alexandra Milgram (bl). **152 Getty Images:** Apic / Hulton Archive (bl). **153 Getty Images:** Peter Stackpole / Time & Life Pictures (br). **154 Corbis:** Stapleton Collection (br). **155 Corbis:** Geneviève Chauvel / Sygma (tl). **157 TopFoto.co.uk:** Topham Picturepoint (tr). **Philip G. Zimbardo, Professor Emeritus, Stanford University:** (tl). **161 Corbis:** The Gallery Collection (cr). **163 Science Photo Library:** Bill Anderson (bl). **164 Corbis:** Bettmann (bl). **165 Alamy Images:** Thomas Cockrem (bl). **168 Corbis:** Hulton-Deutsch Collection (tr). **169 Richard Bowlby:** (bl). **Getty Images:** Lawrence Migdale (tr). **171 Corbis:** Bob Thomas (tr). **Special Collections, Eric V. Hauser Memorial Library, Reed College, Portland, Oregon:** (bl). **173 Albert Bandura:** Department of Psychology, Stanford University (tr). **174 Alamy Images:** Alex Segre (tr). **175 Corbis:** Ocean (bl). **Getty Images:** Jon Brenneis / Life Magazine / The LIFE Images Collection (tr). **178 Corbis:** Christopher Felver (bl). Brian Mitchell (tr) **179 Corbis:** Frans Lanting (bl). **183 Getty Images:** Stan Munro / Barcroft Media (tl). **188 Getty Images:** MPI / Archive Photos (tl). **189 Corbis:** Bettmann (tr). **192 Corbis:** Bettmann (bl). **193 Getty Images:** Universal History Archive/ Hulton Archive (tl). **Mary Evans Picture Library:** John Cutten (tr). **195 Getty Images:** Universal History Archive / Hulton Archive (tc). **Dolph Kohnstamm:** (bl). **196 Corbis:** Monalyn Gracia (br). **197 Courtesy of University Archives, Columbia University in the City of New York. :** Joe Pineiro / Office of Public Affairs Negatives - Box 109 (tr). **199 Corbis:** Bettmann (bl).

All other images © Dorling Kindersley
For further information see: **www.dkimages.com**